Advance Praise

"Traditionally, psychotherapy is carried out by two people sitting in chairs facing each other. However, trauma is about being frozen, about being scared stiff. It is about the feeling that you're unable to move. So it is no surprise that 'talk therapies' have been limited in healing the wounds of trauma and abuse. In this clearly written and well-researched book, Amber Gray reveals just how powerful movement-based therapies can be in contributing to the healing of trauma. In addition, she has applied insights from the Polyvagal Theory to the field of movement and dance therapies.

This book will be beneficial for all therapists as a guide and companion, as well as for those seeking help in resolving their own traumatic experiences."

—**Peter A. Levine, PhD,** author of *Waking the Tiger: Healing Trauma* and *An Autobiography of Trauma: A Healing Journey*

"Amber Gray's extraordinary book is a study in contrasts: wise yet accessible, sophisticated yet practical, singular yet deeply generous. Moving fluidly between the verbal and the embodied, she brings science into conversation with the wisdom of earth, spirit, and culturally-rooted practice. Humbling and inspiring, it invites clinicians into a vital reimagining of trauma work that embraces reciprocity, restoration, and mobilization.

—**Craig Haen, PhD, RDT, CGP, LCAT, AGPA-F,** psychotherapist and cofounder of The Kint Institute

"Our nervous systems are shaped in relationship, and they heal in relationship. In this beautiful and deeply embodied book, Amber Gray reminds us that healing is not only a cognitive process but an experience that unfolds through the body, through movement, and through connection. By weaving polyvagal science with somatic and movement-based practices, she offers clinicians meaningful pathways to support restoration, dignity, and belonging. This work is a powerful contribution to trauma-informed care and to the ongoing conversation about how we help people come back home to themselves."

—**Linda Thai, LMSW, ERYT-200,**
trauma therapist, educator, and speaker

"It's rare that you can feel an author's beating heart in the pages of their book, but this one pulses with Amber Gray's decades of deep feeling for her clients, her mentors, and the work she has so lovingly and dedicatedly developed. Each page is studded with the cut and polished gems of her ideas, images, and viewpoints, resulting in a light that brings the reader to an informed and inspired place. She reframes and reinvigorates therapeutic work, especially with marginalized and oppressed people. A must-read for anyone doing therapy, especially trauma-informed, body-based therapy."

—**Christine Caldwell, PhD, LPC, BC-DMT,** professor emeritus of the Somatic Counseling Program at Naropa University and author of *Bodyfulness*, *Oppression and the Body*, and *Conscious Moving*

Polyvagal-Informed Restorative Movement Psychotherapy

Polyvagal-Informed Restorative Movement Psychotherapy

Roots, Rhythm, and Reciprocity

Amber Elizabeth Gray

Norton Professional Books

An Imprint of W. W. Norton & Company
Independent Publishers Since 1923

Note to Readers: This book is intended as a general information resource for professionals practicing in the field of psychotherapy and mental health. It is not a substitute for appropriate training or clinical supervision. Standards of clinical practice and protocol vary in different practice settings and change over time. No technique or recommendation is guaranteed to be safe or effective in all circumstances, and neither the publisher nor the author(s) can guarantee the complete accuracy, efficacy, or appropriateness of any particular recommendation in every respect or in all settings or circumstances.

This book is not a substitute for medical or psychological diagnosis, treatment or therapeutic support for trauma survivors. If you suffer from any mental health condition concurrent with trauma, such as (but not limited to) suicidality, traumatic brain injury, or psychosis, even though some of the exercises in this book may be helpful to you, advice for managing those conditions is completely beyond the scope of this book. Please seek diagnosis and treatment from your own healthcare provider. Also, if you have any physical limitations, please consult your healthcare provider before attempting the physical exercises described in this book and follow the instructions given for each exercise carefully, since even simple stretching can cause injuries if it is performed incorrectly or inappropriately.

The cases described in this book are composites. Any URLs displayed in this book link or refer to websites that existed as of press time. The publisher is not responsible for, and should not be deemed to endorse or recommend, any website other than its own or any content that it did not create. The author, also, is not responsible for any third-party material.

Printed in the United States of America
First Edition

Manufacturing by Versa Press
Book design by Beth Steidle
Production manager: Julia Druskin

ISBN: 978-1-324-03029-4 (Paperback)

W. W. Norton & Company, Inc., 500 Fifth Avenue, New York, NY 10110
www.wwnorton.com
W. W. Norton & Company Ltd., 15 Carlisle Street, London W1D 3BS
Authorized EU representative: EAS, Mustamäe tee 50, 10621 Tallinn, Estonia
1 2 3 4 5 6 7 8 9 0

To my Mom and Dad. I know you are still listening.

Contents

SECTION II

Practice

Acknowledgments

We are all reflections of our ancestors from family and evolutionary lineage. We are extensions of the natural world around us. We are all mirrors for everyone and everything in this world, that also mirrors us. I heartfully acknowledge everyone who came before or is dreamed out front and is always part of these words and work: two-legged, four-legged, those with wings, roots, paws, scales, and fins.

Over many years, people asked me when I might write a book about "my" work. There is no such thing as "my" work. I wasn't particularly interested until four or five years ago, when I was preparing a lecture and reflecting on my clients' stories and the stories I hear in the communities I've worked with following disasters, complex humanitarian emergencies, and mass historical and current displacements. In these places humanity is very much alive. The immense suffering and the endless courage to share, connect, heal, restore, rise, and keep dancing is real. I only decided to write this book when I realized how impactful and meaningful these stories, their voices, are. The work described here is our work. I have encountered such willingness to experiment and play with the ideas and practices that are polyvagal-informed. I acknowledge the strong hearts, immense courage, relentless willingness, and incredible resilience of the clients and communities whose work this is.

Acknowledging all the people who are part of this: This work reflects the brilliant work of friend and mentor Steve Porges, whose "home play" challenges encouraged me to play with theory and practice and bring the discoveries and stories back. It is rare to know someone of his reach who will pause, listen, and reflect, and who welcomes ideas, experiences and, insights to continually expand the theory and its applications in ways that are beneficial and meaningful for so many. I have been taught, challenged, initiated, and mentored by generous, wise medicine teachers from lineages of both blood and spirit: Whitefeather. Treebeard. Ingrid Llera. ManShoun. Emilie Conrad. Nillias Somby. Tony Lee. Nadine Lee. Sylvia Nulpinditj. Duggan Coburn. Selena Coburn.

My family of origin—mother Mary Jean Jakubowski Gray, father Charles Franklin Gray, and brother Chuck Gray—are strong roots. It is a blessing to be born into a love that is both solid and spacious. I received the contract to write this book the same day I received the phone call that my mother was dying. My father died a few months later. Their deaths delayed the book several years, and its writing happened in fits and starts, alongside the sacred gift of midwifing their deaths and welcoming them as Ancestors. I wish they were here to read it. My husband, Karl John Ferguson, and my dog, Maxi, are very patient beings. Maxi, I owe you a lot of walks! Karl reminded me many times that I had something meaningful to share, and that these are stories, ideas, and very practical things that deserve to be told. His commitment to helping me literally get back on my feet post–spinal surgery is why this book still happened. To be a dancer and a mover faced with learning to walk again and having to reestablish neural pathways I once took for granted reminded me countless times that movement is medicine. I love so many people who are friends who encouraged, believed, incited, advised, listened, pushed back, and offered feedback, idea sharing, time and a space to write, and who kept me dancing. Their names are here, alphabetically, and there are many who are unnamed: Jenny Adams. Conrad Aikin. Susan Aposhyan. Nancy Beardall. Mimi Berger. Sarah Bicknell. Julianne Bodnar (dec.). Kennedy Braden, Karen Brown. Tarrie Burnett. Christine Caldwell. Meg Chang. Stephanie D'Angelo. Deb Dana. Alicia Rencountre-Da Silva. Regan Desautels. Kim Dunphy (dec.). Boby Duval. Zak Ebrahim. Martha Eddy. Kelsey Eidson. Patti Ernst. Mary Fabri. Ashley Fargnoli. John Fawcett. Charne Furcron. Elise Gent. Rosa Maria Govoni. Angela Grayson. Emma Guthrie. Jane Guthrie. Craig Haen. David Alan Harris. Nancy Herard-Marshall (dec.). Kalila Homann. Carter Howell. Brian Isakson. Alex Jordan. Ida

Kaplan. Ryan Kennedy. Annie King. Lynn Koshland. Lalita Lakshmi. Peter Levine. Cathy Malchiodi. B.G. Mancini. Morag McKillop. Sylvain Meret. Ali Mezey. Niloufer Merchant. Melissa Michaels. Michelle Moss. Alice Nkunzimana. Alphonse Nkunzimana. Andrea Northwood. Blake O'Connor. Karen Onderko. Hester Phillips. Jay Radford. Stanley Rosenberg (dec.) Gerald Saggi. Anna Scheuringer. Laetitia Schuett. Zuzana Sevcikova. Nina Simons. Suzi Tortora. Cheryl Stayton. Anna Stillmaker. Mei Lai Swan. Carolyn Swenson. Laura Teachout. George Thompson. Bessel van der Kolk. Jung-Hsu Wan. Heidi Wegner. Jo Woods.

Initially I did not think that I would include illustrations. When I began trying to use words to describe ideas, movements, and practices that are multidimensional, just like our bodies and movements are, dance therapy colleague and friend Sara von Koningsveld offered her talent and time to shape these ideas into figures and illustrations. We are all blessed by the people who support us in myriad ways, and the amazing team at Collectively Rooted, Laura Walsh, Alex Vanderlyke, Dawn Stern, Angela Lin, and Erika Beers, have kept me going in all the other dimensions in my life. Caryn Mirriam-Goldberg and Denise Low are two amazing women whose editorial and organizational insights and literary brilliance and creativity helped shape this book. The team at Norton has been seriously patient through multiple delays; thank you for that, Jamie Vincent, Deborah Malmud, McKenna Tanner, Mariah Eppes, and Olivia Guarnieri.

Foreword by Stephen W. Porges

It is a personal pleasure to introduce Amber Gray's *Polyvagal-Informed Restorative Movement Psychotherapy: Roots, Rhythm, and Reciprocity.* This book is not merely a clinical text; it is a living document—shaped by decades of listening, witnessing, and co-creating with individuals and communities whose lives have been marked by trauma, displacement, and resilience. It also reflects a shared history we have lived in the field of trauma, as the discipline gradually opened to somatic approaches and the organizing principles of Polyvagal Theory. I have had the opportunity to witness this transition—from a field that often prioritized cognition and narrative to one that increasingly recognizes the intelligence of the body. Amber has been an important part of that transformation, particularly through her integration of dance and movement as essential pathways of healing. Her work helped illuminate how embodied processes—and especially the power of movement—can support clients in shifting state, restoring connection, and reclaiming a sense of self. To observe this evolution alongside her has been to see the field expand its capacity to appreciate the body not as an adjunct to therapy, but as central to the process of transformation.

Amber's work stands at a necessary intersection: where science meets lived experience, where theory is informed by the wisdom of the body, and where healing is understood as a relational, embodied process. What distinguishes this book is not simply its integration of Polyvagal Theory into somatic and movement-based psychotherapy, but its reciprocity. This is not a one-way application of theory to practice; it is an ongoing dialogue in which clinical experience refines theory, and theory offers language to illuminate experience.

Polyvagal Theory, first introduced in 1995, proposed that the autonomic nervous system is hierarchically organized, reflecting evolutionary adaptations that support survival, social engagement, and health (Porges, 1995; Porges, 2007; Porges, 2023). Central to this framework is the understanding that physiological state—regulated by brainstem circuits—shapes how we perceive the world, how we relate to others, and how we experience ourselves. These foundational circuits provide the neural platform upon which behavior, emotion, and cognition emerge.

Amber takes these principles out of abstraction and places them within the lived, moving body. She recognizes that trauma is not only remembered—it is embodied. If trauma is embodied, then pathways toward restoration must also engage the body. Her work expands the clinical application of Polyvagal Theory by demonstrating how movement, rhythm, and relational engagement become portals through which autonomic states can shift.

A compelling contribution of this book is its reframing of healing. Amber moves away from language that implies repair of something broken and instead emphasizes a "restorative process." This shift reflects respect for the adaptive intelligence of the autonomic nervous system. What is often labeled pathology—shutdown, hyperarousal, dissociation—can be understood as survival strategies mediated by specific neural circuits. The dorsal vagal complex supports immobilization in the face of overwhelming threat, while the ventral vagal complex enables social engagement and co-regulation when cues of safety are detected (Porges, 2023).

Amber's clinical work demonstrates that these states are not endpoints, but dynamic processes. Through attuned movement, breath, rhythm, and relational presence, individuals can access pathways that support state shifts—transitions in neurophysiological organization that alter how one feels, moves, and connects. Transformation does not emerge from insight alone; it depends on the nervous system's capacity to access and sustain states that support safety, connection, and engagement.

This book also situates these processes within a broader social and cultural context. Amber's work is deeply informed by her engagement with survivors of human rights abuses, refugees, and communities affected by systemic oppression. In these contexts, safety is not assumed; it is relative, contextual, and co-created. This aligns with a core principle of Polyvagal Theory: the nervous system continuously evaluates risk through neuroception, a process operating below conscious awareness to detect cues of safety or threat.

By foregrounding dignity, belonging, and reciprocal alliance, Amber expands the clinical conversation beyond symptom reduction to include the restoration of relational capacity. Her concept of "reciprocal alliance" challenges hierarchical models of therapy and emphasizes mutuality and shared humanity. It reflects the function of the ventral vagal system: to support connection through attuned, bidirectional communication.

Another strength of this work is its articulation of accessible entry points into embodiment. Amber identifies breath, spine, and weight as primary portals—pathways through which individuals can sense and influence their physiological state. These are universal features of human experience. Breath provides a direct interface with autonomic regulation. The experience of weight connects individuals to support and grounding. The spine serves as an organizing axis linking movement, sensation, and interoception.

These portals are complemented by dimensions of space, time, and rhythmicity, which shape how individuals engage with themselves and others. Rhythm plays a central role in coordinating internal physiological processes with external movement and relational interaction. When trauma disrupts these rhythms, individuals may feel out of sync with themselves and others. Restoring rhythmic coherence becomes a pathway to restoring connection.

Throughout the book, Amber honors client wisdom. The composite vignettes are not presented as distant case material, but as contributions to the framework itself. This reflects a fundamental principle: healing is not something done to individuals, but something that emerges within relationships characterized by respect, curiosity, and reciprocity.

From a scientific perspective, this work exemplifies the translational potential of Polyvagal Theory. It demonstrates how a neurophysiological framework can inform clinical practice in ways that are both grounded and useful, while remaining open to refinement. The strength of Polyvagal Theory lies not in rigidity, but in its capacity to integrate new observations and adapt to new contexts.

Amber's book contributes to this ongoing evolution. It invites us to expand our understanding of therapeutic intervention, to reconsider the role of the body in psychological processes, and to recognize the centrality of relationship in shaping autonomic state. It also invites us to listen more carefully—to the body, to movement, and to the cues through which safety and connection are communicated.

In reading this work, we are reminded that the nervous system is not merely a mechanism for survival, but a platform for connection, creativity, and meaning. When conditions support the activation of the ventral vagal system, individuals gain access to behaviors that include play, curiosity, and social engagement—essential features of health.

Amber has offered us a map—grounded in science and enriched by human experience. It acknowledges the realities of trauma while illuminating pathways toward restoration. It offers principles and practices to guide clinicians and individuals navigating the complexities of the human experience.

This book will be of great value to clinicians, researchers, and all who seek to understand how the body participates in trauma and healing. More importantly, it is an invitation—to move, to listen, and to engage with the intelligence of the nervous system in new and transformative ways.

—Stephen W. Porges, PhD

References

Porges, S. W. (1995). Orienting in a defensive world: Mammalian modifications of our evolutionary heritage. *Psychophysiology, 32*(4), 301–318.

Porges, S. W. (2007). The polyvagal perspective. *Biological Psychology, 74*(2), 116–143.

Porges, S. W. (2023). The vagal paradox: A polyvagal solution. *Comprehensive Psychoneuroendocrinology, 16*, 100200.

Foreword by Deb Dana

I met Amber Gray many years ago when Stephen Porges brought us together. He believed we shared a way of seeing the world, and that became the foundation for our friendship. Over the years Amber and I connected online and in person, shared moments of joy and times of grief, worked together when she wrote a chapter for *The Clinical Application of Polyvagal Theory*, dreamed of changing the world, and supported each other while finding our own polyvagal paths. Amber and I carry a deep reverence for the nervous system. At the heart of our friendship is a conviction that the nervous system is wise and its capacity for change unfailing.

I developed the Rhythm of Regulation framework to help therapists, and the clients they serve, befriend the nervous system. By creating a shared language, maps to guide their exploration, and practices to find their way home to safety, I have invited my colleagues to become fluent in Polyvagal Theory and see their work through a nervous system lens. Seeing this work embraced by therapists around the world continues to fill me with joy.

Amber has developed a framework that is grounded in Polyvagal Theory and rooted in our human experience. From the wisdom of her decades of clinical work with human rights trauma, she weaves together Polyvagal Theory, dance movement therapy, and traditional healing practices. She invites us not toward a protocol but toward a framework that, like the nervous system itself, holds both pattern and possibility. In her words, the nervous system "is a gift of our evolutionary ancestors, and it is a pathway to emergence and possibility," and this book truly brings that spirit alive.

Amber and I love maps, and throughout her writing three maps emerge: the historical map that anchors us in our personal lived history, the emergent map that honors what is unknown and still unfolding, and the essential map held in the vagus nerve, tracing the path back to safety. Amber offers us these maps as guides toward healing—from the history the nervous system carries, through what is emerging in this moment, to the possibility of finding the way home.

At the heart of this book is an invitation to all of us: seasoned clinicians and curious beginners alike. Amber's framework is not a method to follow or a single path to healing. It is a way of being present with those who have suffered that honors the body, movement, spirit, and nervous system.

To be present in this way requires a deep trust—in the body, in the therapeutic relationship, and in the nervous system's enduring capacity for change. Amber begins by laying the groundwork—the nervous system, trauma, safety, and self-care—before bringing it to life with practices and stories. She shows us what the autonomic unfolding of healing actually looks like.

We are living in a moment of collective dysregulation. At a time when the suffering in the world can feel overwhelming, Amber offers us something we deeply need: the belief that healing is possible and that the nervous system can find its way. With decades of walking alongside survivors of human rights abuse, and a deep understanding of the nervous system, she gives us a framework grounded in wisdom. Not the wisdom of theory alone, but the wisdom that comes from following the body's lead and trusting the nervous system to find the way home.

In these pages you'll come to know Amber's wisdom. I believe you will be, as I was, struck by the beauty of Amber's words and moved by the stories she relates. When I read this book, I found myself pausing to let the words land, to sit with the practices for a moment before being pulled into the next story, the next practice, the next invitation. The stories stayed with me. The practices felt within reach. The beautifully drawn illustrations brought the nervous system to life. And woven through all the stories, the practices, and the illustrations is

Polyvagal Theory: art and science, body and story, held together in service of healing.

I am deeply grateful to Amber for her work that shows us a way to befriend the nervous system and accompany our clients on the autonomic journey of healing. Read this book with your head and your heart, absorb the stories, hold the maps, and let Amber's words find their way in. Remember, your nervous system is wise. Trust it. Let this book change the way you work and the way you navigate the world.

—Deb Dana, LCSW

Polyvagal-Informed Restorative Movement Psychotherapy

Introduction

Polyvagal-informed somatic psychotherapy and polyvagal-informed dance/movement therapy are the subject of this book. For ease of writing and reading, the terms have been collapsed into "polyvagal-informed somatic and dance/movement psychotherapy" (PVISDMP) and are sometimes also referred to as "the framework."

This book is a map. A historical map, and an emergent map. It's a map of the pathways—Polyvagal Theory, clinical work with survivors of egregious human rights abuses, somatic psychology and dance/movement psychotherapy, and medicine teachings (more commonly known as traditional healing)—that all converged to cocreate this body of work. The heart of this work is emergence, as an emergent process of our autonomic nervous system (ANS). The ANS is both pattern and possibility. It gets patterned by life events and, as a seeker of novelty, is a portal to endless possibility for newness, change, repatterning, and healing. It is a gift of our evolutionary ancestors, and it is a pathway to emergence and possibility. Like a map that connects to the wilderness, there are areas that are yet unmapped and unknown. The theories, ideas, and practices in this book are neither exhaustive nor a final version. They are offered in service of adaptability and evolution, ongoing, just as Polyvagal Theory is.

The simple image in Figure I.1 demonstrates the convergence that is emergence.

This book is a theoretical framework with practices for clinical work with survivors of trauma that is human-rights rooted and relationally and socially oriented and can breathe and grow, that is, is

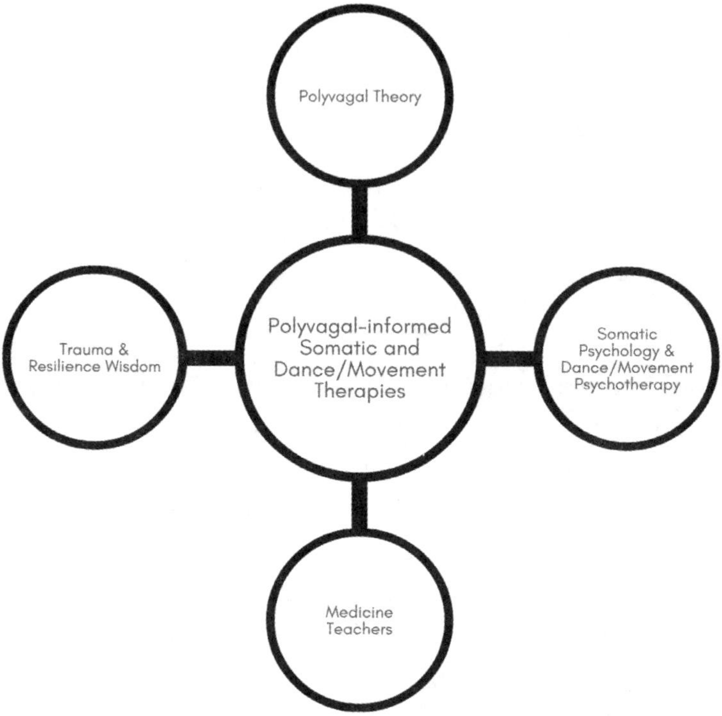

Figure I.1 Emergence

adaptable and flexible. The patterns inform the bones or scaffolding of this framework, which I am continuing to learn in 29 years of this work. The possibility is in the very adaptable and flexible nature of this framework. It is a clinical book based on clinical experience, clinical intuition, and clinical reflection, integrating the Polyvagal Theory into somatic clinical work. Clients have been engaged in the processes, practices, and reflections that formed this framework throughout every step of its cocreation. While my training and approach are somatic, dance and movement based, those are not a prerequisite for applying this work. This book is full of possibility for any clinician wanting to adapt body-based therapies in their work. It is equally applicable to those of us who want to understand ourselves better, as humans with a nervous system, an open heart, and a willingness to change in service of our life path.

Section I, Chapters 1–5, is the framework. These five chapters are primarily theoretical and do include some case vignettes. These chapters highlight the major themes of this PVISDMP framework. Drawing from 29 years of client wisdom and clinical practice with human rights abuse trauma, Section I covers some of the evolving ideas, theories, and practices that contribute to the accumulated knowledge that informs the applied work, that is, the restorative process.

Section II, Chapters 6–11, is the harvest. These chapters describe the clinical application of PVISDMP. It is a harvest of 29 years of learning and practice about the effect of the ANS circuits and their emergent states on human beingness (i.e., our movements, actions, thoughts, and emotions). Each chapter contains descriptions of these harvests: the things I have learned about how Polyvagal Theory supports, impacts, changes, revolutionizes, and humanizes somatic and movement-based psychotherapies with survivors of trauma. The composite case vignettes shared in this book reflects the reality of cruelty, oppression, and suffering that exists in this world far more commonly than is acknowledged. These contexts are much bigger than the work shared here. Somatic, movement, and dance therapies always include many of the same processes all other psychotherapies do. Verbal processing and the processing of traumatic memories alongside more resourced memories are central to this work. For the sake of space and efficiency of content, the somatic, movement, and creative dance components of the work are highlighted in this book, which does not minimize the essential role of verbal processing and the entire traditional clinical process from assessment and intake to closure. Each vignette includes one or more adaptable practices that either evolved from this clinical work or that I learned and adapted for this work and refined with my clients. Readers are encouraged to try them on first, in your own bodies, and find your unique way to share them in your work and life. There is no one way to work "creatively somatic." Your body and your movement are your map.

The case material shared in this book reflects the reality of cruelty, oppression, and suffering that exists in this world far more commonly than is acknowledged. Content warning: This material will be intense, challenging, and painful to read for many of you. It may reflect and remind readers of your own life suffering. All cases and practices have their own headings, and the practices are described in a font distinct from the rest of the book. Please pause and tend to your nervous system, heart, and Spirit before you continue reading.

The chapters are arranged this way:

- Introduction: Orientation to the chapter themes and theoretical content.
- Client case vignettes: The composite case vignettes describe work with clients that both informed and helped create the ideas, theoretical basis, practices, and so on of this framework as described in this book, and practices that can be used to apply a polyvagal-informed somatic and movement approach to work with survivors of trauma.
- Descriptions of the practices themselves.
- Harvests: The lessons learned that reflect client wisdom and inform all the practices shared in this book. The ongoing learning for myself, clients, students, and readers.

This book is also a story. Survivors of human rights abuses are silenced, and their voices are often never heard. Rachel, whose journey of healing and restoration is woven into several chapters, was the first client to ask me to share her story, both her spoken story and her body story, told through a moving narrative she called her "dance to freedom." She, like all my clients, taught me many things, and one of them is how the cultivation of respect, dignity, belonging, and reciprocity in our work is a pathway to liberation from psychological and physical pain, suffering, oppression, and the captivity of fear and trauma. This book intentionally raises survivors' voices as expertise, and their voices are my primary references and sources of wisdom. This is an action of respect, decolonization, reciprocity, and resistance. They are all grateful when someone cares enough to listen to, read, or witness their story. The need for this witnessing has never been more essential.

Section I

Pattern and Possibility

This first section of five chapters represents what my clients, and this work, teach me. It's learning that happens beyond our formal and continuing education to be psychotherapists and to stay current. The themes in each chapter are shared with humility, care, and respect for the clients whose work these ideas and insights come from. The entire section is connected to the idea that the vagus nerve, so central to the ANS, is a living history that contributes to our inner maps that "pattern" us, and an ever-present beacon of possibility, change, and novelty. Chapter 1 is a historical and emergent map. and a timeline of how Polyvagal Theory has contributed to the growth of this work. Inherent in this is how this work has infused aspects of Polyvagal Theory. This chapter also defines some of the concepts that are core to PVISDMP. Chapter 2, "Dancing in Vagus," tracks the vagus nerve and its influential role in the autonomic nervous system as our North Star or Southern Cross, depending on where we are. Written through a clinical, somatic, movement, and intuitive lens, the focus on the ANS is not reductionistic. It is does not overlook or exclude the fact that the brain is taxonomically part of the entire nervous system, that the ANS is part of the peripheral nervous system that includes the somatic nervous system, and that these interconnected anatomical, biological and physiological systems closely collaborate with the endocrine system, respiratory system, and cardiovascular system to bio-intelligently ensure our survival. Chapter 3, "Trauma and the Moving Body," expands trauma-informed somatic psychotherapy approaches by extending somatic awareness to include and center movement, from the tiniest trace of internal movements to dancing in community. Chapter 4, "The Privilege of Safety," interrogates the assumptions that are made about safety in trauma-informed clinical settings and is informed by deep listening to clients' stories and often accompanying and witnessing in the places where the sources of their suffering occur. In Chapter 5, "Self-Care," so often referenced at the end of a conference presentation or as an add-on to trauma trainings is centered as a primary and essential clinical skill. While these chapters are primarily theoretical, they include practices that support their premise and include some composite case vignettes based on my work with clients. While details of individual clients' traumatic experiences are not included, these vignettes reference the all-too-common presence of cruelty in traumatic human experience. They reflect the "terrible knowledge" that exists, always, in our world. The client experiences on which these blended vignettes are based are shared from the brave space of many clients' commitment and courage to restore, liberate, and heal. Please track your own nervous system and tend to your body, heart, mind, and spirit.

CHAPTER 1

The Map

There are no instructions. The map is in your bones.

—RACHEL BLODGETT, SERPENT AND BOW

This book is for clinicians of all backgrounds wishing to integrate polyvagal-informed somatic movement into their work and perhaps a little dance therapy. It sits at multiple intersectionalities: The therapeutic approaches that inform this book include somatic psychology, my primary training; dance/movement therapy, my specialty; and human rights psychotherapy, a term that I came up with one day because nothing else really described the work my clients and I do together. There are other intersectionalities at play here. This book is based on a "wisdom trilogy" of science, spirit, and client wisdom.

In this trilogy, "Science" refers to Polyvagal Theory as it continuously evolves in its depth and understanding of how the automatic nervous system (ANS), the vagus nerve, and vagal circuitry guide us along an evolutionary ancestral trail and an emergent pathway. Since 1999, my immersion in the work of friend and mentor Dr. Stephen Porges, creator of Polyvagal Theory, has constantly fed my clinical curiosity and helped my clients in innumerable ways to return home to their bodies. Chapter 2 explores this framework's intuitive understanding and integration of Polyvagal Theory in a somatic movement and clinical context.

Spirit and science might seem to exist in very distinct realms; however, they are dance partners. If science is one truth, Spirit is another truth. My clients teach me that we need to choose both. This promotes true embodied inclusivity that helps restore a sense of belonging. Much of what science is just beginning to explain in its unique language are ideas, concepts, practices, and deeply embodied, orally transmitted wisdoms ancients have always known and expressed with and without language. Many medicine teachers are also among my mentors, in both the human and more-than-human realm, and their wisdom is core to this framework. How could it not be? Our vagal pathways are a gift from our evolutionary ancestors.

I use the term "trauma and resilience wisdoms" to acknowledge that my clients have the greatest wisdom for their own restorative process, and that trauma and resilience are inseparable phenomena, despite how they are sometimes portrayed as opposites. Years ago, I began using the term "restorative process" because, after listening to and paying attention not just to, but with, my clients, I learned that the oft-used phrase "trauma recovery" can feel like a setup. Survivors don't recover everything (and sometimes, tragically, anything). Many survivors perceive that they recover little or nothing. "Healing" is a well-intentioned term, but it denotes pathology, that is, we are healing from something which made us unwell. Pathologizing human experience is not appropriate in the context of trauma, especially human rights violations. These violations occur in multiple contexts of oppression: intergenerational, transgenerational, and historic trauma; interpersonal or relational trauma; collective trauma; racial trauma; traumatic loss; and all traumas brought upon survivors by an abuse, misuse, or perversion of power. The word "healer" also seems to bestow powers upon the therapist or practitioner, and while our power, when derived from our own empowerment, is essential to the restorative process, language that minimizes the power differential is helpful when we work with those who have been disempowered. "Restorative" names the reality that we restore as much as we can of a sense of belonging and place, dignity, and the many capacities trauma can undermine, such as rest and digestion, sleep, relationships, nourishment, elimination, meaningful work and play, and engagement with life. The metaphor of a house destroyed by a fire, hurricane, or flood is useful here. We can rebuild or fix the house, and it will still be a house, just as we can still be whole. However, the act of restoration does not aim to recover all that is lost or make the house the same, because that is not possible. An improved roof or windows that withstand wind or water, a fireproof safe for cherished belongings, or new colors on walls or siding are all acts of restoring what we can and acknowledging that we are forever changed.

This framework is a map that is client and survivor centered, polyvagal-informed, heart-centered, and practical. It is in our bones. It is the ongoing process emergent from 29 years of work with survivors of political violence, torture, and war from a multiplicity of cultures, who are also my teachers when I can facilitate that space without burdening them. We empower our clients when we allow our own open-hearted curiosity and vulnerability to invite them into the role of expert on their own sociocultural, sociopolitical, socio-geographical, and socio-spiritual reference points. It's important to do this in ways that are not creating more demand for them. It's a nuanced balance of curiosity and our ability to shift back into our own expertise in ways that create the strong container that survivors require and deserve.

Framework Basics

Figure 1.1 highlights the central role the body plays in traumatic experience. It also pays homage to the very multicultural context this work occurs in, which is essential as we clinicians are all called to decolonize our work. Decolonization is not the topic of this book, and an excellent one already exists (Mullan, 2023). The ideas, theories, and concepts that form this book, as well as the shared practices they support, can all contribute to decolonization in psychotherapy. Oppressors always target the body and its primary language of movement, because that is how we are best controlled.

The more I learn from clients, the more my willingness and capacity

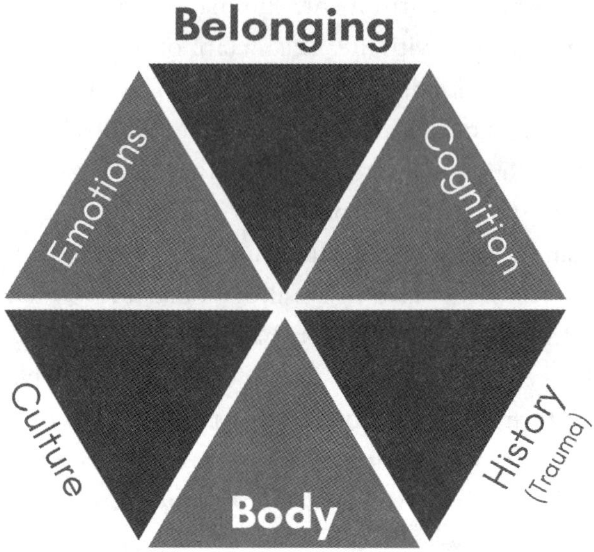

Figure 1.1 The Body as the Base of Belonging

expands to be humble as a therapist and a human. The more I learn, the greater becomes the wholeness and the reciprocity of the human exchange my clients and I share.

In 2008, I was challenged to create a framework for "refugee mental health," a new field then, by a leader at a federal agency that provided much of the funding in this area. He was concerned about a shift to privileging evidence-based cognitive behavioral therapies (CBT) because of their lack of depth in terms of the very physical experiences that form the heart of what causes people to be displaced in this way. He was also concerned about how the centering of cognition might eliminate more relevant forms of therapy, such as creative, somatic, and communal approaches more familiar in the contexts most newcomers come from, which are more holistic, embodied, heart-centered, and communal cultures.

Figure 1.1 represents an alteration to the traditional CBT triangle in service of refugee mental health and, more broadly, applied trauma-informed and survivor-centered somatic and dance/movement therapy (DMT) in a multicultural setting. Originally a triangle, it is now a hexagon, which allows for a more connected and egalitarian image of the relationship between the internal (body, emotions, thoughts) processes and "external" (Belonging, culture, and history) influences that help shape our inner processes and restorative process. At the top, where thoughts sit in a CBT triangle, is "Belonging." This invites a much more global and relevant emphasis on what matters to the displaced person(s) and by extension any community experiencing displacement. Othering, bullying, and gaslighting can all contribute to a sense of displacement in our shared human sense of belonging. A restored sense of belonging might even be a primary desired clinical outcome. "Culture" and "History (Trauma)" are also "outside" the hexagon as essential to fostering reciprocity, dignity, and respect in the restorative process.

The inclusion of culture is essential in this work. I use this term broadly, inclusive of all influences in a person's life that contributes to their sense of belonging. There is much to say about culture. What is perhaps most important here is that we learn and remain open to our clients' cultural perspectives, ideas, beliefs, and contexts so that our work with them is relevant. Inviting our clients to teach us about culture—without burdening them—invites their expertise and promotes reciprocal alliance. We also learn on our own, from reliable sources, so that we don't burden them and can show up with the wisdom and knowledge they expect and deserve from us and offer it in a generous, open-hearted manner.

"History" in Figure 1.1, with "Trauma" in parentheses, is a bit more complex. Studying trauma-focused CBT, I was introduced to the idea that a primary goal of therapy is to help clients put the trauma where it belongs in their life line, that is, in the past. This was a helpful idea for me, based in a Western-centric linear timeline. In service of brevity and clarity, I offer this: Our client histories are far bigger than the "client history" data we may need to collect on our assessment forms and continue to learn in our ongoing reciprocal alliance, which is introduced in a few paragraphs. Our clients' histories are part of their chosen way of understanding and expressing their sense of self. It may include ancestors and nature and all other living beings and more. The therapist develops understanding, acceptance, and acknowledgment that client histories may extend over generations. This way of understanding may not just occur linearly in Kronos (chronological) time, but also in Kyros time, the spiraling nonlinear dreamtime that is still referenced by many societies and cultures. The linear timeline can present the traumas that may have occurred only once or may have occurred across a lifetime as chronological events in a person's lived life (i.e., time on earth) only. They are chronological events, and there are imprints and ripples that reach across time and space touching and integrating with all aspects of a person's sense of self, including relatives, place, ancestry, and communities. These traumas are woven, like a braid, with their history, past and future. Where there is intergenerational trauma there is also intergenerational resilience, and the simultaneous and sequential weaving of trauma and history becomes a braid that also reflects resilience.

Inside the hexagon in same-colored triangles are the pathways of the internal, embodied processes of psychotherapy. Foundational, and therefore at the base, is the human body, the site of all human experience. The body is where clients know, define, and express themselves from the tiniest sensory-motoric micromovement to the largest human movements: migration and life passages such as birth and death. This also, of course, includes and centers the ANS as our body's guidance and governance. Emotions here include the more general and observable expression of affect. Emotions, whether felt for hours or days or months, arise from the neurophysiological states of the body. This also includes the more fleeting surface-level feelings, which connect us to our constantly shifting thought tides. Cognition and all its emergent processes of thoughts, beliefs, ideas and verbal narratives are the other internal process pathway arising from the internal landscape of our body and the emotions that reflect our experience of that landscape moment to moment. This adaptation of the CBT triangle offers a more holistic and dynamic image of this work, and the refugee clients and collaborators who reviewed this were grateful to be seen in a much bigger whole than they had previously been seen.

Restorative Movement Psychotherapy

Initially this work was named restorative movement psychotherapy (RMP). RMP is the adaptation of somatic psychology and DMT for a vast multicultural trauma and survivor-centered context. The name reflects how the term "restorative" became core to this work. It also highlights movement, from DMT, because movement is universally human in ways as mundanely meaningful as chopping vegetables and as expressively beautiful as a moving dance performance or dance party. The idea of dancing can be vulnerable, but movement is a shared experience that can exist on a continuum of stillness to dynamic expression.

This work, as reflected in this framework, was developed working with newcomers to the United States (refugees, asylum seekers, victims of trafficking and torture) who survived war, political torture, and political violence, as well as Indigenous communities in the United States and elsewhere displaced by colonization in their own land, and those enduring long-term racial trauma and oppression here in the United States, as well as in other locations such as Haiti, Guatemala, and Australia.

Because of this clinical community focus, I set out to learn how to make this work as universally relevant as possible. Dance is many things, and one of those things is that it can be a bit scary and vulnerable, while to some it is expressive and pleasurable. Creative expression requires enough relative safety to be able to express oneself fully. There is an inherent vulnerability in being seen in the creative space. As a dance/movement therapist, I was trained to work expressively, but not everyone is privileged with the relative safety necessary to be fully and creatively expressive. This is why *movement* in all its diverse forms has been emphasized in this framework over *dance* specifically.

Primary Portals to the Body and to State Shifting

After several years of working with many courageous clients, I realized that we had "codiscovered" accessible portals to the body that are also pathways to state shifting. A mission of this framework is accessibility. Many survivors of trauma remain in contexts where they cannot access therapy or would not usually participate in psychotherapy due to cultural beliefs, so accessibility is crucial. Stigmas about psychology and mental illness can make all mental health approaches less viable in many settings. The primary and secondary portals to the body are pathways that guide the restorative process. Simply stated, these are pathways that I have observed are accessible to survivors of trauma in many different contexts. Because they allow access to the body, they promote state shifting along various pathways.

"State shifting" is a term that arose in a conversation I had with Dr. Porges in 2008, when we were copresenting in Norway. As part of our preparation, I was sharing my ideas for what aspects of DMT might be helpful to illustrate the clinical application of Polyvagal Theory. Steve asked me an insight-laden question: "What is it that you experience as healing when you dance in ceremony?" Invited to speak and teach to that, the term that arose in my mind was "state shifting." It's not a new term, but this insight illuminated a multilayered perspective on this work and its many parallels and relationships to more traditional, wisdom-based global healing and rite-of-passage practices. In many, perhaps all, ancient mystical, healing, restorative, and celebratory practices, rituals, and ceremonies, it is state shifting that heals, helps the seeker cross a threshold, or indicates a spiritual shift (i.e., in cultures where trance and possession are integral to healing). State shifting refers to a change in a neurophysiological, biochemical state that changes how we feel. Simply put, we go to therapy or movement classes or social experiences or ritual to change how we feel or to feel together in community. It encompasses physical, emotional, cognitive, transpersonal, social, communal, and spiritual realities. Supporting clients to consciously state shift in service of their own regulation is what disrupts the trauma feedback loops that arise from the neurally and somatically embedded imprints of exposures to adverse experiences, and begins to re-establish restorative feedback loops connected to resilience.

The three primary portals are breath, spine, and weight. It was in sifting through various structured practices, which are described in Section II of this book, that I realized this work can be cross-categorized in many ways. Some of the earliest categorizations became primary and secondary portals, and when the work was renamed polyvagal-informed DMT in 2012, the pathways to state shifting for belonging were added.

Breath, Weight, and Spine

BREATH

Breath is a core influence on movement. Breath and movement can be described as akin to a marriage; they support and shape one another. Just try moving without breathing! Breathing can both constrain and expand our movement. In many ways, movement rides breath's flow, and breath shapes and texturizes movement. Watching a dance performance or an athlete is a great way to see how connected movement and breath are. Breath is universally known. From the very practical and necessary, autonomic act of breathing to the more sublime and esoteric interpretations of the meaning of breath in many ancient traditions (such as Kundalini yoga) and more current breath-based practices like Holotropic breathwork (Grof & Grof, 2010) and Continuum (https://www.continuumteachers.com/), breath is well known. In many languages, "breath" and "spirit" are the same word: "prana" in Hindi, "chi" in Chinese, and "pneuma" in Greek. Breath is literally and metaphorically the wave we all ride into life and ride out when we die. In this way, many esoteric and spiritual practices acknowledge breath as the veil between worlds. Breath is core to contemplative practices such as Samatha Vipassana, a basic sitting meditation technique. Each breath is composed of an inhale and an exhale, and many contemplative practices teach about the gap or pause at the end of every outbreath or exhale. This gap is a space of infiniteness because it is empty space, where we are neither taking in nor letting out. It also represents the potential for everything, that is, what's possible. It cusps the end of the exhale and the beginning of the inhale. In school for somatic psychology, I learned that Wilhelm Reich described the inhale as a front-of-body experience, the manifestation, inspiration, and creation side of breath. The exhale, which he described as a back-of-body experience, is the dissolve, or relax, release, and letting go. From a polyvagal perspective, the inhale is the upregulation, and the exhale is the downregulation, and the pause or gap following the exhale that contemplative traditions highlight is a fertile void, a dorsal-rich connection to the universe, mystery, spirit, quiet, and stillness, or however one might see this. Chapter 2 goes into this in more depth. As subtle as breath-based practices can seem, breath shifts our neurophysiological state and biochemistry faster than anything else (Porges, S., personal communication, May 13, 2010), which makes it a most efficient ANS regulator.

WEIGHT

Weight, which is defined in this framework as the physicality of our presence, can seem more abstract to sense. A way to sense weight that has helped many of my clients is this exercise:

Notice all the points or places where your body is making physical contact with whatever surface you are lying, sitting or standing on, or leaning into. Take a moment to sense how much support you are receiving, or not, through these points of contact. You can also notice your weight distribution, for example, is one foot, or back of thigh, or butt cheek more relaxed on or settled into the chair than the other? We often have body areas we hold, clench, prop, or tense even when we are relaxing. This practice will help you sense your weight.

Many survivors of human rights abuses describe how they feel in terms of weight, light or heavy. "Heavy" is often described as "too weighed down" by the burdens of suffering they carry or by sadness and loss. Likewise, "lightness" can be associated with feeling empty in both positive and negative ways; it can also denote dissociative states. At times, a shift from heavy to more levity signals a restoration of embodiment; the reverse is true when one exists in chronic shutdown states, which are often (but not always) expressed psychologically as dissociative emptiness or floatiness. These shifts in sense of weight are cues that neurophysiological state shifts are occurring. Weight, in this framework, has many emergent processes, that is, related physical expressions, such as yield, contact, support, ground, place, and belonging. Connecting to our weight allows us to be in contact with our own body, where we can sense, feel, and access support, locate ourselves (place), and connect to our sense of belonging.

SPINE

The spine may be one of the most important aspects of the body in somatic psychotherapy, and yet many somatic therapies underprivilege it. While focus on the spine is common in yoga and bodywork practices such as osteopathy and chiropractic medicine, it is not centered in most somatic psychotherapies. The spine can be visualized as a backside to our midline. This physically invisible but ever-present midline, around which each body organizes in utero, is supported by the spine. In many ancient cultures and traditions, the spine is the center of the axis mundi of the body. As axis mundi, our spine is the center that connects us to heaven (sky) or divine energies and earth, or earthly energies. As such, the human body always channels these energies. The spine is often known only by its palpable presence in the very back of the body; yet it is connected to our entire body through spinal nerves and pathways. The spinal cord is protected by the bony vertebral column called the spine, and the front of the spine connects to our breath and respiration via the diaphragm, at thoracic vertebra 12. DMT offers unique and well-developed theories about the role of the spine and the sacrum in maintaining physical and mental health. Blanche Evan and Liljan Espenak's work as founders of DMT includes theories, systems of assessment and intervention, and practices that focus on the spine as core to well-being (Levy, 2005). Evan considered the physiological health of the spine reflective of psychological health (Levy, 2005, p. 34), and Espenak (Levy, 2005, p. 47) assessed client well-being through the wheel-like motion of the sacrum, at the base of the spine. The spine is central to many forms of ancient and sacred dance, and in many spiritual traditions is a pathway for spirit to enter and connect with the human body. The wisdom of the spine as a "cosmic riparian buffer" in this framework acknowledges its protective, nurturing, and widely connecting role in our bodies, that is, as a centering, connecting space between the human and spirit world. As such, it is core to PVISDMP and as a pathway of evolutionary history.

A riparian buffer is a unique ecosystem, a vegetated area that can include wetlands that is a protective space between both the water and the land. While this description is metaphorical and somewhat poetic, in most of the world's more sociocentric communities that include understanding one's sense of self as inclusive of the natural world, ancestors, and family, it is not such a far-out idea. Porges and colleagues (1988, p. 353) demonstrated that shifts in pelvic tilt that can promote sacral neutral can increase vagal tone, the measure of a neurophysiological state necessary to promote social engagement. Sacral neutral is the position of the sacrum when it is neither in flexion or extension, nutation (forward) or counternutation (backward), which is ideal for spinal alignment. Fatima Hindi describes the spine as a pathway for interoception: a "corridor for sensory information to travel to the brain, making a pathway for unconscious interoceptive data to be brought into consciousness and processed" (2012, p. 135). The vagus nerve is also a pathway of interoception, so intuitively, working with the spine might also regulate the autonomic nervous system. In this framework, the spine is considered the backside of this framework's "noble pathway" of brains: the deep belly brain, the heart brain, and the brain. These three brains are now known to have rich intraconnected neural circuitry to an extent that each is worthy of being called "brain," hence their nickname as a "noble" pathway. This interoceptive information travels the lamina I spinothalamic pathway (Hindi, 2012, p. 131), an ascending pathway of the spinal cord that is one of the most important sensory pathways of the nervous system. Hindi aligns this spinal pathway with the vagus nerve, also interconnected to the "noble pathway" of brains.

I have never encountered a person that did not have a sense of, and connection to, at least one of the primary portals. These three portals seem to universally be understood as related and relevant to embodiment, movement, physical structure, and well-being. This is important, because all readers will likely already work with one, two, or all of these portals in their work. While this book offers many primary portal–based practices, any integration of them into psychotherapy is a powerful state-shifting invitation.

Secondary Portals

SPACE

The secondary portals to the body, space, time, and rhythmicity, are so named because, while they are present in a client's entire restorative process, they are usually (but not always) more complex and therefore more commonly focused on later in treatment. Space is our earliest relationship in our human developmental process. We relate to space—indeed grow, shape, and form in space—in utero, in the first developmental dimension of horizontality. Space relates to our perceptual and cognitive abilities and tendencies and is also that which we relate to through movement. We as bodies move through space; we are weight moving in, through, and around space. It is this therapist's observation over many years that many survivors of human rights abuse and long-term oppression whose exposure includes captivity (whether physical or psychological) have an altered and often very uncomfortable relationship to space. For some, it is simply terrifying to be in relationship to space. The kinesphere, our personal space bubble, reflects our relationship to space and the environment around us. Konie, describing kinesphere from the perspective of Bartenieff Fundamentals, a framework that strongly influences somatic and movement therapies, states the kinesphere is "the 3-Dimensional volume of space that I can access with my body without shifting my weight to change my stance. From this perspective, our Psychological Kinesphere is the space we can attend to" (2011, p. 5). Many survivors' initial clinical presentation is one of a retracted kinesphere. This complex relationship to kinespheric space, the space around us, and inner or interoceptive space in a body that can feel like a minefield, can make it difficult to work directly and intensively with space early in treatment.

TIME

Time is a dimension that we naturally explore as we develop. Time and space orientation, by definition, are altered or absent in dissociative states, which are quite common to survivors of extreme interpersonal violence. Our movement in time is related to what's known as the "sagittal dimension," referring to forward and backward movement. We move toward what we want; we retract from what we reject. This affects our interactions with and in our environment, based on our appraisal of the safety, or lack of it, in the environment, that is, the space around us. Traumatized individuals continuously and/or sporadically perceive the world as unsafe because their nervous systems have shifted into states of chronic fear or terror. They misappraise the environment as unsafe even when the past danger or threat is no longer present. This is different from chronic exposures that occur in oppressive, controlling environments, where the dangers and threats are ever-present even when not active or visible in the moment.

Our relationship to time, in this framework for the restorative process, reflects this ability to move toward what we choose, or want, in our own timing, and move away or withdraw from that which we do not wish to engage. This ability is undermined by the fear that is core to the experience of being traumatized. Because the time dimension is relational, it is often relatively safer for clients to begin in the vertical dimension in Figure 1.2, even though it's out of sequence developmentally. Verticality and weight, while occurring earlier in our human development, can promote mindful reestablishment of boundaries and allows defenses to deconstruct. In the restorative process, if clients can mobilize and slowly reengage in more active play states with less and less fear present, they can regain enough comfort to begin to reengage with the world. Relationships are fundamental to our humanity, and the perverse abuse of the power differential in relational trauma can make relationships scary. One's sense of self, as experienced through the present-moment experience of weight, may need to be the first portal to embodiment to be restored before one can find the trust (yield) to interocept and rest and relax. Relating outwardly to the world rests on this foundation of space/trust/yield/horizontal and weight/mobilize/push/vertical.

RHYTHMICITY

Rhythmicity is core to PVISDMP. The framework is based on coherence in internal (endogenous) and external (exogenous) biorhythms. Sadistic abusers will intentionally increase suffering for their own vicarious pleasure. This intentional abuse often purposefully interrupts, distorts, and resets important biorhythms, such as digestion and elimination, respiration, and heart rate. This intentional miswiring of these core-to-well-being rhythms literally cause individuals to "lose their beat," which has profound effects on external rhythmicity, that is, how we move in the world. Rhythm and core rhythmicity are worthy of an entire book and are the focus of a chapter on polyvagal-informed DMT (Gray, 2018). For the purposes of this chapter, rhythmic feedback loops are fundamental and core to internal physiological states and external, fluid movement, actions, and engagement with the world, and they are the essence of rhythmicity as a secondary portal. Rhythmicity might be seen as the most integrative of the portals, because when we can align

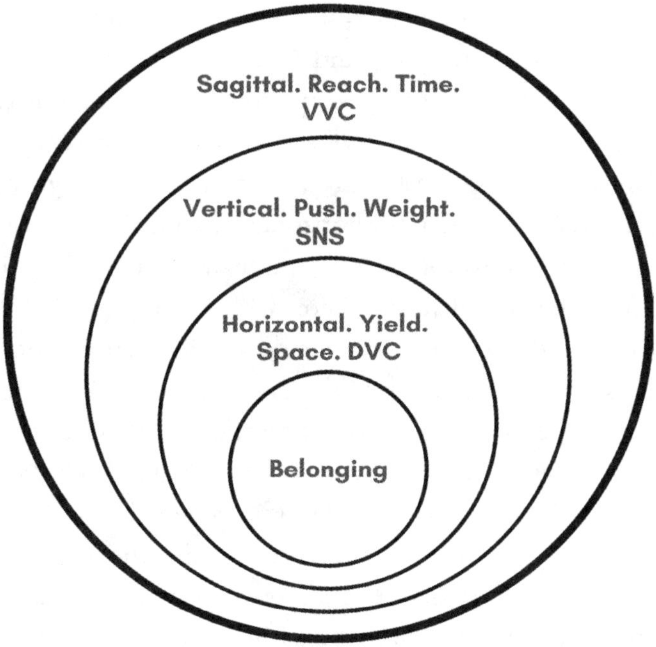

Figure 1.2 Restorative Movement Psychotherapy Basics

our internal and external realities and rhythms, we can move to our natural beat again.

The concentric circles in Figure 1.2 reflect layers of influence on our bodies via human development, species evolution, and as therapeutic processes. Belonging is the heart center of this work, as described above. The remaining terms reflect the influence of Body-Mind Centering (Cohen, 2012), and, body-mind psychotherapy (Aposhyan, 2004), and later on of Polyvagal Theory. VVC refers to the parasympathetic ventral vagal complex, SNS refers to the sympathetic nervous system, and DVC refers to the parasympathetic dorsal vagal complex.

The Three Dimensions and Their Embodied Inquiries and Attributes

Three dimensions underly all our movements and the shaping, action, and movement of our breath, which is fuel for our movement. They are, in developmental order: horizontal, vertical, and sagittal. These dimensions contribute to many planes, shapes, and complexities in human breath and movement. As simple and direct concepts, they are very helpful to clients to understand both their personal development as a moving human being and their relevance to psychological or whole human processes, that is, how people feel, think, act, and move. We begin our lives, in utero and as newborns, in the horizontal or widening dimension. We have not yet developed the physical, mechanical, and energetic structures to move beyond that dimension without support. In our adult bodies, horizontal is the shape of lying down, that is, to rest or sleep. In this dimension, we are the least visible and the most vulnerable. It is in this dimension developmentally that we explore our first relationship to space. Space, weight, and time are concepts central to Body-Mind Centering with the influence of Bartenieff Fundamentals (Hackney, 2015) on Cohen's work. Bartenieff might be described as the mother of many of the movement frameworks that are core to movement therapies.

For humans, the in-utero experience is one of exploration of a hopefully nurturing and nourishing space. Equally, our earliest days as infants and toddlers are an ongoing exploration of space, which we first relate to as we weave the foundation of our embodied life from the environment (space) and our internal sense of the world to inform and shape our developing nervous system, brain, and all their attributes and processes as expressed through the body we will live in our entire life.

The vertical dimension is one we begin to explore fairly immediately. Imagine a young infant rocking to push up on their arms or beginning to push their body and head up into space. Verticality is more visible and less vulnerable because we have more ability to move. In the vertical dimension, we begin to explore our weight. The sagittal dimension refers to the forward-and-back movements that occur as we explore moving through space. We move toward what we want; we retreat from what we don't want. The sagittal dimension has to do with our social and relational capacities. Just as horizontal corresponds to space and vertical corresponds to weight, sagittal corresponds to timing. In this context, timing is the flow and direction of our movement and our capacity to be fully engaged, and present, in our movement.

The Developmental Progression

Dimensions of movement and their psychological attributes are connected to the developmental progression developed by Bonnie Bainbridge Cohen (2012, p. 98) in Body-Mind Centering, using the terms yield, push, reach, grasp, and pull.

"Yield" refers to the most efficient relationship to gravity. A rabbit is a useful demonstration of yield. If you've ever seen a rabbit resting on the earth, looking quite relaxed and connected to the ground, she is recruiting gravity to support her. If a fox trots by, you might see the rabbit launching into the air effortlessly. This absence of effort or collapse is what constitutes a yield. It is our ability to receive the support of gravity and recruit energy from that support when we need to move. The counterpoints to yield are efforting, or bracing or propping, and collapsing. If you constrict all your muscles as tightly as possible and then attempt to leap gracefully, you'll feel what efforting is. Grace and flow are almost impossible. Collapsing is the opposite of efforting. We have no vitality, strength, or muscle tone. It is equally impossible to move efficiently, with grace, ease, and speed, when we are collapsed.

To take a stand. To take our place. To be bounded and self-expressive. This is the realm of "push," which follows "yield" developmentally. It is our sense of self, however we define self—individualistically or collectively. Push is a strong continuum of action, a moving of our weight, that supports our self-definition, our connection to place and ground, and our connection to earth. Push is followed by "reach," when we begin to explore our relationships, relationships to our caregivers and to others around us as well as to the environment and space we move in. Reach connects us to our sense of timing, which pertains to how and when we move in the world.

It is essential to understand that each action or state in all three of these intertwined, developmental actions relies on the previous one for its support, flourishing, and expression. We cannot push with all our presence and strength if we cannot yield. Just try collapsing or efforting while pushing yourself up off the floor. We cannot move volitionally and in our full dimensionality in space if we don't have a well-developed sense of our yield into horizontality and the space around us along with a connected sense of our weight and our ability to move, take up space, and be present.

In Body-Mind Centering, reach is followed by the natural human inclination to "grasp" what we long for and to pull it toward us. In Cohen's work, this pulling into us restores us to yield. In RMP and PVISDMP, we recognize that the pulling toward us is also accompanied by *letting go*, and that letting go is what ultimately invites and allows us to restore back into a more fully expressed yield. This addition reflects the powerful influence of client wisdom on this framework. The act of letting go must be acknowledged, recognized, and processed for us to rest and restore, to yield again. Yield is a deep portal to support: the support of our roots in earth, family, geographical place, community, and all the ways we access and know what supports us.

Figure 1.3 depicts the flow of the developmental progression through the lens of Polyvagal Theory. Those newer to the theory may find these figures become clearer after reading Chapter 2. Yield recruits the deep roots and groundedness of the DVC, and receptivity is the emergent process of being in yield or being yielded. Receptivity is only possible when we are in a flow state and connected to ground, which is possible in a hybrid DVC/VVC state. Push requires energy and movement, so from our DVC yield, we engage the SNS to move. The absence of VVC in the square does not omit the fact that we are in relationship with the environment and experiencing the sense of relative safety that is required for this developmental progression to be integrated and to flow. Each square in this image highlights the circuits of the ANS that are most dominant in this phase of embodied development. The nature elements included here pay homage to the medicine teachings that also influence this framework.

Figure 1.4 shows an interrupted developmental progression through the polyvagal lens. We see the collapse or rigidity that bodies can express when yield has not been fully established. The rigidity or propping that can arise increases SNS input, but the flow or sequencing of movement is thwarted by the lack of rooted DVC ground and integrated ventral flow. The SNS energy or input can become activating or stuck

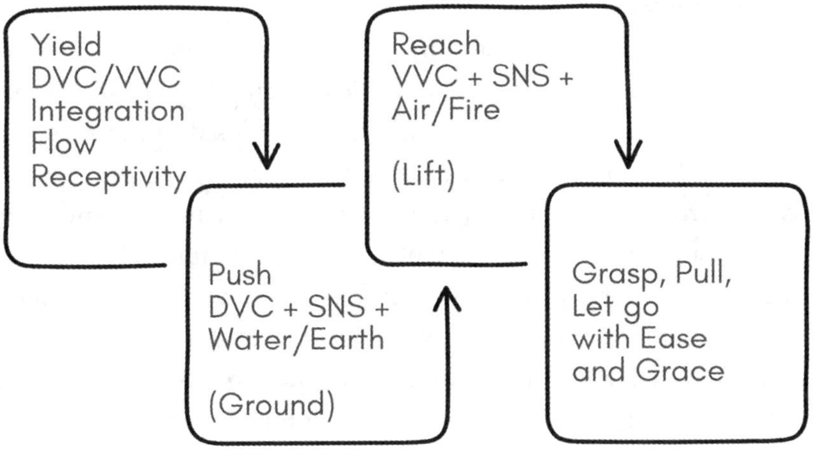

Figure 1.3 The Polyvagal Development Progression in Wholeness

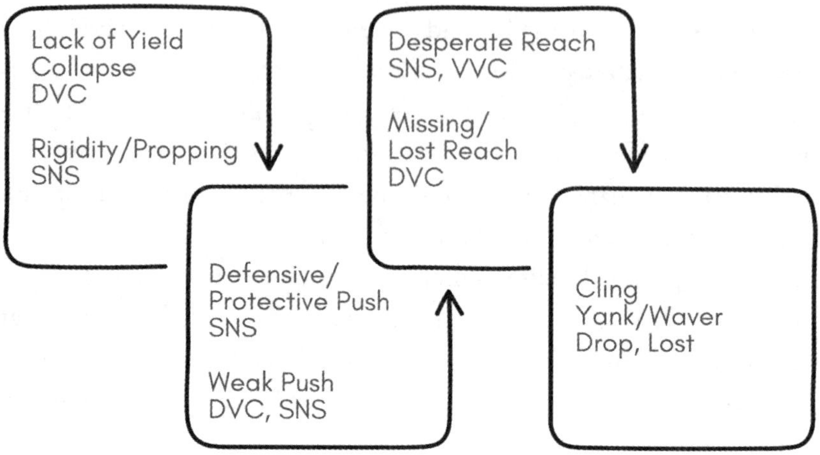

Figure 1.4 The Interrupted Polyvagal Developmental Progression

in ways that create rigidity and tension. As development progresses and without the strong base of yield, our pushes lack strength and can be unsatisfactory as the sequencing of energy that movement is gets stuck, contributing to uncomfortable states and thwarted actions. This continues through the developmental process, and this is why movement in psychotherapy can be reparative and restorative. Through movement, we can access the states beneath the unhelpful stories and begin to state shift in the direction of wholeness. It's important to acknowledge that the choice of the term wholeness in this framework does not suggest a traumatized person is broken. They may feel broken and may express having a broken spirit. Indeed, they may have broken bones and body areas that are injured. In the spirit of, and with deep cultural respect for Kintsugi, the art of golden repair, when pottery is mended by highlighting the remaining cracks with golden paint, the wholeness we always are is still present and available in the brokenness of bodies, hearts, and spirits. In restoring, we are still whole, albeit forever changed.

The Bones of Polyvagal-Informed Somatic and Dance/Movement Psychotherapy

Polyvagal Theory began its influence on the clinical framework of PVISDMP in 1999. While working in a very multicultural context, both in the United States and overseas—in conflict and disaster contexts as well as refugee and internally displaced person camps, and additionally in Indigenous people's reservations and communities—the need to make the work as accessible as possible was immediately apparent. Polyvagal Theory does this. As I learned more and more about the theory and explored and shared it through psychoeducation and the somatic practices that are in this book, my clients and I cocreated PVISDMP practices. This work is still evolving. It's a work in eternal process and progress, not static, just as our vagus nerve in all its meanderings is more potent not as the nerve thing that it is but as the journeys of change, possibility, and emergence it offers. Alongside science, spiritual teachers and practice amplified the impact and meaning of the science. In this process of codiscovery, my clients taught me how their understanding of the science was often shared through proverbs, myths, and cherished spiritual metaphors, symbols, and beliefs. The Dalai Lama is known for his embrace of science and his recognition that there are many parallels in the discoveries by the great mystics and the most prolific scientists. These are the parallel pathways of polyvagal-informed somatic dance/movement psychotherapy.

PVISDMP CORE CONCEPTS

PVISDMP promotes the belief that every human being has the right to inhabit and express their bodies in ways they choose. It recognizes that the subcortical processes that support survival are physiological and biological foundations of actions (behaviors) that promote survival in service of life. In this framework, social engagement is considered a state of wholeness and flow, indicating full social and relational capacities. Embodiment is a continuum, meaning that how any of us are embodied includes influences of our neurophysiology, our culture, including geography and place, and past, current, and future environments we move in. As such, this is a framework that does not endorse interpretation of clients' experiences. Client and therapist are on a journey of codiscovery toward meaning and belonging. Psychotherapy is an experiment.

Therapy or healing is a restorative process based on the knowledge that the ANS-mediated dissolution that occurs in the context of trauma exposure, at an individual level, is life and survival serving. The healing that the restorative process can facilitate is reciprocal: all involved, including indirectly (family members, our community, even extended to those we interact with for a moment, globally) can benefit. Culture and spirit are respected as cornerstones of our shared humanity and therefore essential to this process.

At the core of the work is the belief that movement is the prime state shifter, and that working with the direct experience of our bodies is the most potent and respectful way to work. The restorative process can occur most effectively, simply, and efficiently working through the direct experience of the human body. To shift psychological and emotional state, a prime focus of psychotherapy, our neurophysiological state has to shift. This is a bidirectional process that mirrors the bidirectional information flow of the vagus nerve and pathways. This is how, in the words of friend Deb Dana, state precedes story (personal communication, 2017).

Breath, movement, and rhythmic processes are the most immediate ways to access this direct experience and can be implemented in as many ways as there are individual practitioners, community traditions, and beliefs, in ancient and ever-varied practices. The heart and the sacrum, individually and together, are core to many of the practices that accompany trauma processing. The sacrum, at the base of the spinal column, gets its name from the Latin word *sacrum*, which means "sacred bone." When in neutral, the sacrum can promote vagal tone (1988, p. 353). The heart is the center of this framework innervated by all three neural circuits of the ANS and considered in many ancient traditions a gateway to the universe and the stars. Safety for social engagement, play, and rest and settle, historically not a usual part of psychotherapy, are considered emergent states and actions that are core to the healing that can occur in the restorative process.

Figure 1.5 shows the three concepts that are the heart and the hub of this framework. They are belonging, as described previously, dignity, and reciprocal alliance. If this image could move in spirals, it would more accurately reflect the ways this framework dances. The three circles symbolize spirals that move together, in greater and lesser percentages of connection, depending upon where we are in a restorative process or in daily life. "Dignity" derives from the National Consortium of Torture Treatment Programs (NCTTP) treatment framework for survivors of torture, another significant influence on this work. The NCTTP framework is similar to the phasic approaches for complex trauma that were proposed in the 1990s by early leaders in the trauma field such as Judy Herman (1992). The idea of dignity in the context of torture treatment was originally inspired by the Victorian Foundation for Survivors of Torture's *Rebuilding Shattered Lives: Integrated Trauma Recovery for People of Refugee Background* (Kaplan, 2020). NCTTP emphasizes dignity in the fourth and final phase of treatment, not as a singular treatment goal but as a restoration of a survivor's sense of dignity that permeates as many aspects of their lives as possible. "Reciprocal alliance" is my reframing of the term "therapeutic alliance." As noted above, the word "therapy," in the context of psychotherapy, has as inherent to its meaning a relationship of power between client and therapist, or psychotherapist. In the spirit of the origins of "restorative process," reciprocal alliance acknowledges this inherent power differential and makes the essential ingredient in balancing and equalizing it reciprocity. All therapists certainly need to lean into our hard-earned expertise at times, and many, even most of, our clients appreciate this. In fact, they seek us out or are learning to trust us based in part on this. However, with any experience of trauma that has suppression, repression, and oppression at its core, and that is based on an abuse of power, reciprocity is a powerful and necessary element of the client–therapist relationship to promote a restored sense of belonging and dignity. This term is, in many ways, the heart of PVISDMP, and it is the thread of

Figure 1.5 Polyvagal-Informed Somatic Dance and Movement Psychotherapy

relational connection that is always present in the work. This thread is what restores the client's inherent capacities to be in relationship with self and others, and all things, in ways that are familiar, meaningful, and nourishing to them. The theories, concepts, and practices shared in this book are all pathways to the establishment of this alliance.

While somatic and creative arts therapies integrate the body and arts in ways that can make these therapies more relevant in multicultural and human rights contexts, they still derive from contemporary Western psychotherapy. Grappling with this the entire length of time I have worked with survivors, one of the first threads to creating reciprocal alliance has been the involvement of my clients in the creation of this work. The pathways to restoration that constitute this work are a result of their willingness to experiment with the practices and processes that appear in Section II and share their feedback and experiences, which takes courage and vulnerability.

PATHWAYS AND PRACTICES FOR STATE SHIFTING TOWARD BELONGING, DIGNITY, AND RECIPROCITY

Neuro-Predictability. Neuro-predictability acknowledges that the ANS seeks novelty. Indeed, novelty, that which is new, is likely a primary guidepost for evolution and for emergence. While we know that the

ANS seeks novelty, we also know it has a bias for negativity (Porges, S., personal communication, 2010). What this means is something that trauma clinicians and therapists know very well: Our clients get stuck. They get stuck like an old-fashioned record player needle gets stuck in a groove on the record. They are stuck in outdated and unhelpful perceptions, stories, and ideas of themselves and the world that arise from the extraordinary protective capacities of the ANS. As I often tell my clients:

> Your stuckness, the repetition of uncomfortable symptoms and complaints you no longer want to experience, and the fact you still feel the things you felt in the past even though part of you knows you are in a new time and place, is your ANS championing your survival. Being stuck doesn't feel good or helpful and deters us from our usual and helpful social and relational capacities that guide our connections to others and to life. Your ANS is still reacting to things in the environment and inside yourself that you perceive as unsafe, as dangerous or life threatening.

I often describe the ANS, and the VVC, as "governor" and/or as "conductor of the symphony of the human body." The metaphor of governor helps clients sense how both the ANS and the VVC can offer order to internal experiences that can feel re-ordered and disordered. Creatively describing the human body as a symphony and the ANS (also the VVC/vagal brake) as a conductor who can "bring the bass (ground) up" and "quiet the shrill winds of movement," or any blend of altering instrumentation, can create a clarifying visual for clients.

This is where the concept of neuro-predictability comes in. All the practices in this book offer opportunities for state shifting in helpful directions. The more any of us learn what practices and processes support us to calm, energize, feel lightness and levity, giggle, and be playful, the more we can govern our own somatic responsivity. In other words, we have more mastery over our body's responses to whatever life brings. Our capacity to shift state from uncomfortable, painful, unhelpful neurophysiological and emotional states to feeling ways that are more helpful and hopeful is what neuro-predictability is. This predictability

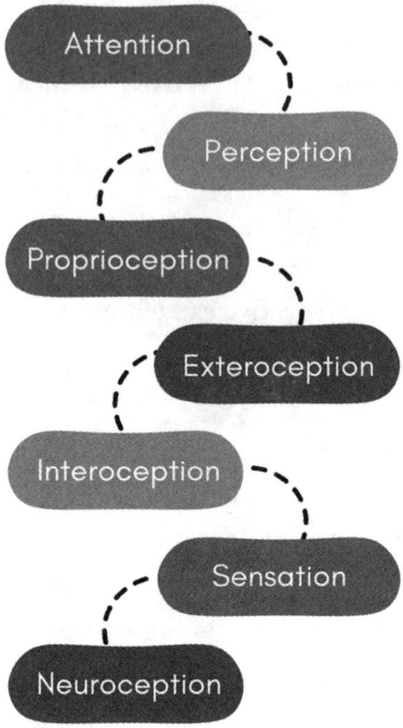

Figure 1.6 Continuum of Awareness

is a metaphor for relative safety, and it is this predictability that erodes clients' persistent trauma feedback loops and helps establish restorative feedback loops.

Interoception. Interoception is part of this framework's continuum of awareness, as seen in Figure 1.6. Interoception relies on interoceptive signals that are transmitted to the brain via multiple pathways in the body, including the lamina I spinothalamic pathway of the spine, the classical viscerosensory pathway, the vagus and glossopharyngeal nerves, chemosensory pathways in the blood, and somatosensory pathways from the skin. While interoception is an embodied scientific phenomenon that can be quantified by these five specific pathways in the human body, it can also be defined as everything we sense and know beneath our skin. It is a way of knowing that is well-defined in some Indigenous wisdom, and in this context, this knowledge can extend to acknowledging the mystery that exists all around us. This sense of mystery, covered in Chapter 10 on core rhythmicity, connects to the PVISDMP concept of our "inner wisdom pool," which refers to our unique cache of accumulated knowledge, an idea for which the Kreyol term *konysans*—a deep inner unspoken knowing—best reflects this type of wisdom. *Konysans* is a knowing that is intuitive, felt sense, gut instinctual, and spiritual, for those for whom spirituality is meaningful. Many traditional and ancient practices have terms that name this old way of knowing that in modern neuroscientific terms is expressed in the terms "neuroception" and "interoception." A defining feature of trauma is that it interrupts, disrupts, and sometimes severs our interoceptive capacities. We can no longer "hear" ourselves; we no longer trust our bodies. In the most severe cases of interpersonal trauma, the body becomes the betrayer because survivors no longer recognize themselves in the confusion and complexity of fear- and terror-induced feelings and actions they live every day. A survivor once said "I have become so unpredictable I don't even know myself anymore."

Sensation. Sensation is most often how we are aware of our inner landscape and interoceptive knowing. Sensations are physical cues that help us identify and name what we are feeling. They are most accurately described as textures (gritty, smooth, bubbly), weight (heavy, light), and anything sensory (what we touch, taste, hear, see, smell, e.g., soft, burning, etc.). Sensation can be considered the key informant of what we know, which always originates with what we sense, because sensation is always the root of what we perceive, feel, think, and do. Sensation cues us to the interoceptive pathway to and from our inner wisdom. Exteroception is the information stream coming in from the outer world. Subconscious neuroception, interoception, and exteroception spiral together to inform how we perceive the world, including environment, people, and events. Perception sequentially informs how we pay attention and what we attend to. Awareness is broad, a generalized sense of what's around and within us; attention is more specified and refined, and in this framework is the conscious oscillation from our inner landscape to the client's, as well as our tracking of the environment or outer landscape while also tracking the client and their ability to track themselves and the environment. This continuum is important in trauma work because trauma is not considered a pathological condition or disorder but a survival strategy that supports reordering of the world based on how attention was initially shifted. This is covered in depth in Chapter 3, "Trauma and the Moving Body."

Microempowerments, Micromovements, and Micromobilizations. "Microempowerments" is a term created by a client whose story I share in Chapter 4, along with the practice that gave rise to this term. Empowerment is always a hoped-for outcome in a human rights approach to psychotherapy and a restorative process. Microempowerments describe the actual feeling in our body of noticing when we are more present, feel a bit stronger or grounded, or find more courage and find our voice. Small state-shifting practices that help cultivate our ability to foster our own neuro-predictability create microempowerments, and I often tell clients that, small as they are, many moments and experiences of these weave together to become our healing and restoration.

Micromovements are those tiny movements such as trembling lips, a flutter of the eyes, or a pulsing or rippling anywhere in the body that are often overlooked. They are also tiny movements like a wiggling of the toes or fingers or a momentary twitch that moves the skin, or a limb. Emilie Conrad, who created the movement practice known as Continuum, did innovative work with micromovements before it entered the somatic psychotherapy field. Christine Caldwell, creator of the Moving Cycle, also encouraged the integration of noticing and paying attention to micromovements early on. Dance and movement therapies have tended to privilege bigger and more expressive movements, and while many somatic approaches to trauma therapy invite attention to micromovements, they often don't work with the full flourishing and exploration of the movement. Micromovements are the smaller, intrinsic movements that support and buoy our larger, more expressive and everyday movements. Tonic muscles, or "background" muscles, are the ones that support our posture and often send micromovement signals. Tonic muscles can be "shut down" functionally from the overwhelm and activation caused by trauma, which is why many survivors lose their capacity for fluid, efficient movement, and/or experience a lot of pain and constriction even where there is no physical injury. Phasic muscles are the larger muscle groups that we tend to be more familiar with that are instrumental to our movement. Connective tissue also moves and is often what we see when we notice pulsing or rippling that appears just under the skin surface. Because connective tissue, and in particular fascia, plays a key role in the transmission of hormones and neurotransmitters, it plays a role in the communication of our feeling states. Fascia is an inner web of connective tissue that both contains (it literally wraps and gathers our voluntary, big red muscles—otherwise our muscles might droop off our bones like brisket) and is a vast web of inner connection. According to researcher Robert Schleip, fascia and the autonomic nervous system are intricately connected (Minasny, 2009, p. 12) and house at least 250 mission nerve endings. Fascia can become hard and sticky when inflamed or injured, and conversely, tension in the fascia can create inflammation. Fascia is directly related to micromovements because it is part of the inner tissue that creates those movements. The pain clients feel and associate with musculature may be in their fascia. The vagus nerve communicates changes in the fascial web through interoceptive and proprioceptive sensory feedback, so it's a central part of our awareness.

"Micromobilization" is a uniquely polyvagal-informed movement therapy practice that therapists can implement in sessions. It is our invitation to clients to shift our attention toward something, which may create a barely perceptible or outwardly invisible movement only the client feels, or that we as therapists may sense in our own bodies as a shift in our felt sense. Micromobilizations can refine our capacity to pay and sustain our attention to people or things that matter to us. Being distracted or not being able to focus are common complaints from my clients. Micromoblizations are often the most accessible way for clients in true shut down from terror states to promote shifting out of immobilization. True clinical shutdown is challenging to shift. Movement is the prime state shifter, and to avoid overwhelm and activation of fear, intentionally inviting clients to engage in "premovement," that is, to sense and begin to move the impulse that precedes a movement, or to just be able to initiate a wiggle of the fingertips, to take slightly longer or deeper than usual breaths, or make a slight tilt of the chin to pay attention to something in the space can initiate movement out of shutdown and stuckness. Micromobilizations can also appear spontaneously and are noticeable when a client suddenly has a glimmer of light in their eyes, or makes momentary eye contact with the therapist, or when we hear their longer, deeper breaths. This level of subtlety can offer more relative safety than larger movements or attempts to engage relationally with a client who has been harmed by a twisted, perverse, power-abusing human interaction and relationship. I invite micromobilizations by inviting clients to notice if they can sense or hear their breath for a few moments and then let this go. They can also open closed eyes for a few seconds and then close them again. Repeating this several times begins to "wake" up the ANS through slow arousal which inspires movement. It's not unusual in polyvagal circles to hear being in a ventral state privileged as the optimal place to be, and this has influenced psychotherapy in some unfortunate ways. Clinicians can "go for the goal" of social engagement and relationality too quickly and too big. The pathway toward belonging and wholeness does not always follow the hierarchy of evolution that created our ANS. Its states are not always emergent in a straight line, that is, going from shutdown to active mobilization in fear to safe enough for social engagement. It is a sidewinding and indirect path that may take many turns through not just up- and downregulation but also through sideways and diagonal state shifts. Micromobilizations are a safe-as-can-be way to codiscover with our clients which direction will offer us a pathway out of fear and terror-based states and begin to interrupt trauma-based feedback loops. This is described in a case in Chapter 6.

Self-Reciprocity. Self-reciprocity, akin to self-regulation (Chapter 5), reflects the premise that therapists' self-care is an essential clinical skill. It derives partially from Indigenous wisdom as taught by a Larrakia mentor and teacher, who attempted to help me understand what deep listening really is. Originally a First Nations and Indigenous concept, it is a depth of listening that incorporates the whole body. Body is not just physical; it exists in many realms, from rooted in our physicality to transpersonal and connected to the cosmos. Each layer is actively engaged in the listening. It is not my place or ability to teach deep listening from this perspective. To learn more about deep listening, Miriam-Rose Ungunmerr Baumann's YouTube video (https://www.youtube.com/watch?v=tow2tR_ezL8) is a beautiful introduction to its meaning and practice. Self-reciprocity is a concept and practice that arose when teaching PVISDMP in an Indigenous community in Australia. Just as we can be in relationship with others in a way that is beneficial to all, we can be in relationship with ourselves, however we define self, whether we end at our skin or extend to the stars. This relationship begins with our willingness and ability to be still, and to listen interoceptively. A self-reciprocity practice is included in Chapter 5.

Core Rhythmicity. "Core rhythmicity" refers to the myriad rhythms we human beings are. We are polyrhythmic, like the most ancient and sophisticated forms of music. Just consider some of the rhythms and movements in our bodies in the space of one minute:

> Neurons in the brain fire 5–50 times per second.
> Our heart rate is approximately 60–80 beats per minute.
> A standard respiration rate is 12–20 breaths per minute
> Blood pressure feedback loops (vascular rhythmicity) occur every 15–30 seconds
> Beta waves in the brain have a frequency of 12.5–30 Hz (hertz, cycles per second), or 750–1,800 per minute.

A defining feature of trauma is the dysregulation of our usual rhythms. When we are internally dysregulated, we move differently in the world. Oppressors create this intentionally: To oppress, they control the body and the movements of the person and peoples oppressed. Whether it's through detention, death threats, or systemic and pervasive racism, homophobia, and/or discrimination against disabled people and any of our human communities, the effect on our ability to move freely affects, how we act and move through our lives. This ripples into relationships, decisions, and all aspects of our daily living. Likewise, when our endogenous biorhythms are interrupted, distorted, and disrupted by oppression and violence, as occurs in political torture, we can no longer express authentically because we cannot move the way we move. We literally lose our beat, that is, our core rhythmicity. Any practice or process that regulates the ANS restores our core rhythmicity, which is covered more in Chapter 10.

Bioplasticity. Bioplasticity is PVISDMT's reframe of neuroplasticity. In Chapter 4, the concept of neuroception is expanded as it relates to the environmental context that influences our neuroception and perception of relative safety. Part of this expansion includes the term bioception (Conrad, E., personal communication, 2006). Bioception reflects Emilie Conrad's belief that our human bodies are extensions of our natural world, and that we nourish and are nourished by this connection. In her body of work, called Continuum, our human bodies and experiences are part of the ever-unfolding wave of evolution. We are always being created and innovated. Neuroplasticity describes the brains adaptability to alter its structure and function throughout our lives and has replaced an older and now outdated theory that stated the brain was static after puberty. That the brain is centered seems to reflect the human fascination with the brain, and the mind, the latter sometimes seen as arising from the human's more advanced brain than that of all other species, and sometimes, as in the Cartesian mind–body split, seen as elevated beyond the physical brain. Both ideas contribute to the idea that humans with our great brains are superior. Bioplasticity recognizes our whole body connection to the world of all living things. It draws from more indigenously referenced worldviews that sees the human as an interconnected strand in the web of all life. As such, its perhaps not just our brain that can change with novel experiences, but our entire body as the physical expression of who we are.

CHAPTER 2

Dancing in Vagus

Everything in the universe has rhythm. Everything dances.

—MAYA ANGELOU, FACEBOOK, OCTOBER 25, 2011

The Vagus Nerve and the Autonomic Nervous System

Our vagus nerve is central to the neural circuitry of the ANS. It is one and many pathways: It is a single nerve, and it is its many wandering branches. It is named "vagus" for its nomadic tendencies, as "vagus" is a Latin term meaning "wandering." Wander it does, as one nerve with two neural circuits (ventral and dorsal) that are a major part of the parasympathetic nervous system. Figure 2.1 shows a fraction of the many parasympathetic tributaries, streams, and pathways that travel alongside the sympathetic nervous system (SNS). The SNS is often represented as separate from the parasympathetic circuits. They are not completely separate. However they are arranged anatomically and however they function biologically and physiologically in our bodies, they are connected energetically as pathways of a shared wilderness. These pathways release and inhibit energy that, with the peripheral somatic nervous system, informs, shapes and creates our movements; from each subtle breath we may not even notice to all other expressions of movement, including mass migration.

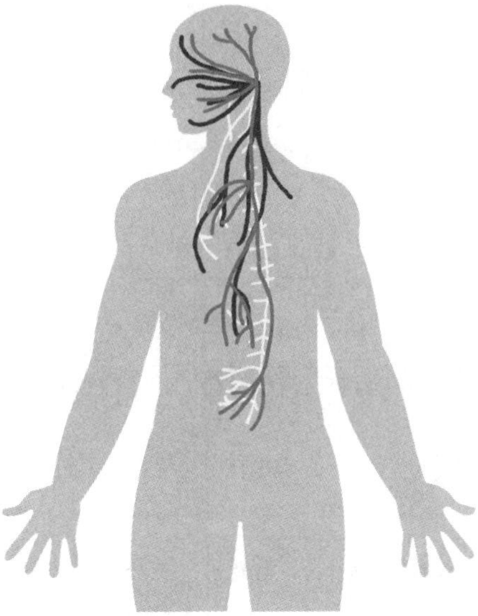

Figure 2.1 The Autonomic Nervous System

The vagus nerve helps pattern us, and its nomadic paths offer potency for change and possibility—for emergence. Our autonomic nervous system is an ancestral trail and an evolutionary pathway, a living gift from our evolutionary ancestors, which includes our human as well as our more-than-human lineage. This framework's nicknames for the vagus nerve are "ancestral nerve" and "nomadic nerve." "Ancestral nerve" acknowledges that our ANS is the ongoing expression of the evolution of the mammalian nervous system. It also reflects the many ways we are interconnected with the world of all things: other mammals and all living creatures, whether two-legged, four-legged, winged, rooted, scaled, or finned. There are now many books, articles, and courses, and a great deal of online information available about the vagus nerve, the vagal circuits, and the ANS. From the perspective of this framework, the vagal circuitry, as part of our entire nervous system and in collaboration with our biochemistry, muscles, bones, and entire body moves us and forms the basis of our perception of the world on a continuum from unsafe to safe, or relatively safe, the subject of Chapter 4. This continuum is a palette of many variances in neurophysiological states that reflect our neuroception (Chapter 4) of relative levels of safety and unsafety and that contribute to what we sense, feel, think, and be.

A Trail and a Path

The vagal circuits are both trail and pathway. Trails are remnants of the past. Wildlife trails, historic Native American trails, and logging roads are all trails. They all show that these areas have been walked and traversed before. The trails remain because they were walked for so long that they become an almost permanent part of the landscape. They can, however, be altered, changed, and removed. These trails are made wherever they are for many reasons: practicality, time, and access to water, for example. The more they are walked, the more they become part of the landscape. This is also true of our ANS, descending from earliest ancestors—who courageously evolved and sometimes successfully became a new species and sometimes died out—and from our own personal ancestral and familial lineage. The human neural circuitry "tracks" these old trails. This tracking is evident in their age: The dorsal is around 500 million years old, the SNS 400 million, and the ventral 200 million. Each arose at a specific time for a specific need in evolutionary history, discussed later in this chapter and explored in depth in Section II.

Our vagal circuitry is part of our vagal complexes. "Circuit" refers to the specific nerve pathways of the ANS. There are three of them. The dorsal is parasympathetic and is the oldest part of the vagus nerve, located below the diaphragm. The sympathetic nervous system came next in our evolution. It originates in the spinal cord and emanates out to target organs like our heart, kidneys, and so on. The parasympathetic ventral vagal circuit is newest; it's the nerve pathways of the vagus nerve above the diaphragm and is known for connecting our face to our heart. The dorsal and vagal circuits are part of the dorsal and vagal complexes, which connect to patterns of recall that are below consciousness. Both the dorsal and ventral vagal complexes refer to the brain stem area that plays a crucial role in how these parasympathetic circuits regulate various bodily functions like digestion and elimination, heart rate, respiration, and even the facial muscles that help regulate our social and relational capacities. The ventral vagal complex includes the social nervous system (cranial nerves 5, 7, 9, 10, and 11) that helps orchestrate our social and relational capacities through all the ways we connect to others: our voice, through vocal prosody. Our eyes and smiles through facial expressivity and gaze. And the way our head tilts when we listen or pay attention to someone. This ancestral trail contributes energy to our remembering; it "feeds" the imprints of exposure and of restoration that become movement patterns rooted in trauma and in resilience. This is why we startle every time we see a red shirt even though the injury done to us by someone in a red shirt happened five years ago. It's why a particular cologne or movement style or tone of voice causes our hair to stand on end or our belly to flutter and feel nauseous or we start to dry heave. This is the pattern of recall that is created in the moment of exposure, which is the subject of Chapter 3.

The field of epigenetics is uncovering and revealing the potency of trauma across generations. The concept of intergenerational trauma, coined and researched by Yael Danieli, or Dr. Maria Yellowhorse Braveheart's "historic trauma," have long described the individual, familial, communal, social, and collective impacts of oppression, colonization, genocide, and human rights violations. Dr. Danieli's work focuses on Holocaust survivors, and Dr. Braveheart's on Indigenous communities of America. Intergenerational trauma becomes an imprint in the vagal trails that continue to promote survival strategies rooted in the ANS circuits and their emergent and patterned states. Intergenerational resilience is also transmitted through these trails. This book is testimony to all the ways the body serves as portal and pathway to healing and restoration, because resilience is also a neural ancestor gifted us by all the layers and eons of not just survival, but "thrival." The ANS and our vagal circuitry are historic ancestral evidence of how connection, cooperation, and collaboration promote life, suggesting that "survival of the funnest" may also be part of our phylogeny.

The ANS is also a nomadic path. Paths are not completely distinct from trails, as a well-worn path eventually becomes a trail. The term "path" also denotes movement toward the future. A path is both the trail we leave behind and the yet-uncharted route in front of us that guides us. The vagus nerve is a nomadic nerve that is part of a much larger neural ecosystem with many interconnections. Nerves, like veins and arteries, are reminiscent of the natural environment and systems we emerge from. Nerves look like tree branches, coral reefs, rivers, and streams that snake their way to larger bodies of water, like ponds, lakes, and oceans. While our connection to the natural world is not the focus of this book, it is essential to remember that the origins of our nervous system are in this natural world we rely on for our existence and are part of. Our nervous systems formed because of our evolutionary ancestors' movements through and interactions with the environment. We can sense, feel, and know through our fleshly connection to the earth and all her elements that evolution is not over, and we are not at the end of the evolutionary trail. We are an expression of how evolution is ongoing. Our nomadic vagal circuitry is also a pathway of emergence. As part of our autonomic, peripheral, and entire nervous system, the vagus nerve, with its origins in the brain stem, influences on our biochemistry, and connection to our whole body, potentiates healing, change, possibility, and liberation.

Memory and Emergence

Emergence is core to this framework. We emerge from and into and toward experiences. We are always emerging. Chapter 3 discusses emergence through movement. While our lives may feel stale or stuck at any time, and many clients are neurophysiologically stuck in truly immobilized states, our ANS is a path that can guide us toward something new. The memories and symptoms or complaints we work with (or experience) are the pattern. In this way, the ANS is both pattern and possibility.

The nervous system seeks novelty, that is, what's new, and what has the potential to meet the new with curiosity. It is the patterning, the fear, exhaustion, and trauma that influence our neuroception, so we meet novelty with fear and uncertainty. This subcortical process, as described in Chapter 4, feeds our perception; therefore, where we aim our attention will affect the choices we make. If we are curious, we may follow a path of emergence, emerging into something new: the possibility. The healing. The change. If we meet this novelty with fear, which is more likely when the nervous system biases toward the negative, it stays stuck in these trails. This is often why clients come to see us. In this latter case, state shifting is the catalyzer of the change toward emergence that makes healing possible.

Predictability is one of the metaphors for relative safety, or as safe as can be, that is essential for this work. Section II contains many state-shifting, pattern-disrupting, polyvagal-informed practices to restore clients' (and our) sense of predictability that, from a somatic or embodied perspective, is a sense of being connected to, engaged with, and able to self-regulate our own body and movement toward safety, comfort, and even liberation.

The Nature of Our Autonomic Nervous System

For my clients who have varying degrees of understanding about, and interest in, the ANS or Polyvagal Theory, nature is both a literal and metaphorical way to share the central role their nervous system and body are playing in their life, their well-being, and the very moment we are in together. Most of the cultural contexts my clients come from are more sociocentric or communal in nature than this mainstream U.S. society where I see them. Obviously, this society has many cultures, so this isn't a blanket statement, although the United States is known for its strong ethos of individualism. Chapter 4 explores this a little more deeply in relationship to safety.

The human nervous system is connected to our sensory systems; therefore, our senses are a portal to our ANS. These connections are living, breathing, ever-moving pathways of communication among nerves, hormones, the various regions of the brain, muscle tissue, bone, and movement, our organs, and more. The lower, or older, part of our brain processes sensory information. Often conceptualized as more primary and referred to as the reptilian brain, there is wisdom in this slower, older part of the brain. It regulates the autonomic functions of our body such as respiration, heart rate, and digestion, and processes sensory information. And our senses are how we first know the world. Prior to our abilities and capacities to think, feel, and connect what we feel inside to what we are going to do, or move, or act, or be, we sense the world. A warm touch. A soothing voice. Glittering lights that cause us to squeal with delight, curious about the movement, brightness, or color—unnamed though it is to a very young life. Connecting to nature is one of the most accessible ways to discover, or rediscover, who we are as human and how central our ANS is to our connection and belonging in this world. Here's one way to do this.

THE NATURE OF ANS PRACTICE

Think of a place you love to be in nature. Or better yet, go to that place if you can. When you arrive, take a moment to pause before entering the space. Whether it's a place you will lie down, sit, stand, or move—pause. Notice with all your senses what you see, hear, smell, taste, and feel on your skin. Elders remind me to ask permission before entering a space and be willing to accept a "no" and move along. If you adopt this practice and sense it's okay to be here, settle into this place.

Once settled, take time to become aware. Awareness is broad; it is casting a wide net with our attention. Once you are aware, notice the entire landscape or space around you, from far away to near. Begin to oscillate between this broad awareness and focused attention. Focused attention means we notice some specific things in this natural setting: a blade of grass. A dewdrop. Maybe the colors in a stone. We pay attention on a continuum, from the most focused fine-tuned attention (e.g., studying a tiny bug or dewdrop on a blade of grass) to noticing all the green in the space around us, which might include grass, tree leaves, flower stems, or a house's shutters. The broader we cast our attention, the more we engage with the spaciousness of awareness. This practice is similar to micromobilizations because it supports clients to refine their attention in ways that increase their capacities for focus, and for paying attention to where they are in the present moment, which can foster a relatively safer and more satisfying connection with the environment.

Continue to oscillate your attention between detailed and panoramic, occasionally practicing very broad awareness of the entire landscape around you.

This practice trains us to have a quality of attention that reflects our presence, which by transmission supports our clients to seen, to feel as safe as can be, and can promote their sense of being present. It also enhances our capacity for attunement. This practice is the basis of an important clinical somatic skill I call "fluid attention." Fluid attention is our capacity to both oscillate our attention from one thing to another sequentially and to hold multiple points of attention at the same time. It's a somatic tracking practice. Fluid attention reflects therapeutic presence.

Now focus on one thing in the environment and spend a moment casting all your attention there. Begin to meet and greet this thing with all your senses. What sound does it make? What colors and textures do you see? Can you hear it? Perhaps it's a leaf that rattles in the wind or water bubbling in a stream. Even if the sound isn't that obvious, listen to its voice. Touching it, how does your skin sense this thing as temperature, texture, contact? If it's safe to taste it, what does it taste like? If not, can you imagine its taste?

Take time to really get to know this thing in a favorite place with all your senses. As you do this, notice how you feel. Tracking the shifts in how you feel is what's called tracking state shifting. You are also tracking changes in your physiological state because these changes—an increased or decreased heart rate or breathing, a relaxed or tense muscle—are the roots of what you feel.

The root of these changes is like shifting tides that are occurring in your autonomic nervous system. Connecting to a natural place in this way offers direct access to our nervous system and is an efficient and meaningful way to get to know both the patterns and the possibilities of our nervous system. The more we practice, the more we can reflect on how and when our heart rate or respiration changes; when our skin feels clammy; when we feel scared or excited; and so on. We can notice if there are specific cues or events or people or situations that ignite these changes. And we can begin somatic and movement-based practices such as those in this book, to consciously shift states and be able to "self-promote" our own well-being.

As an additional practice, if you are open to engaging your sensory imagination—which is a powerful bridge between the past, the present, and future possibilities—take a moment to observe this thing that you've chosen with all your senses at the same time. This is focused attention. Allow yourself to play with this question: What can this object in nature—this tree branch, seashell, stone—teach me about my sensory nervous system? The sensory nervous system connects to both the autonomic and the somatic nervous system. Jot down or journal or doodle whatever comes up, in a free-association, free-flow, creative tracking style. Trust your gut. Don't think about it, and don't edit yourself. Just write, or draw or color, whatever thoughts , images, symbols, words, phrases, etc, that arise.

Here's an example.

Figure 2.2 A Bed of Pine Needles *(Credit: Dang Nguye, Unsplash)*

One of my favorite places in nature is among the pine trees. I like to sit and rest in a bed of pine needles. Figure 2.2 is a picture of a bed of pine needles.

In this recent exploration with pine needles, I noticed the pale beige-brown of their color because they had been on the ground since last season and were no longer green. Touching them, they were brittle and dry and could poke my skin, so I felt a little sting. They smelled different from the pungent green of live pine needles. They had an earthy smell that was a little bit spicy and a little bit musty. Lying on them, I felt my body automatically breathe and exhale deeply. I noticed that I relaxed. I began to drift off into a nap—a rest-and-settle pattern of mine when among pine trees. While I did not taste the pine needles, I can imagine they'd have an astringent taste, partially from my memory of once biting one. This memory causes a little surprised jolt in my body, because I don't love astringent flavors. This creatively demonstrates how the ANS is pattern, that is, it is part of the whole-body experience that remembers because it holds some imprints of past experience that affect what we feel (like distaste) now. It is its wandering, nomadic nature that can connect and reconnect. This allows us, when timing and context are safe enough, to create new and emergent neural pathways, feelings, and experiences. This is the possibility.

Here's a way to playfully explore the idea of possibility through the many pathways the vagus nerve is. This practice is helpful for clients who see the world more metaphorically and are not as drawn to learning science. Because it is a playful activity, it can also help clients who are stuck in patterns of mobilization activation, that is, mobilization in fear, the primary state arising from the sympathetic nervous system of the ANS. This process can help them sideways state shift to playful expression of an engaged mobilization and connected state, that is, a hybrid ventral and sympathetic state.

Nature is a mirror of our own inner landscape. For this practice, I pretend that a scattered clump of pine needles is an image of my ANS, and it can even be an image of the interconnectedness of my entire nervous system. After observing a pile or clump of needles, I pick them

Figure 2.3 A Bed of Pine Needles With Three Arrangements Circled *(Credit: Dang Nguye, Unsplash)*

up and toss them back on the ground, I observe and imagine how the image of the just-fallen needles might look like a neural circuit or circuits, depending on how they land. I get curious about what it might teach me about the ANS. I toss the handful of pine needles several times and notice how they land in many different arrangements, and how each time, there are some breaks or disconnects. There are also places where they still connect. Even with the breaks between individual needles, there is a lineage or sequence of connection that connects them all.

Take a look at both Figure 2.2 and Figure 2.3 to see this. Figure 2.3 represents the newly tossed pile of pine needles. This time, there are three circles on the picture to show three new arrangements of pine needles. While I did not actually toss these piles you can see three different examples of pine needle arrangement in this specific place.

It's an adventure with the imagination and the autonomic nervous system that can encourage playfulness. As an extension and reflection of the natural world we evolve from, the ANS is an ongoing and constant dance between the environment (including the natural world, and human created environments such as offices, kitchens, and cars) and us. Our inner landscape or terrain senses the outer landscape or terrain we are moving through, and the ANS is, in Dr. Porges's words, the "intervening variable," or the space in between. This is neuroception, which is covered in Chapter 4.

Our ANS shapes the patterns that inform how we meet the world. As we interact with the environment, the ANS can signal danger or life threat based on environmental cues rooted in past experience. And it is emergent, which means a new experience—a comforting touch, a beautiful image, or soothing words—can shift how we feel in a way that we experience as delight, discovery, connection, reassurance or awe. This state shift heralds a recruitment of the vagal brake, when the ventral vagal circuit is in a metaphorical "governance" or "conductor" role. This is covered more in depth later in this chapter. Our perception of the environment shifts, and we feel different inside. This may not fix the "breaks" in the ANS, and it may create new connections, just like tossing the pine needles does. This is the emergent nature of our ANS, which parallels the natural world, constantly shifting to pattern, de-pattern, and re-pattern in ways that can elicit meaningful, hopeful change.

Our nervous system has many pathways of communication depending upon what happens or how we meet the world. Each time I toss the pine needles, I notice the points of connection and the points of disconnection. There is always a place where they are connected, and this represents the streaming of information of a "humming" ANS. Whether it's pine needles or a coral reef or a forest of trees, our nervous system echoes the shape of the branches and waterways of the natural world. This is a helpful way for clients to get a sense of their own nervous system when the actual science is not accessible. Many of my clients are delighted to look at a book and learn about the nervous system, and just as many would rather embody the experience of the nervous system in this way. The point is for them to understand how engaging with the environment and the world in new ways can change the way they feel, and this change is a state shift, and that state shifting is both an emergent process of our ANS and a pathway to their restored capacity to consciously state-shift in ways that are regulating, healing, and hopeful.

Ancestral Nerve: The Vagal Lineage

Mother Nature is the original ANS map. The evolution of the mammalian nervous system is thoroughly described in several books: Stephen W. Porges's *The Polyvagal Theory* (2011), Deb Dana's very practical clinical perspective *The Polyvagal Theory in Therapy: Engaging the Rhythm of Regulation* (2018), and Stanley Rosenberg's *Accessing the Healing Power of the Vagus Nerve* (2017) all describe this evolution. The ANS is both a gift from the natural world and a reflection of it. Writing about it as rivers and coral reefs may seem metaphorical, and there may also be scientific merit to this. The evolution of species surviving (and not) in a variety of natural environments is threaded into our physical bodies, including our ANS. The practices shared in this chapter have supported many clients to understand the impact of their constantly changing environments, relationships, and interactions on their nervous system. As covered in Chapter 4, these practices are explorations of the relationship of inside, outside, and in between.

Our Autonomic Triad: A Story of Evolution

This chapter's description of the ANS, the vagus nerve, and its many pathways are based on extensive clinical experience and the dedicated application of Polyvagal Theory to work with survivors of human rights abuses. *This is what polyvagal-informed means: grounded in science and understood or interpreted through a somatic, movement-based clinical lens.* Scientific research begins as inquiry born of intuitive hunches. The accuracy of our own experience of our bodies is valid data.

The evolution of the vagus nerve is a story of ancestry and lineage. It is also a story of nomadic emergence, because it is still moving. This evolution is both the trail behind us and the path before us. It is etched through evolutionary time by the incredible courage of our evolutionary ancestors experimenting with life. Some survived, some did not. Entire species arose from these experiments that both shaped our nervous system (and all aspects of our physical bodies) and were guided by its unfolding.

The oldest branch of the autonomic nervous system is the dorsal vagal circuit (DVC). This circuit is part of the parasympathetic branch or pathway of the ANS, which is around 500 million years old. The reptilian world has its own version of this circuitry; the mammalian nervous system has an "updated" version. The dorsal is named for its relationship to the ventral. Dorsal means back and ventral means front. The dorsal circuit emerges from the same area in our old or reptilian brain, called the medulla oblongata, as the ventral, but it emerges behind the ventral. It is fascinating and apt that these two branches are named relationally, given their powerful influence on our experience of human relationships. The medulla oblongata is part of the brain stem, and it regulates our autonomic functions such as breathing, heart rate, and digestion.

The three neural circuits of the ANS each contribute to a primary neurophysiological state. A neurophysiological state can perhaps be described somatically as an energy that will give rise to an action that is in service of our survival. This energy reflects the primary survival strategy that emerged evolutionarily to protect the species it emerged in. Without this strategy, the species may not have made it, and there would have been a full stop in that evolutionary pathway.

Dorsal Vagal Circuit: The Wise Old Vagus

The dorsal vagal circuit emerges from the dorsal nucleus of the cortex and travels slightly behind the ventral vagal branch. It travels alongside the heart and innervates or connects to it at the sinoatrial node, an area of specialized muscle fibers in the right atrium of the heart that initiate the heartbeat. This innervation is a vagal brake because of its ability to immediately slow heart rate down when we perceive life threat and immobilize in terror, the primary neurophysiological state arising from this ancient circuit, and shut down, the survival strategy arising from this state. These strategies are also referred to as actions, or in the case of shutdown and freeze, inactions in this framework. The DVC continues traveling downward, innervating the stomach, and the viscera, and connecting to a vast neural network of deep nonverbal bio-intelligence that intuitively must be our gut instinct.

When we "trust our gut," it refers to deep in our belly, subdiaphragmatic, and, as such, is our *deep belly wisdom*, or *inner wisdom pool.* It is the wellspring of our primary, sensory bio-intelligence. The DVC is both the seat of terror and the seat of bliss. Referred to as the old vagus, this ancient circuit is also the wise vagus. And because it is oldest in evolutionary lineage, it seems possible that many of its fibers might originate in this deeper inner space.

It is the seat of terror because it is the neural circuit that immobilizes us when we feel terror associated with the subconscious neuroception and arising conscious perception of life threat. In that moment it becomes the dominant governance of our ANS. Imagine waking up in a cave after seeking shelter from a storm and realizing it is the home of an apex predator, like a cave bear. Faced with the growling, drooling, hungry predator, you'd confront (almost) certain death. Terrified, our DVC is recruited, and we immobilize in terror. The biochemical cascade to brain function that co-occurs with the rapid neurophysiological state shift to terror shuts us down. This causes the primary state known as immobilization in terror, which leads to shutdown. It is primary because it emerges instantaneously and subconsciously from the DVC's override of the newer neural circuits. Consciously, we perceive life threat and a subsequent registering of terror. This neurophysiological state shift results in a very slowed-down heart rate and respiration, loss of tonicity in muscles, and evacuation of our bowels. It is part of an extreme slowing down for survival. It is a brilliant, ancient strategy of feigning death to ward off the potential predator or threat. This is mercy: We are flooded with endorphins, which increase our pain tolerance, so we suffer less when faced with death. Vasovagal syncope can sometimes be a consequence of this neurophysiological immobilization and subsequent shutdown state.

Vasovagal syncope is caused by a trigger in the environment that causes your heart rate and blood pressure to drop suddenly, which leads to reduced blood flow to the brain, resulting in a brief loss of consciousness. In DVC shutdown, the loss of consciousness may be more extended. This is why dissociation is often a behavioral imprint of shutting down. Any future triggers in the environment that remind us of that moment of exposure can cause the same neurophysio-biochemical reaction, reinforcing trauma feedback loops.

This shutdown is a profound survival strategy or (in)action. Shutdown as an (in)action bypasses the SNS. In other words, we don't retrace the hierarchy of evolution. It also seems related to the old behavioral term "peri-traumatic dissociation," which described dissociation in the moment of exposure. This is considered a risk for the increased likelihood of traumatization. Somatically, dissociation reflects a subconscious, dysregulating state shift that has become a patterned survival strategy to help us continue surviving after actual exposure, based on the original imprint. Dissociation is often associated with shutdown and freeze reactions only. The SNS can also create dissociation because of its intensity. Clinically, these dissociative responses present differently. When the SNS is involved, a client can be spaced out, flat, and exhibit many of the more common features of dissociation with the neurophysiological expression of the SNS—rapid heart rate, fluttering eyes, fast respiration, twitching limbs.

The DVC roots the autonomic nervous system. Rooting is our deepest connection to the earth. Connecting to earth, we connect to gravity, and this is how we are shaped to move. Gravity is the first and most constant lover; her embrace is always there for us. Gravity connects us to weight and its emergent process of yield. This is how we know our place and find a sense of belonging. The DVC promotes a sense of yield. It is metaphorically the ocean that buoys the ventral vagal circuit, which is often described separately. They are not separate, however. They are connected, and they co-carve many neural pathways of both pattern and possibility. Yield is a state of receptivity that perhaps epitomizes the way the DVC supports the VVC and their ongoing bidirectional communication: trails and pathways in service of not only our survival but also as taproots to place and belonging. And to our shared humanity. Together in their unified neural dance, they promote yield to root and settle and be receptive to support, to access mobilization and movement (SNS) when needed to survive or for play, and to rise (VVC) into connection and relationship.

Many clients understand the DVC as the foundation of our deep wisdom pool and a wellspring for our intuition. It is a portal to the ancient, and while most often associated with its ability to shut us down for survival, it is also the portal to states associated with nourishment, union, and harmony, like those that are exalted in many spiritual practices. These more relational connected states are traditionally considered a hybrid (hybrid = two primary states together) of DVC (immobilization) and VVC (safe enough for connection and feeling our wholeness). This is true, and these states would not be possible without the DVC and its deep roots in our reptilian ancestors and kin, who know the sensation of warm earth on their bellies. In contemplative practice, we can be in states of nourishment, like active or passive rest, solo, that is, by ourselves with nature, or it can be a deep sense of peace that we cultivate within ourselves and with our own breath and heartful, bodyful, mindful practices. In other words, the relationship does not need to be with other humans. Intuitively, the DVC alone must have its own ability to create states of stillness in the presence of safe-enough environments, or where our own inner safe environment/climate feels safe enough, to slow us down in service of "rest and digest." From an elemental perspective, this is the deep roots, the earth connection of our body. It is also a portal to our human understory through evolution, spirit, and all the ancient wisdom they offer.

Sympathetic Nervous System: Spine as Initiation, Movement, and Uprising

The SNS is the sympathetic branch of the ANS. This system is multicircuited and is referred to throughout this book as a circuit for consistency. The SNS is thought to have emerged in early vertebrates around 400 million years ago. Its emergence marks a time when a new survival strategy was needed because immobilization—hiding, feigning death, shutting down to complete stillness—was not enough protection or defense. Think of a brightly colored fish in the ocean when a hungry ocean dwelling predator sees it. It cannot stay still because it is too visible and will become dinner. The domain of the SNS is movement and it evolved when movement became necessary for survival. We recruit the SNS when we need to move. Alone, it is energy for activation. When we perceive danger (which is different than life threat), we feel fear. This mobilization in fear, an activation, is the primary neurophysiological state arising from the SNS. It fuels the action of fight or flight as well as freeze, a DVC/SNS hybrid state. It is this feeling of fear that arises from the neurophysiological state shift that increases heart rate first, followed in milliseconds by respiration, blood pressure, and the shifting of blood to our limbs to enable us to move. A flash of fear can become a subconscious trigger that recruits the SNS and increases heart rate, catalyzing all the neurophysiological and biochemical changes such as surges in cortisol, norepinephrine, and adrenaline (epinephrine) that energize us to move. Mobilization in fear or activation to protect and defend is the primary neurophysiological state arising from the recruitment of the SNS.

While the SNS is a distinct branch in the autonomic nervous system, it is connected to the parasympathetic in the way that the pile of pine needles is always connected, no matter which way they land on the ground. The SNS originates in the spinal column and its cord. It branches out to all the target organs such as the stomach, kidneys, and heart. The human spine is an origin place for human movements.

In utero, prior to the development of our spine, our breathing and movement is jellyfish and starfish like. Pulsating and radiating from our navel center, we ripple to breathe and move. When our spine develops, we begin to explore movement through tiny pulsations of the spine. These pulsations are small spinal pushes and reaches between our head and tail, and they initiate more dynamic, dimensional movement with our whole body. With the SNS's origins in the spinal cord—and its outreach to target organs like heart, kidney, lungs—movement becomes the center of the ANS, and the spine becomes a moving center. It "bridges" the DVC and VVC. In this way the spine and the SNS are a crossroads of the ANS. A crossroads is a potent meeting place that invites the new—and movement is always new. As axis mundi, the spine is the energetic verticality between heaven and earth, meeting the horizontal dimension humans walk while on earth. We rise from horizontal to vertical just as the SNS "rises us" above the dorsal. This rising is the connection between these two branches. One shuts us down and helps us calm, center, and ground and nourishes us in union. The other moves us toward relationship.

Ventral Vagal Circuit: Wholeness and Flow

The VVC is flow. This highly myelinated vagal pathway is above the diaphragm, and the streaming of communications in this region—which includes the heart, lungs, striated muscles of the face, middle ear muscle, and esophagus and extends indirectly to the appendages—is faster due to this myelin sheath. This fatty sheath is like high-speed internet compared to the slow-moving, nonmyelinated DVC, which is more like dial-up internet. This heart-to-face pathway is uniquely mammalian, and so it is both poetic and true that what we feel in our heart is reflected in our face. Our gaze, facial expression, smile, neck tilt, and posture all reflect our heart. The VVC is, in many ways, a

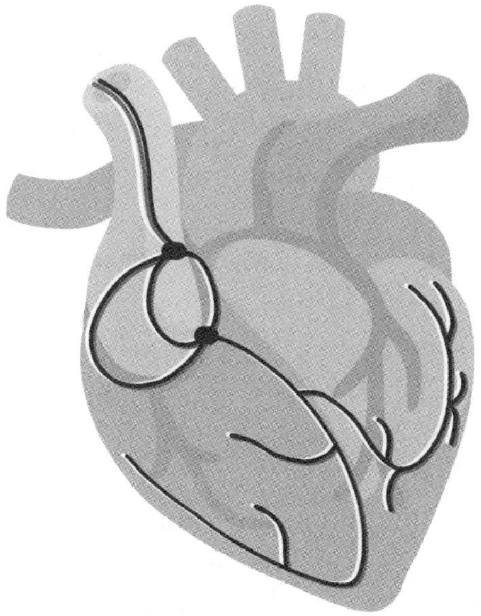

Figure 2.4 The Heart as Hub

governing circuit. It is also a "conductor." When it is recruited to govern the flow of the ANS, it is literally inhibiting the inputs or energies supplied by SNS and the DVC, like a conductor quiets the brass and percussion sections so the wind section can be heard. This supports the larger ANS in its conducting role. It also innervates the heart in the sinoatrial node, which is known as the vagal brake. This is where its primary action is to inhibit the SNS sinoatrial neural fiber innervation when the environment is safe enough to support states of wholeness. That the heart (see Figure 2.4) is innervated by all three neural circuits of the ANS centers the heart as choreographer of our movement, emotional regulation and psychological wholeness.

The VVC is often referred to in isolation, but it isn't. By virtue of its structure, location, physiology, and action, it is core to our social and relational capacities. The VVC is the circuit that, when recruited, creates a state of relative safety and flow that allows us to be socially engaged and feel whole.

Like the DVC, the 200 million-year-old "new vagus" VVC also originates within the medulla oblongata, but in the nucleus ambiguus. It travels in front of the DVC alongside the carotids and esophagus and ascends the groove that forms between the esophagus and trachea to innervate the larynx, crucial to our breathing, sounding, swallowing and singing. It's connected to the social nervous system of cranial nerves 5, 7, 9, 10, and 11 that are part of the extended ventral vagal complex. These cranial nerve pairs help our mouths chew, kiss, and suck. These pairs help our face recognize pain and touch sensations in our face such as hot or cold; they control facial movement and expressivity, tear and taste production; they help us swallow and move the tissue of our throat to support vocalizations; they sense pain in the throat, filter safe from unsafe sounds; regulate heart rate affecting heart rate variability; shrug the shoulders and tilt the head, and support our shifting, moving posture. Think about how central our face and our facial expression is to human connection, and how we orient to and get to know one another. Facial expressivity in another human cues us to whether we are attracted to them and vice versa. The idea of the neutral or poker face long advocated for therapists is passé, given that our face is where our clients read our kindness and accessibility and search for cues that promote their own sense of relative safety.

The VVC vagal brake is particularly important because when the brake is "on," this promotes vagal tone. The SNS also innervates the sinoatrial node. Vagal tone is the VVC inhibiting this neural feed that increases our heart rate. Vagal tone is a scientific measure that indicates a neurophysiological state that promotes enough safety for social engagement. Often detected through heart rate variability (the fluctuations of time between your heartbeats, which in this framework relates to our heart's natural capacity to vary its rhythm in response to physiological, metabolic, and physical needs) or respiratory sinus arrythmia (a normal variation in heart rate that occurs when inhaling and exhaling), vagal tone can be considered a measure of our integrated flow and sense of wholeness. Vagal efficiency is a newer concept that refers to our ability to restore vagal tone after times of stress, distress, depletion, suffering, and fear. When the world places demands on us that take us out of our natural rhythm, our capacity to restore is a function of vagal efficiency. Therapy, and somatic and movement therapies, are particularly helpful to maintain our vagal efficiency because movement always includes posture change, even if it's miniscule. Any time we shift posture we state shift, and this can promote vagal tone. This does not always mean we are automatically healed or in a safe enough state for social engagement. It means we begin state shifting in the direction of feeling safer.

The Noble Pathway

This intricate ANS pathway, and the longest and most meandering vagus nerve, like the belly, heart, and brain, is also refered to as a noble pathway in this framework. The belly brain was proposed "as a fact" by neurobiologist Dr. Michael Gershon in 1999 (p. 3). The idea of a heart brain is not new; one of my first Indigenous teachers made sure I understood that our true intelligence is fed when we are developing in utero in the fetal curled shape because our hearts and brains are proximal.

The energetic connection made possible by this proximal spatial relationship contributes to true intelligence, the heartmind intelligence, because our feeling and thinking worlds are integrated. It is interesting that Polyvagal Theory illuminates that the ventral vagal circuit's bidirectional pathway between heart and brain is the pathway of fastest information conductivity. Neurocardiology researcher Dr. J. Andrew Armour introduced the concepts of the heart as sensory organ (vs. the previously held idea that it was just an involuntary muscle pump) and of a functional heart brain (Sneijders, 2024, p. 1) with a vast intrinsic nervous system. Known to have pathways of communication in each brain, the vagal pathway offers efferent (away) and afferent (toward) communication along this noble pathway. This is part of our interoceptive wisdom, our access to our *konysans*, the inner wisdom pool whose wellsprings is our deep gut intuition, in the dorsal realm.

Primary, Hybrid, and Blended States

The three circuits of the ANS, the DVC, SNS, and VVC contribute to primary, hybrid, and blended states when recruited by environmental and internal changes and demands. These states can all be emergent—for instance, those that are recruited in the moment of exposure as described in the following chapter—or they can be patterned. Patterned refers to how the imprint of that exposure, also described in Chapter 3, becomes the "bias for negativity" the ANS gets stuck in, contributing to and creating the complaints, symptoms, and conditions arising from the trauma feedback loop that therapists work with. The primary state of the DVC is immobilization when we feel terror. This ensures our survival when facing life threat because we no longer move and are less interesting to predators. We shut down to increase our chance of survival. The primary state of the SNS is mobilization in fear, or activation. This SNS state is one of energy to mobilize and move. This ensures our survival through movement—action to flee and to defend and protect, that is, fight, which are the two primary actions arising from a state of activation. This activation becomes the movement that gets us out of the way of danger.

The primary state of the VVC is safe enough to support social engagement, flow, connection, and wholeness. This is an integrative state that is governed by the VVC and supported by the other two circuits. We can relate and socialize while being relaxed and calm, or enthusiastically energized, and we can move volitionally to interact, or not, with the environment, spaces, and people around us. The VVC's recruitment supports a receptive, grounded, and open-hearted yield state. Yield is an action that supports all our movements. Social engagement as an action arises from this safe-enough-to-relate state, and wholeness acknowledges the overall function, impact, and reach of the ventral vagal complex, governing and conducting, to keep the ANS humming and our neurophysiological, emotional and psychological states, and movement, flowing.

This framework also puts forward the idea that the DVC promotes a state of immobilization that supports the actions of deep rest and settling. This is a harmonic state that nourishes us. In this framework it's called the continuum of nourishment.

Hybrid states are the neurophysiological and biochemically induced emotional and psychological states that arise from the recruitment of two neural circuits due to the demands of our inner climate or the outer environment. They are sometimes called blended states in other contexts. Hybrid is preferred for PVISDMP to distinguish it from the other blended states that emerge from the recruitment of three neural circuits, referred to as blended states in this framework. It's important to note that primary, hybrid, and blended states can all become patterned; in other words, they can reflect the trail from the imprint of exposure in our ANS that creates and contributes to clients' ongoing symptoms and complaints from a seemingly neverending trauma feedback loop. They can also all arise emergently in the moment as a new reaction to danger or life threat. The language used in this book is chosen for distinction and consistency. The DVC and SNS together cocreate a combined immobilization/mobilization state, which invokes the action/inaction of freeze. Freeze differs from shutdown because sympathetic activation is happening at the same time as the DVC immobilization. The oft-used metaphor to describe this is an automobile brake and accelerator pedals being pushed at the same time. This can happen when we are in extreme or sustained states of activation that overwhelm our system, and the parasympathetic DVC brake is recruited to restore homeostasis. The SNS's engagement intuitively must recruit varying degrees of energy and acceleration. A freeze state also describes an archer who is poised to release an arrow. There is no fear; there is intense focus and stillness supported by energy and alertness. The archer's freeze is active, but their still focus—a fearless focus—keeps the energy tightly contained to hit the target. This SNS energy of mobilization without fear also promotes the more playful side of activation and energy. Freeze occurs on a continuum as well, so this state and action is called the continuum of freeze.

The SNS and VVC together cocreate mobilization without fear, a play-inducing state. Play, the action, exists on a continuum, from gentle sensual play to competitive fierce play to erotic play to lyrical fun and childlike play. As such, these play states are also emergent; the "percentage" of input from each neural circuit is influenced by the context and environment. Volleyball requires a very different type of energy than sexual foreplay. Dancing requires a very different type of combined mobilization and safe-enough energy compared to boxing, running competitively, or running into the ocean joyfully to dive into the waves.

The DVC and VVC together can cocreate nourishment states and actions such as rest and digest, rest and settle, or intimacy and harmonious union. I often describe this as taking a siesta after a delicious meal or falling asleep in the arms of our beloved after lovemaking. It is more than that, however. It is also a state of union we can achieve through meditation, contemplative practice, ritual, and ceremony, and I believe it pertains to trance states common in many traditional healing rituals and ceremonies. It describes the states of oneness we can experience in the natural world when forest bathing or sitting in an outdoor hot tub or camping. I wonder if spiritual masters can attain this state almost solely through recruitment of the DVC, the wise old vagus. This seems plausible when the mind is so quiet that we are rooted and centered in our body, relating solely to our own internalized sense of peace, quiet, or stillness, or connected deeply to Spirit through prayer, meditation, or movement. I imagine the sacrum is in the fluid, still point of sacral neutral to an extent that our spine's interoceptive pathway is more open so we can access our own deep wisdom pool without the distractions of the external world or a busy mind.

Emergent states are those that arise in our daily lives from a novel exposure or experience, whether pleasurable or adverse. Emergent is used in this framework to highlight that there is a continuum of neurophysiological and emotional/psychological states humans experience that are immediate and/or transient. They are both mundane and subtle, and dramatic and intense. Some of them are unnamed because we can move through them very quickly at times. None of these states are static, and all emergent states, particularly those that involve more than one circuit, move. Patterned states refers to the states that amplify the trauma feedback loop that creates symptoms, complaints, and behavior or action changes. The neural circuits involved are recruited continuously to subconsciously shift our neurophysiological, biochemical, physical, and emotional states in response to ongoing fear-provoking changes and demands in the world around us. This creates ANS dysregulation, and while this is in service of our ongoing survival, it segregates us from our sense of wholeness and belonging. To constantly be subconsciously reminded of the initial exposure and imprint and feel it all over again is what being traumatized is. Any neurophysiological state, when novel, is emergent. We can experience them once or a few times in a lifetime, and of course what's once emergent, with enough opportunities to "replay," can also become learned or patterned. The movement patterns arising from trauma imprinting and patterning become survival strategies and can occur individually, or as a dyadic, family, communal, and/or collective strategy.

Appeasement and fawning are currently a popular and important subject in trauma work, especially from a decolonizing perspective. They merit more coverage than this acknowledgment. In this work, appeasement is the most common blended and patterned survival strategy clients refer to and exhibit. This is likely due to the context in which their exposure occurs and the nature of the forced relationship in human rights abuse secondary to war, organized violence, and torture, which is different than other contexts for forced relationships. Faced with danger, life threat, or both as the perpetrator alters their methods of abuse to increase suffering, survivors can employ the emergent strategy of appeasement that arises from recruitment of all three circuits. Clients describe experiencing immobilization, mobilization, and relationality all at once. One of my clients described this as feeling frozen deep inside her body, breaking out in a cold sweat, and at the same time feeling her heart rate increase while heat spread in her skin. This, in my clinical observation, demonstrates the moving, shifting nature of blended emergent states and actions. Another client described being very dizzy and spaced out and at the same time being able to focus on the face and the hands of the perpetrator and tracking them that so that he could engage in ways to please the perpetrator and reduce harm. This action regulates the perpetrator's nervous system. Appeasement is often described as a state, but that is inaccurate. It is a survival strategy or action that can arise emergently and often becomes a necessary pattern of survival strategy. As a patterned action, it is one that anyone who lives in fear, is oppressed, and/or lives in a society that is built on institutionalized racism will engage and express out of survival necessity. Appeasement can be both the trail, a reflection of a prior neurophysiological state imprint, and the path: an emergent response to danger or threat that necessitates managing the perpetrator's state so that the person being abused survives.

Appeasement is its own complex topic worthy of interrogation through a polyvagal, social justice, and rights-based perspective. Appeasement can be so nuanced that it's barely noticeable to an observer. Related to this, many members of a dominant culture who are predominantly white descendants of colonizers have developed a well-conditioned practice of not noticing, which perpetuates the environment that requires members of our community to appease those holding power in any relational interaction. This is a complex reality that is built on the foundation of institutionalized racism in U.S. society, and this is why Jennifer Mullan's (2023) aforementioned book *Decolonizing Therapy* and several other books (e.g., *My Grandmother's Hands* by Resmaa Menakem [2017] and *Decolonizing Trauma Work: Indigenous Strategies and Stories* by Renee Linklater [2014], among many others), are essential reading for all therapists. Rae Johnson and

Nkem Ndefo's 2021 article "When Agreement Is Not Consent" offers a comprehensive explanation of appeasement. This racism permeates health care, mental health, education, and all major facets of American society. When the environment always, often, or many times sends signals to someone that they are less than, in danger, or threatened, the very real embodied experience of oppression, anger, and fear—and impacts of bias and racism—means the ANS must constantly recalibrate through fear and life-threat states so that its human body can navigate the unsafe terrain and survive. Many of my clients talk about how tracking the perpetrator's needs, especially when they were being violated, helped them tolerate their dysregulating nervous system while they attempted to escape pain, and sometimes, the perpetrator. This is a complex emotional experience that contributes to extended shame and isolation. "Placating," which is the preferred term for this framework, seems more accurate than the more ubiquitous term "fawning," for my clients. Placating is a soothing of the other's nervous system in an emergent or patterned state–driven act of survival. One client described it as "using the right words and attitude to calm the perpetrator down" to decrease the client's risk. Some clients describe it as part of appeasement. This may be due to the specific context of political torture and war my clients have survived. Fawning, a people-pleasing response, derives from the meaning of the term as exhibiting excessive flattery or affection, often inauthentically. That the survivors I've worked with don't use or relate to this term doesn't undermine its relevance to other survivor communities from different contexts of interpersonal and relational trauma. These survivor-centered language distinctions have helped my clients and me to understand the origins, meaning, and relevance to the restorative process of their state-shifting patterns in a survivor-centered, trauma-, and polyvagal-informed practice.

THE NOMADIC NERVE EXPLORATION PRACTICE

This is a practice to track your vagus nerve pathways. It is a creative process I use with students to teach both the general anatomy and neurophysiology of the ANS and vagal pathways. It is also a practice to prime intuitive awareness and understanding of our own ANS, neural patterns, and states. It's a creative, intuitive process.

Optional: Get a piece of paper, some Sculpey clay or other modeling clay, pen and paper, your favorite instrument—anything that helps you be creative. Get as physically comfortable as you can, lying down or sitting. Do any practice that helps you settle.

Rest your hand behind your head, in the occiput—the cradle at the base of your skull. This is near the origin of both vagal circuits, the dorsal (dorsal cortex of the vagus) and the ventral (nucleus ambiguus). Place hands on each circuit's origin place, either simultaneously or sequentially. Pause. Sense or intuit what's there. You may imagine sounds you can make or sing; images, symbols, words, even gestures or movement sequences. Play with this as creatively as you enjoy. If you want, take a moment to draw, sculpt, write, color, sound, or move what you sense here.

Continue this very same process while visiting each of the neural circuits. You can trace the pathways the way you sense or intuit them between each circuit, or not. I invite students to trace the VVC by tracing the space from the occiput along their neck (the VVC passes alongside the carotids) and then bringing their hands up to their face to massage around the eyes, mouth, ears, and all through the face and neck, connecting physically and energetically to the nerve fibers of the VVC. Then trace one hand down to the heart, imagining you can touch the sinoatrial node—the "kiss of the beloved"—where a VVC fiber inhibits the SNS fibers to maintain our heart rate variability, vagal tone, and flow. Repeat the process of engaging intuitively and creatively with these areas; it does not matter if you trace the exact anatomical area. You can look that up in an anatomy book or on a reputable website. Or see Figure 2.1 for a simple scaffold.

From the VVC, you can choose to go in order of reverse evolution and find the SNS, which is roughly between your T1 (your first thoracic vertebra) and L2 (your second lumbar vertebra). It originates in the spinal cord. It can be hard to palpate, so you can also lie on your back and imagine this area massaging the floor. If you can touch this area, give it a little energetic massage to honor its initiation of your movements.

After repeating the creative, intuitive process, return your hands to the origin place—the medulla oblongata and the DVC origin of the dorsal nucleus of the cortex—by placing them once again in the occiput and imagining you can touch deep into this area of the reptilian brain. You can also do this immediately after tracing the VVC, which is out of reverse evolution order but tracks the pathways of the vagus nerve more seamlessly. Trace down your body imagining the vagal pathway behind the VVC, winding around the heart (with its own neural fiber innervating the sinoatrial node), spiraling below your diaphragm and connecting through a sheath of fiber into your viscera and guts. Figure 2.4 shows this.

Many students like to place one hand on their belly and the other on their sacrum, cradling the pelvic bowl, or cradle, area. Either way, rest your hands into the DVC and repeat the creative process, drawing, sculpting, singing, moving, dancing, reciting, writing poetry, or scribbling your sense of your DVC. Take some time, if you enjoy creative process, to create a choregraphed dance, a song, a poem, art—anything.

This process helps clients and students develop an intuitive sense of their own personal ANS. This, in turn, helps cultivate the skills of tracking the nervous system so we familiarize ourselves with our own ANS states and patterns. This embodied exploration also helps us awaken possibility. Most scientific inquiry begins with intuition, which is an emergent process of our interoceptive capacity. Many clients discover sensations in the ANS circuit exploration that help them understand the feeling states and actions that arise when they are recruited. This is a useful beginning to our ongoing work together and galvanizes their connection to the source of how they sense, feel, taste, touch, hear, and see the world.

CHAPTER 3

Trauma and the Moving Body

> Movement, to be experienced, has to be found in the body, not put on like a dress coat. There is that in us which has moved from the very beginning: it is that which can liberate us.
>
> —MARY WHITEHOUSE, "PHYSICAL MOVEMENT AND PERSONALITY," 1999

One college summer I worked in Maine. I often walked a paved path by the ocean in the mornings. Frequently, a woman whose name I never learned would ride up to me on her bike and say, "Movement is life." I always enjoyed these brief proclamations from this free-spirited woman who epitomized that time period of the 1960s and 1970s. We rarely conversed, but I still remember her face, posture, twinkling eyes, and enthusiasm when she spoke. Her words remain with me and many a client has heard them too.

Movement Is Life

Movement is central to life, and more urgently so in a society that has increasingly created situations where sitting for long hours is commonplace and accepted in education, employment, and elsewhere. In fact, at the time of writing, following a global pandemic that moved most of us online for extended periods of time, movement can seem like something we have to plan to do instead of the essence of who we are.

Emilie Conrad, creator of Continuum, states, “Movement is not something we do. It’s who we are” (personal communication, July 12, 1999). The human body is movement. We are polyrhythmic, and our rhythms are ever-changing, which is emergent change. Each moment of our embodied living offers a cross-section of rhythms, pulsations, and vibrations. Our breath and our heart rate are distinct and interconnected rhythms. All of our rhythms fluctuate in response to change around and within us. The rhythms we sense and feel are just a fraction of all the rhythms and pulsations that are occurring in our bodies that inspire, support, and maintain the movement we are.

Evolution. Human development. Migration. Art. Dance. Music. Birth. Death. Everything is movement. Even stillness is movement. Movement exists on a continuum from deep “pools” of stillness (called “still pools” in this framework) to dynamic, large movements—like dancing, running, and bold gesturing—of the physical body. Movement describes the pulsing light of a star, long dead. Its light, through movement, reaches us from many light years away. Movement describes the forced migration of several hundred or 4 million people, fleeing persecution or disaster. Movement also describes the mass migration of birds and butterflies, the sound of a hummingbird’s super-quick wings beating, and the cilia along a paramecium as it glides through our inner fluid.

How Trauma Moves Us

Trauma affects our movement. It stills it, freezes it, shifts its various expressions. The body can develop new trauma-based movement patterns that can overwhelm our usual movement patterns, which are biologically and culturally informed. Movement patterns consist of nonvolitional movement, that is, all the neurological and biological wiring that is subconscious and that we don’t need to consciously direct to move. In simple terms, it's why we can open a door or turn on a car or pick a book up without thinking about all the micromovements and neurobiophysiological streams of communication that create the movement. How we move also has volitional elements, and a dancer is an illustrative example of this. If you've ever seen a dance performance, you'll know that dancers use their movement to communicate. They can move slowly and spiraling or fast and staccato. How they move—which combines breath, muscle tension, energy flow, facial expression, tempo, and so much more—will influence our emotional and aesthetic experience. This is volitional movement, and we all do both. We use movement to communicate how we feel, and it's how we get practical things done. It's life.

From the individual to the collective, trauma is an embodied, somatic experience. If we consider each body as a community of biological, neurological, physiological relationships, the interdependence of all the rhythms and inner micromovements that contribute to and create our body movement and daily movement and life movements is affected by trauma. Most of what all mental health professionals work with is an interruption, disruption, destruction of our natural and usual life rhythms and, therefore, movements.

The idea of trauma entered the mainstream of psychology in the 1980s, when the diagnosis of posttraumatic stress disorder (PTSD) first appeared in the *Diagnostic and Statistical Manual of Mental Disorders* in its third edition (1980) , although the Greek roots of the word "trauma" (τραύμα), meaning wound, date back to the mid-1700s (Kolaitis & Olff, 2017, p. 1). As the trauma trajectory continued, and many more forms of therapy and approaches to healing emerged, evidence grew that somatic (body-based) therapies, once overlooked by a dominantly cognitive and behaviorally focused medical community, have critical importance. The role of somatic therapies and creative arts therapies as central to trauma therapy, recovery, or restoration is emergent and grounded. There is already ample literature about somatic approaches to working with trauma. Dr. van der Kolk's book *The Body Keeps the Score* (2015) is a significant documentation of the science supporting the central role the human body, our soma, plays in both the consequences of trauma and the paths to healing. Dr. Porges's books *Polyvagal Safety* (2021) and *Our Polyvagal World* (2023) equally document the central role the body and the ANS play in both experiencing and healing from trauma.

In the current trend in somatic trauma therapies, movement itself is not usually centered. Movement, as the thread that connects us all through breath, behavior, and action, offers a more dynamic understanding of both the effects of trauma and the restorative process for survivors of trauma. One bridge between human communication and movement is spoken language, and working with the body requires us to use words that direct our attention to the immediacy of our physical experience. This is a reason why body-based therapies are so powerful and increasingly acknowledged as essential to the restorative process for survivors of trauma. Physical sensation is the language of the body, and sensations help scaffold and shape our movement. As a brief example of how sensation is used in this work, I invite my clients to describe what they are feeling in physical sensation–based words. Often, they use feeling words such as "calm," "content," "worried," or "stressed." In order to guide them to the physical sensation underlying those feelings, I invite them to notice, name, and note. Here is an exercise:

To do this now, notice a physical sensation in your body (hint—sensations are not feelings). Often people will use words like "calm," "grounded," or "at ease." To find the sensation, ask yourself: Where is my body telling me this is how I am now, and how does my body let me know I am calm? Sensations are texture, temperature, density, and other physical attributes, such as warm, hard, gritty, soft, and tight.

Once you identify or recognize the sensation, name it. Write it, draw it, or say it aloud. For example, the sensation I am most noticing is tingly. It's both cool and warm. It's in my belly.

Because language is central to human connection, relationship, and healing, it merits noting that many of the common ways of describing the experience of trauma are not always helpful. For example, "trauma recovery" is used ubiquitously to describe trauma-focused work. The term “recovery” seems like a setup to many of my clients, because survivors do not recover everything. They certainly may recover some of what was lost, or how they used to sense, feel, think, and act, but they are forever changed. The acknowledgment and acceptance of this is a focus of polyvagal-informed somatic and movement therapies because the imprints trauma leaves become the patterns in our autonomic nervous system; patterns that we default to in service of survival. These imprints and patterns contribute to the physicality of trauma.

“Restorative process” is a term I coined 20 years ago when working with survivors of torture as an alternative to “trauma recovery.” There are many reasons why the typical language of describing trauma was not helpful or effective for my clients. All us humans experience neurophysiological reactions to our perceptions of danger or life threat, and these reactions become the patterns that psychotherapists know as symptoms or complaints. They are often reorganized into diagnoses.

Many of the typical diagnoses are not relevant for cultural reasons. In the early days of trauma treatment, the most common diagnosis for trauma—PTSD—emphasized behavior and affect, which did, and does not, adequately express the ways clients suffer because the enduring physicality of trauma was not centered.

Survivors of egregious human rights abuses, interpersonal trauma, historical and intergenerational trauma, racial trauma, and long-term oppression live in layers: Layers of fear and terror alternate with layers of hope and strength. This is why trauma and resiliency cannot be separated. Understanding that this relationship is body-based and rooted in the dance of the autonomic nervous system (ANS) is the basis of this framework.

For many years now, somatic approaches to trauma have correctly stated that trauma is not the event—it’s what happens to the body. The simple illustration in Figures 3.1 and 3.2 is one I use both when offering clients psychosocial education and when teaching my students. Central to the experience of trauma is the exposure (the traumatizing event or events) and the movements that occur in direct reaction or response to the exposure. It’s important to understand that our immediate reactions to these exposures are not something we choose or are responsible for; these reactions are our bodies and our autonomic nervous systems acting in service of our survival. This reaction will vary widely based on what I call "how we meet the world" in the very moment(s) of exposure, which can be fleeting or lifelong. The figures simplify a very complex and nuanced process. Movement is at the heart of how we meet the world.

An exposure to trauma is perhaps a car accident, an attack by a dog, or an intruder. The murder of a family member. The war and all that experience contains, whether we live it for a few days or years. Exposures can be a single event or extended and ongoing, often referred to as chronic and/or cumulative. Clients and students will often ask if one type of exposure is "more traumatic" than another. This is difficult to answer because certainly, when we read or hear about the terrible things that happen to others, some stories will impact us more than others. This is based on our own prior adverse exposures, how we met and moved through them, how they still imprint in us. As Deb Dana says, "story follows state" (Sunseri, 2019), and we are affected by the story because of how it shifts our state. At the level of biological and physiological processes of the human body, there is no story. There is only the immediacy of what we sense and feel in our body. In the moment of exposure, our ANS, in concert and connection with our brain, our extended nervous system, endocrine and other systems of our body, will recruit survival strategies afforded us by our nervous system. The ANS doesn't have a story or understanding of what's happening. It is our survival promoting "wiring."

An example I often use in my classes is a bus accident. If we are all riding a bus, and the bus begins to veer and an accident seems inevitable, each person on the bus will have a different reaction. In such a case, a reaction is automatic. We don't control it. Reactions arise subconsciously and directly from our neural circuitry, that is, our neuroception. And they can be life-saving. A response also involves our neuroception, and it involves more of our awareness. It isn't about strength or weakness, right or wrong. It's our capacities at the time.

Back to the veering bus. Each person presents a complexity of internal sensations, feelings, ideas, and movements. Some of us may be having an excellent day and feeling great, and therefore we are resourced and our inherent strength is more accessible. Others may be physically or emotionally or mentally depleted and not feeling well. Whether we flunked or aced an exam, had a fight, or made up with someone we love—these are all elements of the state we are in when we meet the moment of the bus accident. As is the context: Are we in the front or back of the bus? Do we see everything that is happening or nothing at all? For some, seeing everything would be terrifying. For others, it might help them stay present as they track what's happening. Perhaps they have experienced an accident before and have a sense of "I've got this—I can see what's coming and I think we'll be okay." For others, seeing or not seeing may determine if they maintain that awareness, or react in fear or terror.

For simplicity's sake, there are three primary emotional responses directly linked to our ANS: (1) feeling safe enough for social engagement, (2) fear, and (3) terror. To distinguish these further, fear and terror are reactions, because they are truly survival based. Social engagement, which is based on our perception of safe-as-can-be, is a response that promotes feelings of calm and connectedness, because we maintain a level of presence that is necessarily absent when we react in fear or terror. Social engagement is what I call a state of wholeness and flow. In the moment of exposure, we might call this staying present with thoughts, feelings, and our body, to varying degrees. The hybrid and many blended states of our ANS can support different actions and strategies that affect how we meet the moment.

How we react or respond is a function of what we feel, which rises from what we perceive. Perception is conscious and is based on our subconscious "automatic" neuroception of the situation and environment, a focus of Chapter 4.

Very simply put, if we perceive danger, we feel fear, and the 400-million-year-old sympathetic nervous system (SNS) circuit is recruited. This circuitry arose when movement and mobilization became necessary survival strategies for evolving life. This is the defensive, protective fight-or-flight activation state, and it's a state that initiates movement in service of survival.

If we perceive life threat, the 500-million-year-old dorsal vagal circuit (DVC) of the parasympathetic branch of the ANS is recruited, and we feel terror. The DVC's primary survival strategy is complete shutdown. This is *no movement.* A behavioral expression of this total shutdown is peritraumatic dissociation, a behavioral health term that has long been associated with increased likelihood of traumatization. These are the primary states (mobilization in fear/fight or flight/activation and immobilization in terror/shutdown) arising from the ancient wisdom of our ANS circuitries. The strategies they support involve movement, even when it's the absence of movement. A very common hybrid state is freeze, which is a blend of DVC and SNS. We may react in fear initially, and the intensity of that reaction may recruit the DVC/parasympathetic system to restore homeostasis. We are momentarily or sustainedly frozen with a lot of charge inside of us. In terms of movement, we want to move and may not be able to. It's important to understand that these are not static experiences; they are moving experiences. While any of us may react initially in a pure primary state, we may instantly begin to fluctuate the levels or degrees to which any of the three neural circuits are recruited to state shift us in service of survival. In this way, our nervous system, and in particular our ANS, dances.

These reactions are the setup for traumatization, however they appear in a person's movement, actions, symptoms, complaint, and diagnoses. Clinically, I've observed that extended time spent in any fear- or terror-based primary, hybrid, or blended state can result in clients feeling and acting stuck in those states. This is how the ANS imprint becomes a pattern and becomes a well-walked trail. If in the moment of exposure we manage to stay connected to another person, perhaps calming them down as the accident plays out, or to ourselves, we may recruit these older strategies with an infusion of our social and relational capacity. One client's way of staying connected to self was to repeat over and over silently and occasionally aloud, "I am going to be okay." Hearing himself say that allowed him to focus on his ability to keep walking through a war zone in service of his flight to freedom. He maintained some conscious awareness of what was happening while he fled gunfire and militia. This may even increase our likelihood of survival. For example, in the bus scenario, we might move to another

Figure 3.1 Setup for Traumatization

Figure 3.2 Setup for Resilience

place in the bus or crouch down, if we have time. Conscious awareness and decision-making is what makes this distinct from a purely SNS fight-or-flight reaction, and it promotes more resiliency.

The imprint of how this plays out in the moment(s) of exposure will influence the likelihood of traumatization, promotion of our resilience—or both. This is what the simple illustration in Figures 3.1 and 3.2 attempts to show. Trauma and resilience are like a braid; they coexist. That is why a prior exposure and successful survival of a bus (or transportation) accident might make us more vulnerable in the moment, or it might be protective, and sometimes, it will do both. It's all in who and how we are when it plays out.

This book is an offering to how we can recruit the wisdom of both the body and the ANS, and the dance both continuously do together, which is expressed as movement, in service of promoting resilience in the restorative process for those who have emerged in varying states of traumatization, however they are expressed, labeled, or diagnosed. For years, these reactions were pathologized, and the ongoing expression of them (i.e., the symptoms or the behavior) were seen as maladaptive. I would suggest the ongoing expression of them is adaptive movement that is continuing to respond to the imprint of past events. This adaptive movement, however it's expressed or understood, is instrumental in the work we do with clients to calibrate their ANS, bodies, and movement to the present.

Movement can amplify and complicate these approaches. An oft-uttered phrase among dance/movement therapists is "Movement is our primary language." This is true, and there are many contexts that shape our signature movements. PVISDMP recognizes our autonomic nervous system (and our entire nervous system) as the biological and physiological underpinning of our movement because anytime we move, the nervous system responds to the feedback. *There is movement.* In this spacious theoretical and practical framework, we know that there are many portals to movement and many layers to how and when we move. Our nervous system moves us and responds or reacts to movements (including lack of) around us. This polestar of our anatomy is a neuro-memory of our mammalian evolution and in communication with all other bits of our body: muscles, bones, blood. We are seen and express ourselves through movement arising from inner signaling of the nervous system.

Somatic psychotherapy is powerful work that raises clients' awareness of body processes and patterns, their roots in past experience, and how somatic practices that integrate breath, simple body-based techniques, and varying degrees of movement can aid the restorative process. Movement is not hierarchical; it is developmental, evolutionary, and emergent. Expanding the idea of somatic therapies with even more invitations to explore movement, rhythm, and even its expressive counterpart and expression, dance, offers clients a far more varied and diverse field of potential to heal.

For those unsure of using dance in a therapeutic context, dance is not just the refined movement of a well-tuned artist's body performing advanced choreography. It is also not only the many magnificent ways dance is core to Indigenous and traditional society and culture globally. Rather, dance is something every human has the capacity to participate in because everyone has rhythm. Not only that, but dance is something that occurs within every human. To those who say, "I cannot dance because I don't have rhythm," I invite you to feel your heartbeat. That's one of our core, endogenous biorhythms. The ANS, and likewise the vagal circuitry, dance. This is poetic and it's also literal. The constant streams of communication, the surges and interruptions of our physiology and biology, are choreography. Some of it, we initiate consciously. Some we don't. Because dance movement therapy (DMT) sits uniquely at the crossroads of somatic psychotherapies and creative arts therapies, and utilizes movement as its primary language, movement is a way clinicians of all theoretical orientations can integrate somatic and DMT practices into their work. Section II offers many possibilities for this.

REINA: THE POWER OF MOVEMENT

This brief case snippet demonstrates the power of movement. A client who survived three years of daily torture in an underground prison described a pain in her heart that was both physical and emotional. This pain radiated out to her left shoulder, and in this first session together, we worked with that pain through breath and movement. As a recently graduated and enthusiastic dance/movement therapist, I saw (and heard, through the way she described the stuckness in her shoulder and the pain that inhibited it from even the smallest shoulder roll movement) a simple, tiny movement potential and decided that by the end of the session, we would get her shoulder to roll. I encouraged her to roll her shoulder backward, out of the stuck, forward-folding shape it had occupied since she fled her home country and left her children behind. This immense grief and guilt became a literal pain in her heart that froze her shoulder. When she finally rolled her shoulder, she let out a large gasp-like exhale and winced. I asked how she felt, and she simply said, "Okay." The session ended quietly; I wasn't certain of what happened, but I noticed it felt a bit stiff and awkward in the space between us.

What I learned when she canceled the subsequent session

(and the two after that) was that it was too much. She felt overwhelmed, had an asthma attack, and remained in her house, without leaving, for almost a month.

She came back, and I learned that I had moved too fast. Movement is a direct pathway to the nervous system, and her ANS activated and she felt "flooded." At that time, I had just been introduced to Polyvagal Theory so did not appreciate that it was the ANS that cued us to the too-stimulating pace of our work. Most of the practices in this book, equally for practitioners and clients, arise from these learnings. They are rooted in all the ways the body can restore balance, wholeness, and a sense of belonging. This book is a testimony to her, and all my clients', courage.

The following exercise is a simple way in which I invite people listening to a lecture or talk I am giving to connect to the power of the body (embody) and to experience how movement is affected by, and affects, how we feel. How we feel, our psychological and emotional state, arises directly from our physiological state, governed by our ANS.

EMBODIMENT PRACTICE

Here is the procedure for embodiment practice:

Stand or sit somewhere you can be physically comfortable. You'll be here about two minutes.

First, imagine you are sitting or standing in a very confined space. I usually imagine I am in a box, which is confined but not scary. If this is an experience that is too real for you, or that becomes too uncomfortable, please don't do this.

While you imagine you are in this confined space, close your eyes if you can. If you cannot, look down at the ground. What do you feel? Notice your muscle tone and tension. Notice your posture. Notice if the longer you imagine you are confined, your feeling state changes. Feelings (calm, anxious, irritated, etc.) reflect what we notice in our body (neurophysiological state, such as rapid heart rate, sweaty, cold, and clammy). Use all your senses to imagine your confinement to this box; what would this confined space taste, look, smell, sound, feel, and be like? Keep tracking both your body (neurophysiological) and emotional (feeling) states.

Open your eyes, let this go, and notice how you feel. Let this go.

Now imagine you are in the most open environment you can imagine. Perhaps a wide-open field of wildflowers, an expansive horizon, or a favorite place you feel unencumbered. Again, as you use all your senses to conjure up this environment, notice how your body and feeling states change. How is your muscle tone and tension, posture now? How is your breath and heart rate? This somatic awareness offers an embodied example of how our bodies and feelings are connected.

To add movement, repeat this process. When you imagine you are in the confined place, try to move. Notice if this is easy or challenging. Do the same while imagining you are in the open, free space. In each imagined experience, how do you move? Are you stiff, fluid, relaxed, tight? Which feels familiar?

This seemingly simple practice usually demonstrates the potency of the imagination: When we imagine different environments, our neurophysiological and body states change, and so does our movement. It is also through movement that we can sense and see this, in our own bodies and others. This change is the ANS expressing itself through the actions of the body it is embedded in.

No matter what symptoms or complaints a client brings, or we experience, it will alter our movement. We become more still. We have stuck, tense, painful places in our bodies that limit our range. We cannot settle; we cannot rise. We no longer leave our house or even our room; we stop flying in planes or going to movie theaters. The fear or terror that underlies traumatization changes our movement. These changes manifest from the levels of the tiniest physiological micromovements to our ability and willingness to move from one place to another.

Movement is a language, a pathway, a portal to the restorative process for therapeutic work with survivors of trauma in a human rights, social justice framework. In this context, where clients present from a variety of countries or cultures, speaking many languages and being aligned with many different religions or spiritual practices, movement offers a more complete method to bridge the implicit with the explicit, which is core to trauma work.

One of the most significant understandings that comes from research on trauma is the nature of memory. In trauma, memory is disorganized and disconnected; indeed, the scramble of what happened that results in the classic loss or confusion of narrative is because "trauma memory is sensory motoric and image based" (Terr, 1992, p. 182). What that means is that shards of implicit sensory information, like color or light or smell, remain encoded in our biology and physiology like patterns of movement themselves, as somatic markers (Damasio, 2005, p. 196) in the amygdala and as imprints in the nervous system that affect what we remember and change how we move in the world. Much more recently, Dr. Ruth Lanius's work (2024) on autobiographical and traumatic memory illuminates how traumatic memory is an intense reliving of sensory fragments (movement, color, sound, images, smells) of the past and is a body-based experience. Her research suggests that sensory and body-based approaches to trauma are more effective than verbal processing alone. For many of my clients, migration, as a movement that interrupts all their sense of relative safety, is a formative experience that colors the rest of their lives. Most of them can never go home again. For many survivors of trauma, even if they are not geographically displaced, they describe being displaced from their body, that is, it no longer feels like it is their body. This is the ongoing assault of the exposure channeled through the ANS, our body, and its movement that protectively tells us we are still not safe. This can feel like internal oppression, and this is amplified for those living in ongoing oppression. For this, and for our clients, movement initiates the path to liberation. In the next chapter, oft-used ideas and concepts such as safety and neuroception are recalibrated in service of therapists' understanding of the responsibilities we have to stewarding that path forward.

CHAPTER 4

The Privilege of Safety

THERAPIST: If you're okay to continue with this intake, I'd like to ask you some questions.

CLIENT: I would like to ask you some questions first.

THERAPIST: Okay.

CLIENT: Where are you from?

THERAPIST: I live in Denver.

CLIENT: No, I mean, where are you from?

THERAPIST: Do you mean where was I born? I was born in Chicago.

CLIENT: No. Where are you *from*? Where are your people from?

THERAPIST: Oh, my Mom is from Michigan originally and my Dad from Pennsylvania.

CLIENT [SIGHS]: No, your people. Where do they come from?

THERAPIST: Oh. You mean my ancestors?

CLIENT: Yes.

THERAPIST: My mom's people came from Poland and from Scotland, Ireland, and Canada. My dad's people are from England, Wales, Germany, and his father was also Native American.

CLIENT: Thank you. That's what I needed to know. Now I know who is in the room with us.

This abbreviated excerpt from an actual assessment/intake illustrates a rather unusual and helpful "intervention" by a client who needed to know more depth about the person who was about to ask them a barrage of questions. The usual clinical structure for assessments is a one-way series of questions to help the therapist come up with diagnostic impressions, if not a diagnosis, and begin to formulate referral and treatment planning. While I always invite clients to ask me questions, this was most unusual and most illuminating. It was one of my first invitations to recognize that the environment I am responsible for as a therapist extends far beyond the obvious. It was then I began to contemplate how neuroception is constantly being shaped by sociocultural, sociopolitical, socio-geographical, and socio-spiritual influences that are unspoken and not known to all—and that the idea of safety as a starting point has some flaws.

Why Assuming Safety May Not Be Safe

Polyvagal Theory is often referred to as the science of safety. Indeed, one of the most illuminating contributions of this theory is how central feeling safe is to a flourishing human (mammalian) life. Safety, which in these contexts refers to feeling safe versus actual safety (because actual safety, i.e., safety in the environment and relationships, is not fully under our control) is also central to trauma treatment. When "complex trauma" was first proposed as an alternative diagnosis to PTSD (Herman, 1997), phasic approaches to treating traumatized survivors were soon emphasized as the most effective treatments. The suggested diagnosis of complex trauma arose from a realization that for many clients, in particular adult survivors of childhood abuse, PTSD did not accommodate all the troubling issues and symptoms of these survivors. The inability to regulate emotions, somatic or body-based symptoms and complaints, and relational issues were criteria missing from PTSD but included in the proposed complex trauma diagnosis. While this diagnosis did not make it to the fifth edition of the *Diagnostic and Statistical Manual of Mental Disorders* (*DSM-5*), awareness of the complexity of trauma and the many ways culture, context, and other conditions influence symptomatology has helped clinicians develop more nuanced cultural reference frames for working with survivors. There are now many treatment models for complex trauma, and in all of them, safety is always the focus of the first phase.

This use of safety assumes some things that are essential to consider when working with survivors, especially those of us who work with survivors in multicultural, social justice, international, and other contexts. True safety in the environment is beyond any of our control. The perception of safety, that is, our ability to feel safe, is a function of neuroception, that subcortical, subconscious process that our ANS gifts us. While we can certainly design, alter, and enhance some aspects of the environment to increase its feeling safe enough, we can have no idea, until we know our clients well, what type of environment will help them to neurocept, and therefore perceive, a safe enough space.

An example of this is in our (Gray & Porges, 2017) book chapter "Polyvagal-Informed Dance/Movement Therapy," which introduced this polyvagal-informed therapy using the case of a young man, Alphonse, who was completely shut down from the horrors of war he experienced in his home country. It illustrates how our work could begin only when we changed our environment. His initial clinical presentation was of a young man who would not speak or make eye contact, whose body was limp and lacking vitality, and who appeared to pay little to no attention to me or anyone attempting to engage. We began our work together in my large movement therapy space, a room rich with color and texture. I very intentionally decorated it with textiles from countries my clients came from, plants, and other bright things that I perceived as cheery and comforting. After several sessions, recognizing how agitated Alphonse always became in the space, my intuitive hunch moved us downstairs to a room that I experienced as bland and uninteresting. It was our underused, undecorated foyer. Once a living room in the Victorian-era home, our offices were intended to create a more homelike rather than clinical environment. This room wasn't yet in use. It had a few pieces of neutral-colored furniture, a neutral-colored rug, and a table. When we began working in that room, he immediately retreated under the table. I oscillated between remaining outside his "perimeter" and slowly, slowly advancing toward the perimeter until my hand or elbow and eventually more and more of me was also under the table. Our work together shifted significantly (Gray & Porges, 2017, p. 125), and eventually he began to allow bits and then eventually all of himself to leave his table hiding place. In doing this, he shifted from a true dorsal vagal shutdown in terror to tiny doses of a SNS-governed fear mobilization, a neurophysiologically activated state that is survival oriented and therefore not relational but gave us a starting place because we could move. These small, neurophysiological shifts that became small movements helped birth the PVISDMP concept of micromobilizations that precede micromovements. I believe the richly decorated space, which my other clients appreciated, created too much stimulation for his ANS. Alphonse neurocepted threat.

"Neuroception" is a term that, fortunately, is becoming more commonly used and understood. As Deb Dana writes, "Neuroception is a 'wordless experience.'" Quoting Porges, she continues, "It is the response of the autonomic nervous system not only to cues in the world around us but also to cues from within our bodies" (Dana, 2018, p. 36). Deb's work brilliantly highlights the importance of our learning to track and honor our own neuroceptive tendencies and appreciate their role in our sense of safety and commitment to survival. In this case, my neuroception offered me a hint in the form of an internal cue that inspired a sense, and then an idea, that we might benefit from a move to a different room. Nervous systems communicate through transmission: We sense other people and how safe or not they might be to us through this subconscious process that is an evolutionary gift.

Relative Safety

What does neuroception mean for promoting a safe-as-can-be space so that our work at least begins to promote a sense of relative safety in our clients?

"Relative safety" is my chosen term as it seems the most concise term for describing the reality of safety in the therapeutic relationship, or what I now call the reciprocal alliance. I first heard the term "relative safety" from Anngywn St. Just (personal communication, 1999), an expert in social trauma. It seems more apt for the reality that many clients face. Anngywn defines it as "being as safe as we can be in an unsafe world." I have slightly altered this definition to "feeling as safe as we can feel in an uncertain world." This distinction has been incredibly helpful to my clients because, in their words, it reflects my understanding of their reality. It also reflects my knowing that the space between our sessions is where most of the important work happens, which is why working at the level of the ANS is essential. Clients' ability to recognize their nervous system patterns, bring awareness to their neuroceptive tendencies, and then learn to self-regulate through state-shifting practices that promote greater ease or comfort in the time we are apart is the heart of this somatic work. Clients engagement with "homeplay" between sessions and our consistent reciprocal check-ins about their inquiries, practices, and experiences during session is what disrupts trauma feedback loops and promotes and integrates restorative feedback loops. As Deb Dana says, befriending the nervous system and understanding and increasing awareness of our neuroceptive patterns is what makes change possible.

Dr. Porges (personal communication, October 13, 2022) insightfully calls the ANS an "intervening variable" between us (inner), the environment or others (outer), and the in-between—the relationship, energy, or space that is created in the synergy of two or more meeting. How we react or respond to the interpersonal and environmental cues we pick up through these interactions arises from our neuroception of the environment. The in-between is mediated by our ANS. Perception is a conscious process that arises from subconscious neuroception, which produces the sensory information we receive, which we then translate into emotional and cognitive meaning. If we perceive the environment as safe, the in-between will seem relatively safe enough that we can welcome, connect, and relate. If we perceive danger or life threat, our neurophysiological reaction will promote mobilization or immobilization, in service of survival. Chapter 2 describes these neural circuits and emergent and patterened neurophysiological states.

This idea of the in-between is a modern scientific explanation for ancient wisdom. A Larrakia spiritual mentor from the top end of Australia called this the third space. In his community of spirit and healing, "third space" refers to the presence of other—all that is unseen and perhaps unknown. It is unique to each interaction, meeting, and context. It is created in the process of relating and healing. In his, and many sociocultural and socio-spiritual contexts that retain traditional wisdom, this third space is essential to "two-way learning" and "two-way relating," which are at the heart of reciprocal alliance. These concepts reflect the bidirectionality of human relationships that establish reciprocity. "Two-way" refers to the essential role and place each human (or more than human) holds in any relational process. This is akin to the clinical concept of intersubjective space, albeit more spiritual and mystical in nature. I have found that being able to refer to the third space is reassuring in its familiarity for many of my clients, who represent many cultures and spiritual traditions. This seems important for clinical settings that include a truly multicultural community of clients. In traditional behavioral health, it has been historically common to omit religion and spirit from clinical practice. Working with survivors of extreme exposures to adversity, especially human-made and human-intended, the inclusion of spirit and anything that connects to a person's faith may be a cornerstone of their healing.

A Polyvagal-Informed Environment

Returning to the case example from 2017: It's natural that our personal preferences will inform how we decorate our therapy spaces. We cannot assume that our tastes, which are certainly useful for our self-regulation, will suit our clients or supervisees. Since my experience with the young man, I have made a few simple environmental adjustments that promote relative safety in the environment of my office.

I have found it very helpful to keep a large cupboard where I can store things—smaller pieces of art, musical instruments, textiles—that

I can bring out for each client. I keep my space relatively neutral with muted ocean colors and realize this is wisdom therapists have used for a long time. My preference to have as much color as possible may not be the norm. Beyond the basics of decor, a polyvagal-informed therapy space can increase the likelihood clients will feel as safe as possible. I adapted a few simple processes to create this space:

1. I choose artwork that is much simpler and more neutral than my usual preference and is easy to move. I once had a client who was activated by one of my paintings, so I had to take it off the wall and turn the image towards the wall so it was not visible before his sessions. Since then, I make sure all paintings are in a place where they are easy to move if necessary.
2. I use a lot of props and used to choose bright colors, imagining they bring a cheeriness to the space. I learned from several clients this is often not so. I now ensure:
    a. I have space to store all props.
    b. Any props too large for storage are covered with a neutral-colored cloth or tucked away.
3. I keep plants to a minimum. I was surprised by a client who was activated by "too many plants." I used to keep supplies like watering cans, water glasses, and teacups out so that I would remember to water the plants or offer my clients water. All these things are stored away, too. In two-way relationships, as in reciprocity, we all benefit from our interactions. This has helped me rely on myself more than an external object to pay attention to and complete these rituals, which can promote mindfulness and presence.
4. As I work with a lot of children, I have a large sand tray and objects as well as plush toys. I used to keep quite a few out. I now store all the plushies in large baskets and have stored the sand tray under a table. Curtains hide the objects, which sometimes are provocative to my clients.

While these are basic suggestions and likely commonplace, its useful to highlight them in a context and time when demand for mental health services from well-trained somatic and trauma-informed practitioners is rising. In a polyvagal-informed world, all environments such as schools, hospitals, and medical, legal, and social facilities would be thoughtfully constructed, painted, and decorated to welcome a broad diversity of people. It's important to recognize the reach of our work as clinicians. Our clients safe-as-can-be experiences can become ripples that incite similar spaces elsewhere while their ANS transmits the gift of relative safety.

The Space in Between

The core of this work happens between sessions, when clients' nervous systems, bodies, hearts, minds, and spirits are navigating the world. I learned this from a client who seemed like a perfect clinical success, who experienced a dramatic shift in his environment that exposed his vulnerability and demonstrated how quickly our repatterned ANS can revert to fear and exposure-based patterns and layer even more of the same into new patterning.

JEREMIAH: THE SET-UP OF ASSUMING SAFETY

Jeremiah lost every single family member in the diamond wars on the continent now known as Africa. He came to the United States alone as a refugee. We worked hard for eight months to process his deep grief and fear of an uncertain and lonely future. After our very intensive work, he was ready to find a job. It was important to Jeremiah to be able to support himself financially, and he dreamed of a future where he would support a wife and children—his own family. He was persistent in his job search, but, month after month, he remained unemployed. He began

> to consider that one reason was communication. He thought his accent was affecting his job search. His native language was very lyrical, and he could sense it was difficult for some people to understand him. To shift this, we turned our sessions into mock job interviews, and he landed a job with the U.S. Postal Service. Jeremiah loved his job. His job loved him. This man, who had lost his entire family, would often say to me, "It makes me so happy to be delivering news from loved ones to their family members here."
>
> Jeremiah was quickly promoted. This promotion included a move to a new and more upscale and reportedly (per his manager) safe neighborhood. On one of his first days delivering mail there, he could not find an address and asked someone for directions. The person told him to get out of the way and called him a terrible, derogatory, racist term. When he next returned to therapy, he was broken and crushed. He had been moved from a multiethnic to a very homogenously white neighborhood as a promotion to a "better" and "safer" neighborhood. He kept saying, "I feel as betrayed as I did back home."

The experience amplified the shame he felt at not being able to save his family, at his unique way of speaking (in the U.S.), and at his not knowing the address. We backpedaled a bit and did some deeper work to shift his internalized sense of relative safety. This meant visiting some of his most difficult memories of war and loss that he had not previously shared with me. Each time he became activated or began to shut down, we came back to his sensory, interoceptive experience of pride in his present-day job he had earned and loved, and his joy at delivering "bundles of love." We codiscovered the state-shifting practices that regulated him as we navigated these corridors of terror. This is not easy work, as it requires learning to track the ANS and recognize our patterns. In instances where one flees an environment of persecution and violence and ends up in one where systemic racism and oppression are dominant, the environment is a wild card. We cannot always be with our clients; hence the idea that the most important work in service of reestablishing a safe-as-can-be internal environment is the ability to shift ANS patterns rooted in trauma to emergent states connected to hopeful and helpful human and social interaction. In some ways this might suggest that the work is on them, which adds to the burden of injustice they are already carrying. Our tending to the space in between (sessions) is our accompaniment all along the restorative process.

The Work in Between: The Third Space Made Real

To support this transitory space between sessions, it can be helpful to link elements of our office that we know clients appreciate or orient to for safety and comfort with things in their home, work, or any oft-visited environment. This is illustrated in an excerpt from work with another client.

MELISSA: GROUNDING TO SPACE

Melissa arrived in the United States terrified of leaving her home. She came from a country with extreme laws for women, where she was a women's rights activist. She had seen my card, noting that I was a dance/movement therapist, at the refugee resettlement agency, and asked to work with me as she wanted to learn "yoga to relax and exercise to help me feel strong." We began with simple yoga-inspired postures and movements—always seated as she was not comfortable getting on a mat or the floor—that addressed areas of tension or pain. For example, her legs felt weak, so we would inhale and lengthen our whole body upward from our seated position in a "stretching from chair to sky" shape (Figure 4.1a) and then, on the exhale, slowly fold at our hips, reaching our hands to touch our toes (or as close as we could get) and breathing and stretching the back of our legs long and strong (Figure 4.1b). Any familiar yoga asana, favorite stretch, or learned exercise or dance step can be adapted to a chair, or standing against a wall, or any posture the client feels okay in, to amplify a sense of support. Section II of this book is filled with such practices, all adaptable.

Once Melissa had learned some yogic postures and stretches she could practice at home, we began to work with her terror of leaving home. We designated a safe-as-can-be place in her home, a big comfy chair placed in front of a window where she could see trees and birds and felt "peaceful, calm and strong." The chair reminded her of the chair that she sat in during our sessions. We agreed in session each week how far she would try to venture from this chair. We began with just a few steps, then the edge of the room, through the door, to the edge of the next room, and eventually to the front door, and so on, until she could walk to a store two blocks away, which took about three months to accomplish. We practiced these journeys together and created "postures of preparation." She always sat in this chair and centered herself by practicing our specific yogic sequences, or postures of preparation connecting her in the present moment, in her home, to our in-session work. These postures and movement sequences were named for the issue or complaint we were addressing, such as "strength pose," "relaxation stretch," "back-softening stretch," and so on. After each session, we determined together how far she would venture out the next time. It took eight months for her to feel relatively safe enough to drive a few miles. Eventually, after a

Figure 4.1 (a and b) Stretching From Chair to Sky

year, she was driving a friend and herself to NIA (neuro-muscular integrative action) classes—the exercise that made her feel strong.

Through the lens of the ANS, movement in the form of yoga helped Melissa regulate her nervous system so she could begin to move more freely in the world. Working with posture is polyvagal-informed: shifting and changing our body shape promotes vagal tone, a scientific measure of capacity for social engagement, and can promote integration and flow toward wholeness. In the words of this client, reflecting to me her understanding of the neurophysiological changes that were happening as she moved and felt her strength growing, "I felt like I will be happy to be with people again." Weeks later, describing her previously hard-to-find interoceptive experience: "Inside me feels like the dawn or dusk when we do our prayers. It is at this time that Allah is closest to us. My inside body softens, and I feel myself smile." This very sociocultural and socio-spiritual description of her inner landscape and inner climate demonstrates how movement shifts our neurophysiological and therefore emotional and psychological state.

PRACTICE: SPACE-PLACE-PACE

Because entering our space is one of the first steps our clients literally take to work with us, it should be supported by as much environmental ease as possible. "Space-Place-Pace" is a simple practice that I learned from my teacher Dr. Christine Caldwell. I have adapted it several ways, and one of them is a beginning to every session.

I have one door into my office, so clients always enter there. Previously I had my own chair, as many therapists do. I have let this go.

There are three options for sitting, and clients choose which one they want. Depending on all the things that affect how any of us feel, clients may choose a different (or same) seat each time. I ask them to settle and see if there is anything in the office they want to change. (Hence the space to store things.) We take time to do that. I invite clients to make sure they are sitting where they want to be and facing where they want to face and adjust anything needed. I also take time to intuit where I should sit (almost never directly facing a client and at varying distances, depending on my sense of the space between). I invite my client to let me know if I might sit closer, farther away, or at a different angle. This may sound tedious, but done every session, it is a way we can use our power in our therapy space to encourage clients to be empowered to do this between sessions. I call this practice, and the final practice of this chapter, microempowerments. Microempowerments are an essential pathway of PVISDMP. Any practice that begins to promote state shift in a direction that promotes clients' relative safety and a sense of bravery and voice is a microempowerment.

Our clinical demeanor is also a strong influence on the space between us and will directly impact that intervening ANS variable. This may sound obvious, but it is surprising how many therapists still verbally assure clients, "You are safe here," that "you can trust me," and don't consider the setup they are possibly creating for their clients. By definition, when someone is living in a state of traumatization, there are always times (and it may be all the time) when they don't feel safe. It's wonderful if therapists can create a safe enough, or brave enough, space to encourage and nurture the process of therapy to restore and heal survivors. And because it's the time in between sessions that is most relevant in a client's life and that offers the most potent opportunities for healing, feeling safe in therapy and then experiencing reoccurring loss of safety between sessions can feel like failure. These failures add to the sense of loss, shame, and betrayal a survivor already experiences. Safety is a birthright for all, and it's a privilege for few.

This is a both/and. It's disrespectful to assume safety for clients, because inviting them into the therapeutic space is inviting them into a healing context that derives from a Western frame, which may be different from their own. In many examples of therapy that are rooted in a Western medical framework where the healer (therapist, physician) is an expert, that don't allow flexibility and adjustment, one can argue we are bringing clients into a white supremacist framework (Okun, 2021). I also disrespect my clients if I fail to recognize their sociocultural reference points for safety—family, community, meal sharing, worship—that may occur outside our relationship and that they may or may not have access to them. Being safe as can be is cultivated slowly through respect and reciprocity. The power dynamic that exists in our relationship with clients can be comforting to some, who are accustomed to seeking the help and guidance of an expert or doctor. This power differential may be scary to others who have experienced human rights abuse, oppression, and subjugation at the hands of another, especially if the other was a professional (e.g., doctor, dentist, psychiatrist). The suffering of many of my clients was enhanced by the involvement of psychologists who assisted perpetrators to break down their psychic stamina, or dentists who inflicted intense pain on them, as they are often used to increase the suffering of those being persecuted. Such violence is more common than many of us might like to imagine. The presence of overwhelming power, in any human rights violation, is intentionally terrifying.

Microempowerments to Promote Relative Safety

"Microempowerments" as a term arose in work I was doing with a client whose case also exemplifies the importance of acknowledging that a sense of relative safety may be embedded in cultural practices we may not usually discuss or offer in therapy. Our work helped me understand the role of clients' sociocultural processes in their empowerment. This vignette illustrates the responsibility we have to welcome our clients' worldviews in the service of relative safety.

SARAH AND MICROEMPOWERMENTS

Sarah, also a victim of the blood diamond wars, had been used by soldiers in a rape camp where she was held for almost a year. She would shut down when any reference to her time in the camp, or the wars, came up. I spent much of our sessions grounding and orienting her to promote state shifts out of this immobilization. It was difficult for her to engage with the practices we tried in our sessions. I decided to focus on her accessible remembered and active resources, and invited her to tell me stories that connected her to prewar memories.

One of Sarah's favorite memories was of gathering water with other women in her community. She emphasized the importance of carrying water properly, so as not to lose any, and how the women would compete playfully when carrying it back. This gave me an idea. I invited her to teach me how to do this, and this story became the first of a shared storytelling process. We went back and forth teaching each other skills (she, carrying water, swaddling a baby; me, driving a car, making coffee). These stories became a dance we cochoreographed in an increasingly mobilized playful shared dance, literally begun in our chairs, and finally becoming a full-fledged dance around my therapy space. After each session, which included more and more movement, our relationship strengthened, and she was able to engage in more conversations about her suffering. I learned more details of her experience in the camp, essential for her asylum hearing. We began small, and I recognized that each increment in movement and our connection was a microempowerment, enabling her to slowly regain her relational and social capacities. A microempowerment is a moment—sometimes fleeting—of felt sensed strength. Of a sense of oneself, however expressed and understood. Of feeling whole again. I often tell clients that each moment of microempowerment is a thread that will eventually become part of a woven tapestry of healing and wholeness. In Sarah's case, microempowerments became micromovements that became gestures that became movements that became a shared dance. Changing body shape, or posture, recalibrates the nervous system by engaging the whole peripheral nervous system, autonomic and somatic, which can promote vagal tone, vagal efficiency, and flow.

After several months of this work, and after receiving asylum,

> Sarah realized she needed a cleansing ritual to clear herself and her children. I always search for someone from clients' communities with these capacities, but there was no medicine person from her religion in our community. She decided I needed to facilitate the ritual. I attempted to explain why that might not be an appropriate role for me. When she insisted, I offered to continue to search for someone. After the session, the interpreter pulled me aside and said, "You are the only person she has shared her secrets with. If she requests you to do this, please do. You are the person she is beginning to trust in this city." In polyvagal terms, she was neurocepting enough safety in our relationship to invite it to a new level of relationality, on a path to reciprocity, which is also a risk in a therapeutic relationship. We spent the next several sessions with her, and the interpreter who was from the same tribe and familiar with the ritual, teaching a willing colleague and myself what we needed to do. We cocreated the cleansing ritual with our interpreter.

This sociocultural process was far more meaningful to Sarah's sense of relative safety than anything else I might have offered. Our storytelling dances spurred a continuum of mobilization without fear-based states that allowed us to playfully move, dance, settle, and reflect together in the continuum of play. Movement became the pathway to social engagement, following the trail of our neuro-ancestral lineage. Her neuroception supported a sense of safe-enough that she perceived me as an ally. When this happens we are in a collective nervous system that coregulates through transmission. The collective nervous system includes the many layers of "-ceptions"—socioception, geoception, culturoception, and so on—that uniquely shape our own neuroception. My willingness to engage in a practice that was part of her internal cultural architecture and a reference point for her understanding of healing and community fostered the reciprocal alliance that is core to bringing a human rights and social justice lens and core to our work. The human nervous system is a root of our social and relational capacities, and sociality is a shared state that fosters humanity.

Socioception and Culturoception

Because the human nervous system extends beyond our bodies, not as anatomy but as energy for connection, the intervening variable or third space that informs neuroception is relevant in a much broader environmental context than is usually portrayed. An Indigenous Australian medicine teacher, following a class we co-taught, described the ANS as the stellar bones of our energy body. Our ANS influences how we feel because our feelings are rooted in our physiology. Our neuroception of the environment creates conscious and/or sub conscious state shifts that become these feelings. This teacher asked me "how much of the environment do you believe we neurocept?" In his worldview and way of seeing and believing, we are always neurocepting everywhere, in the immediate surroundings to the very same stars we come from.

"Socioception" and "culturoception" are terms emerging in the polyvagal-informed field today that describe the powerful influence our social, cultural, political, geographical, economic, familial, and other influences have on our neuroception. Neuroception, as a subconscious ANS neurophysiological process, may be inherent when we are born and is also most certainly shaped by the environment we are raised and hopefully nurtured in. My colleague and friend Niloufer Merchant is expanding the concept of neuroception to incorporate the larger systemic influence on our nervous system which she refers to as culturoception. She defines culturoception as "Neuroception of the socio-cultural context that impacts the autonomic nervous system" (Merchant, personal communication October 7, 2025). This calls for attuning to not only the individual experience, but also the collective experience of historical, intergenerational, political, cultural, and societal experiences which influence our nervous systems. Bioception is a term coined by Emilie Conrad, founder of Continuum, which acknowledges our relationship to the natural world around us. By biocepting, we sense our connection to all other living things. Geoception is a term that arose when teaching this work in an Indigenous community in Australia, when my teacher asked his question. Geoception reflects the potency of place, in the broadest most inclusive sense, to our sense of relative safety. The land we live on, our home and the things in it, the time and place of our birth and death, and our relationship to the cosmos and Ancestors, all become part of our inner geography as we develop and therefore are intricately woven with our ANS. Figures 4.2 and 4.3 attempt to express how connected and mutually influencing these concepts are.

Our neuroception is the understory of our ANS that cues us whether we are relatively safe, or in danger or life threat. Explaining this to clients, I will use the image in Figure 4.2. This figure shows how these three primary neurophysiological and emotional states, and by association all other emergent states, emanate from our heart center, where each neural circuit innervates the sinoatrial node to influence our neurophysiology, biochemistry, and ANS states. The heart is widely considered the center of our emotions. Many clients are fascinated and grateful to learn that these emotions arise from nerve fibers connected to their survival championing ANS. Because their feelings often contribute to their feeling "crazy," isolated,

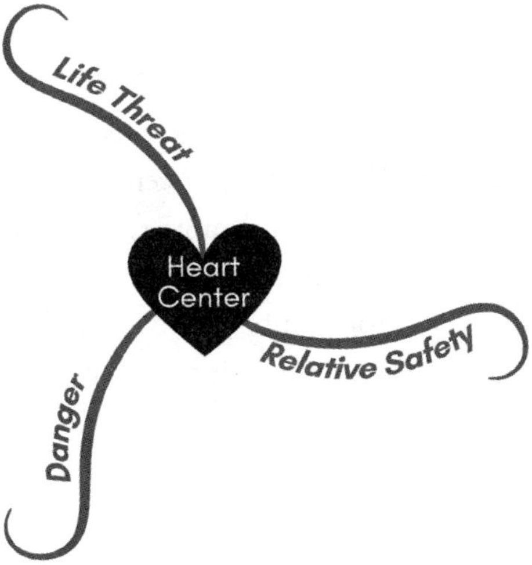

Figure 4.2 Neuroception Pathways

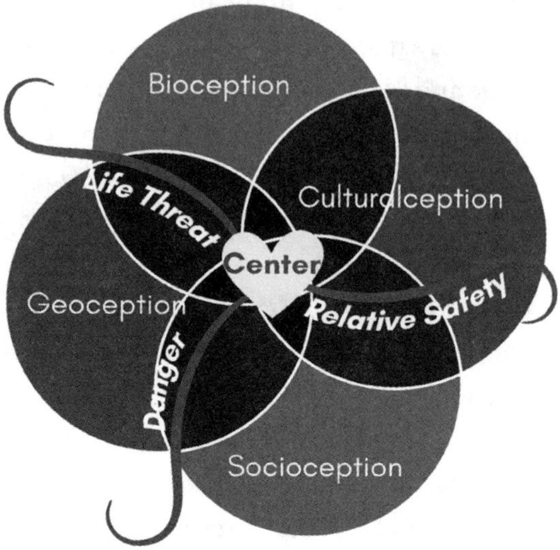

Figure 4.3 Influences on the Shaping of Our Neuroception

misunderstood, and many other uncomfortable ways, this information is reassuring. Figure 4.2 also acknowledges that being centered and recentering through our heart center, which is often a moving center, a theme of Chapter 5, is both an expression of and a pathway to feeling safe enough.

Figure 4.3 endeavors to show how these layers or waves of influence—culture, society/social influences, geography, and biology—are constantly influencing our ANS. From our center, depicted as a heart, the center of the noble pathway and the mother beat of all our biorhythms, we can spiral in and out of our inner landscape and the environment, space, and inhabitants around us. How we do this, how we move, is always influenced by our neuroception, which is in turn contributing to our multiplicity of neurophysiological states, perceptions, and stories based on our perception of relative safety, danger, or life threat. This perception arises from our neuroception.

Our essence is equal; all human beings have a shared history that is expressed neurophysiologically and biologically. While it is scientifically accurate to state that we neurocept our environment, it bears emphasizing that our environment shapes our neuroception. Human development is a dance between our inner and outer environments. We internalize the ways we are cared for, responded to, or not, and our inner climate and landscape inform how we move through, and even send ripples into, the environment. All our actions affect others. The ripples of our ANS are transmitted to those we are sharing an environment with at any given time. It matters when we reach across the apparent borders of difference that the culture or society any of us come from can appear to create.

In service of recognizing how we as clinicians and fellow humans interact with and inform relative safety in our work, please consider these two questions: (1) What sociocultural messages are embedded in my environment, and how do I sense them? How do they affect me? (This question relates to our bodies.) (2) How do I contribute to sociocultural messages that might create less safety for another person? (This question relates to our contributions to the environment that "feeds" all the perceptions.)

Neuroception Microempowerment Practice: Shifting to Comfort

It was with Sarah that I first practiced a very simple neuroception-refining practice I now refer to as Shifting to Comfort. This practice helped prepare her for our movement practices, and it is now a staple in PVISDMP. Even the tiniest shift in our physical comfort can invite the neurophysiological and biochemical cascade that moves us in the direction of relative safety. I believe this is a function of our interoception, which might be defined as everything we sense and know from inside our body through physical sensation. In the continuum of awareness, neuroception precedes interoception and becomes part of the formation of our perception of whether we are safe or unsafe (see Chapter 2).

PRACTICE: MICROEMPOWERMENT—SHIFTING TO PHYSICAL COMFORT

Take a moment to notice how physically comfortable you are.

Pause.

Now take a moment to practice increasing your physical comfort. What in this moment will help you feel more physically comfortable? Notice the internal cues, for example, how perhaps uncrossing a leg or shifting your weight might reduce muscle tension or ease pain. Notice the external cues, for example, whether you need to move to another area of the room, change what you are sitting on, and so on.

Pause.

Take another moment to change anything else that will increase your physical comfort.

This practice is the basis of the polyvagal-informed somatic concept of microempowerment.

Each microempowerment is a thread to our own sense of resource, strength, safety, and presence, and contributes to the restorative process and journey to wholeness. The more threads we generate and cogenerate with our clients, the more we weave a metaphorical blanket—a feeling, a place inside us, our sense of place and belonging—that increases in frequency and duration. This is what healing and restoration are. In this spiraling cotransmission of ANS to ANS, client to therapist to client to therapist, we cocreate ripples that refine our neuroception. We are co-regulating. In this spirit, you readers are invited to consider another question, not just now but ongoing: What ripples am I, have I, and will I send out into the environment, and how might they affect others? How will they return to me? This question reflects our commitment to safe-as-can-be "-ceptions" for all and perhaps can expand our clinical co-regulation so the "co-" includes community and collective as well.

CHAPTER 5

Spiraling In

SELF-CARE AS A CLINICAL SKILL

Yesterday, I was clever, so I wanted to change the world. Today I am wise, so I am changing myself.

—RUMI

I am often asked what the most important clinical skill is that therapists need to know to work with complex trauma. My answer is consistent: self-care. Self-care is self-regulation, self-compassion, self-love, and self-respect. To tend to one's own sense of well-being and wholeness is an act of self-compassion, which fosters self-love. Often compassion is treated as that which we send toward others in service of kindness and connection. My advice to all therapists working with human suffering is to send a "bazillion" more times compassion to yourself than toward anyone else. It begins in our own bodies, hearts, minds, and spirits and seeds love. It is cliché but true that how we treat others begins with how we treat ourselves. Nervous systems communicate across the space between them; the seed bed of self-compassion and self-love we grow in our self can seed the same in others. Respect is at the heart of this work; without respect, there is no reciprocity. To embody self-respect is to offer our clients the deepest form of respect possible, because we transmit it to them. Yes, we must also demonstrate respect toward our clients, and in my experience, the absence of self-respect that reflects the shame so common with interpersonal trauma needs the light of the presence of self-respect in another to find it in oneself. Self-care is also a moral and ethical obligation to our clients, and to our own families, friends, and beloveds.

Self-regulation is, of course, a skill we learn through how we were and are coregulated. In early human life, it is essential that our caregivers coregulate us, our tiny bodies and developing brains and nervous systems, because the human species takes approximately 25 years to fully develop (Arain et al., 2013, p. 451). Self-regulation and coregulation might be described as a coevolving spiral: Our ability to self-regulate is rooted in, and always blossoming from, our coregulatory relationships. We know that a lack of healthy or appropriate or complete coregulation early in life has consequences. This is not a topic of this book; Dr. Porges (2011) writes on it extensively in his seminal book *The Polyvagal Theory*, and colleagues Marilyn Sanders and George Thompson (2021) brilliantly describe it in detail in their book *Polyvagal Theory and the Developing Child*.

At times, colleagues have suggested that the concept of self-regulation is flawed, because it is a skill that emerges from coregulation; therefore, there is no such thing as self-regulation. I would suggest this is a limited perspective because it is rooted in a Western sense of self. Having once witnessed a Naga Sadhu bury himself up to his neck in sand and remain there for several days, appearing calm, peaceful, and present, I believe self-regulation is a human capacity that is rooted in many things: ancient spiritual beliefs and practices, our own history of positive coregulation, and other aspects of our development and life. More egocentric or individualistic societies (and the United Sates is considered the most egocentric) celebrate individualism, which can be quite unfamiliar in collectivist or sociocentric cultures (Harris, 2002). Each societal form has its benefits and challenges in terms of what a clinical and personal sense of self and agency is. The recognition that a sense of self does not always end at the skin—and may include ancestors, the natural world, family, and even the cosmos—is an essential starting point to accept that coregulation is self-regulation is coregulation, on and on. It's a spiral. That we indisputably learn self-regulation from coregulation does not mean self-regulation does not exist. They are intricately and eternally connected in our learning and in our ongoing capacities as human beings.

Both concepts are core to self-care as a philosophy and as a practice. Early in this work, I recall many colleagues who rolled their eyes at the idea of self-care, describing it as "soft." I was certainly not aware of its central role in this work until my own dances with burnout. PVISDMP is client- and survivor-centered. The expertise in this framework is client experience, as courageously shared in many years of clinical work. One client in particular, who was also one of the inspirations for reciprocal alliance, taught me that my self-care—all therapists' self-care—was a moral obligation and an ethical commitment to them, our clients.

RAJANI'S WISDOM

Rajani was a mother of three and the loving wife of a husband who had been detained and tortured for many months in their home country. During his detention, their eldest son lost an arm in a bombing. Following his release, the family fled. The second son was literally born in flight, without any medical support; the third was born a few years later in a refugee camp. Shortly after the youngest's birth, they arrived in the United States. During this harrowing journey, Rajani kept her family together, loved and cared for. Her cultural role as mother and wife was extremely important to her; she cherished it.

Over several years I worked with the father and eldest son, and the two younger sons participated in a children's creative arts therapy group. Over the years, I observed that Rajani appeared tired and stressed. She began to hunch over and was not as enthusiastic as usual. I invited her to therapy, and she finally agreed following a diagnosis of fibromyalgia. Knowing I worked with the body and movement, she thought I might help her with pain reduction and stiff joints.

We had worked together for eight months, and in that time, I had become the clinical director and had more administrative tasks and almost the same caseload. When I arrived at work one day, I checked my calendar, and she had booked the last two afternoon sessions. Irritated, I asked our administrator why she allowed this (it was very unusual) and why my client had requested this. She only said she had been "insistent."

Unsatisfied with this answer, I went about my day, sensing growing irritation as my client's two sessions approached. I really didn't know what to say when she arrived. I was mad. Mad she was taking up two sessions in my busy, busy day; mad I didn't have a solid explanation for why she had booked two back-to-back sessions; and mad that other clients weren't able to get a session in my increasingly hard-to-book schedule.

Rajani arrived on time. We sat down. I was working hard inside to offer my usual kind, soft brow and welcoming face. In my utter humanness, I really wanted to say, "What were you thinking when you booked two sessions in one day?!" Here is how our conversation went:

ME (A): Hello, Rajanai. As always, it's lovely to see you. I have been so curious all day why you booked two sessions with me in one day.

RAJANAI (R): I actually came to tell you to go home.

Dead silence. I can only imagine what my face did. Inside, I recall feeling a gush of warmth like a splash of hot oil inside my face. I did not have a clue what to say. I was new enough as a therapist that I was straining to keep composure while I read the "how to be a perfect therapist" book inside my head.

A: I'm sorry. I am not sure I understood you.

R: I booked the last two sessions of the day so I can tell you to go home.

A: I am sorry—I am still confused. Why would I go home? You booked two sessions. Something important must be going on. This is your time.

R: Yes, and that's why I am here.

[Pause.]

I know you. I have known you since my family and I arrived here. You have been everyone's therapist. You brought my husband back to me. Now, he is a gentle and kind lover again. You helped my eldest son get a robotic arm, and now he can participate in so many more things at school. He has friends and enjoys his life. You helped my youngest sons belong in a group, and now they are thriving in school. We are a happy family. [Pause.]

When we first arrived, I remember how you greeted us here. You always floated down the stairs, smiling, and offered us water. You said hello with warmth. Now you come rushing down the stairs, dropping things. You look tired—you have circles under your eyes. You have gained weight. [At which point she gathered a bit of her hip flesh and pointed to mine. I could feel my face flushing and imagined it was fuchsia by now.]

Now that I am your client, I believe I can remind you of what you always tell me: I must take care of myself to keep being a mother and wife, especially after everything I went through. You also must take care of yourself so you can do your job. So, I would like you to go home.

I was floored. I had no training, no template, no notion about what to do with this conversation. And I was really irritated now.

A: Rajani, you know I cannot go home. You have a session, and I always have work to do.

R [CUTTING ME OFF]: Amber, I also have a message from our [her country] community. We had a meeting last night.

> My stomach plunged beneath the floor, and I began to feel upset. She spoke quickly.
>
> R: The meeting wasn't about you, but we talked about you because you have helped so many members of our community. [Ours was a fledgling torture treatment program and for over a year, I was the only clinician, so I had worked with many of the members of the community from her country.] I have a message from all of them:
>
> You are our reference point for everything that is good and true in this world. If we lose you, we lose everything.
>
> I did not know what to do or say. I was stunned. It had never occurred to me to consider how the community of refugees and survivors of torture I worked with might think of me between sessions, or even after our work was complete. I saw so many clients that I focused on our time in therapy, not in between.

In the end, I went home. I learned from our continuing conversation that Rajanai had cleared my going home early with my boss, our executive director (who was concerned about my overworking and clear exhaustion but didn't have the interpersonal skills to approach this). She also gave me very explicit instructions for what to do. These instructions ranged from walking my dog to cooking our favorite meal for my husband with my sexiest lingerie under my clothes. Her instructions gave me insight into who she was, as mother, her most cherished role, and wife, as the woman who held her family together. I suddenly had an insight into my client and what it meant to be woman, mother, wife, friend that I had never even thought of in our work together. This realization was deeply moving. Reticent to leave early and aware of how much I had to do, I did leave and drive around the block, planning to return. She was standing on the porch. My client knew me with a depth I did not expect, and this is something I now consider with each client. How do they see me? What do they learn from my actions, inactions, things said, unsaid, how I appear, how I present, say hello, say goodbye? This is when the idea of true reciprocity in therapy was seeded in a way that would revolutionize my work and become the experiences that inform this book.

Coregulation Is Self-Regulation

Along with being the most important clinical skill, self-regulation for self-care is our personal and professional commitment to our clients. This is what Rajani taught me. It is disrespectful to show up in any state other than fully present, which does not mean being perfect or ignoring the very real things that go on in our lives. It also does not mean being unaffected by the depth and intensity and horror of our clients' experiences. It means taking full responsibility for the work we have agreed to do, being honest about who we are and how we are feeling on any given day, and learning to track and befriend our nervous system, and state shift so that we are as authentically present as possible.

The nautilus shell is a powerful symbol for this. It is often used to show the spiraling nature of life and is considered a classic example of a logarithmic spiral. Nautilus shells begin with four chambers. As the shell grows, housing a larger and larger nautilus, the number of chambers increases to up to 30 (Figure 5.1). The nautilus fills and empties these chambers of water to control its own buoyancy, allowing it to sink or rise depending on its needs. When it outgrows its shell, it does not abandon it; it grows a new chamber at the tail end of its spiraling protection. Folklore about spirals is ample and includes the notion that no matter how large a nautilus shell grows, it will always source its center for nourishment. Whether or not this folklore is accurate, it is a powerful metaphor for self-care, and for life. Perhaps, like this poetic representation of the nautilus shell, our resilience is in our ever-spiraling-from-center ability to grow, and as mammals gifted with the magnificence of our complex and capable brain, ANS, and heart, to keep learning as we grow. Our resilience is equally rooted in our ability to adapt to our personal and collective growth, as the nautilus fills and empties its increasing chambers. In the spiral shape of all life, perhaps

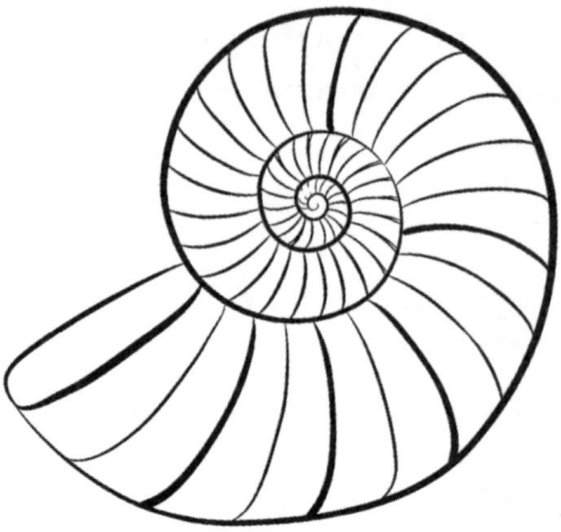

Figure 5.1 Nautilus Shell

we know exactly enough to tend to ourselves and have everything we need in our center.

The nautilus inspired a self-care practice I call the Moving Center (Figure 5.2). Because the human body is movement, and is 70% water, our center also moves. While human bodies have an anatomical and energy center, our watery composition means that any time we shift our relationship to gravity, our weight redistributes. Like the nautilus

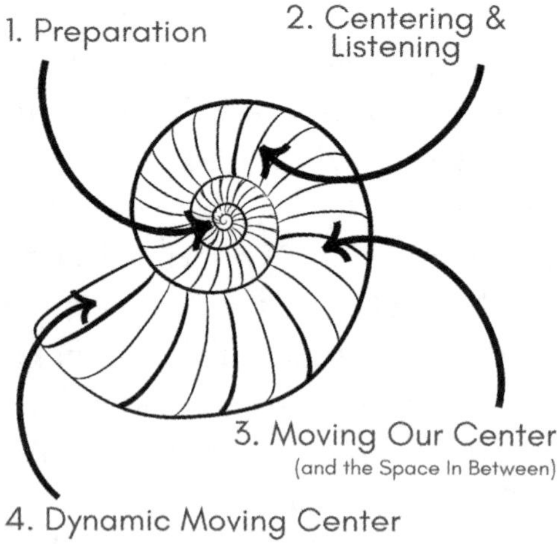

Figure 5.2 Moving Center

moving water from chamber to chamber, our human bodies weight shifting is the movement of water, which moves our center. Dance, gymnastics, and other dynamic movement arts, practices, and athletics work intentionally with a moving center. This practice, which has many optional layers, acknowledges and honors this.

MOVING CENTER PRACTICE

Layer 1: Preparation

To practice, find a space in your home where you can lie down, sit, or stand and perhaps even move (stretch, dance, asana, or just wiggle) a bit. You can put a mat or blankets down if you want to lie down. If you choose to sit, find something comfortable and supportive to sit on. Because there are several options, or layers, to this practice, and depending on your creative preferences, you may also want something to write, doodle, draw, or color in or on, and even clay or Sculpey if you like to shape things with your hands. If you enjoy movement and dance, cue up some music that you like to move to.

Once you have your supplies and space organized, choose your shape, or posture. Lie down, sit, or stand. Practice Shifting to Comfort

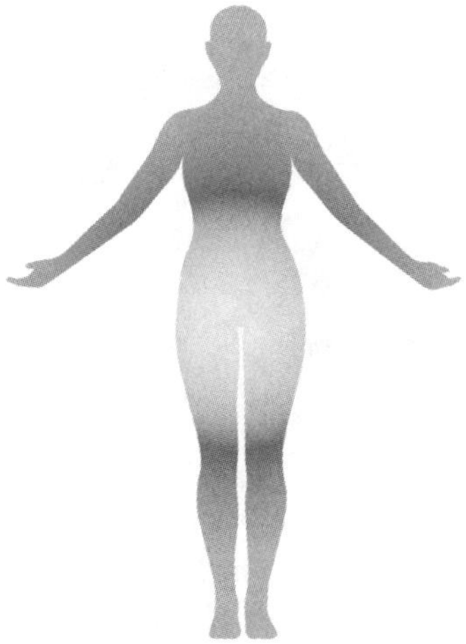

Figure 5.3 Preparation

from Chapter 4. That's a useful way to prepare for any somatic or movement practice.

Layer 2: Centering and Listening

Find your center. It doesn't have to be your anatomical center; it can be anywhere in your body, as Figure 5.4 shows. If it's comfortable for you, place one hand (or both) on your center. Take a moment to pause and sense into your center.

The bones, connective tissue, and blood vessels that become our arms develop from the same neural tissue type as our heart; the lateral plate mesoderm (Prummel et al., 2020). Body Mind Centering proposes that our hands are also an energetic end point in the human body, meaning they, along with the feet, pelvic floor, and head, are areas where the energy that becomes our movement enters and exits. In this way, our hands can metaphorically and perhaps even a little bit literally be considered an extension of our heart.

In this spirit, invite your hand to sense your center: What's in there? Use your imagination: You might sense colors, symbols, textures, images, allies, and ancestors. Reciprocity is an important concept in

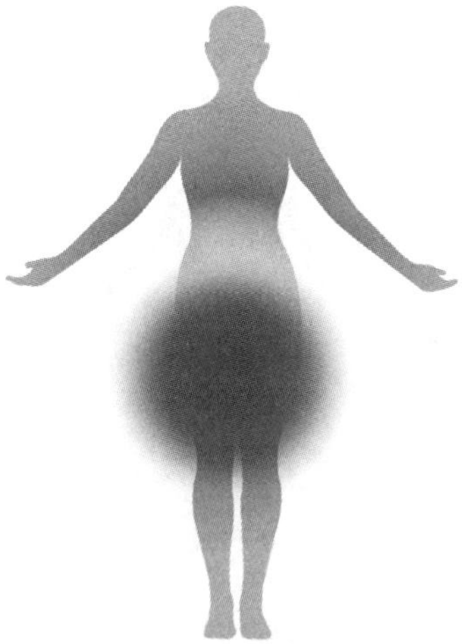

Figure 5.4 Centering and Listening

Polyvagal Theory, and in human relationship. It's our capacity to be in and maintain relationship that is mutually beneficial in some way for all who are relating. If you want, take a moment to document what you sense through drawing, scribbling, sculpting, or writing.

Simultaneously, and reciprocally, while you sense your center, you can send energy to your center. Just as we place a hand on a friend's shoulder or back to comfort them, let your hand offer energy (calming, healing, empowering, etc.) to your center. I call this practice self-reciprocity. Self-reciprocity is a PVISDMP term signifying our capacity to connect to our own embodied sense of self; to listen interoceptively to ourselves. In our busy world, it can be hard to find even a few moments for this depth of self-listening and self-reflection.

Once again, take a moment to document or describe your center.

Layer 3: Moving Our Center and the Space in Between

There are several ways to elaborate this practice. One is to notice if your moving center has moved to a different area of your body. If it has, place one hand on your new center while maintaining contact with your original center. Sense and receive, send and offer, in both centers. Our body is a community of many parts, rhythms, energies, movements, and feelings. Being in dialogue with two centers simultaneously amplifies our natural polyrhythmicity, which is part of the art of our unique mammalian complexity and innovation. You can continue to document what you notice or, if you want to integrate movement, the second-layer practice invites movement.

Sense the space in between your two centers. Figure 5.5 shows what this space in between might look or feel like. Using your breath, begin to breathe into this space. Let this breath become movement. The movement may be quite still, outwardly invisible. It may be tracking internal sensations moving, like the color and dance of coral reefs under a still ocean surface. Or you may experience tiny micromovements between your centers. Invite your body to expand and grow these micromovements, as much or as little as is comfortable for you. You can also remain still while tracking this space between. Stay comfortable.

This moving between moving centers, initiated by micromovements, is often a relatively safer way for people to begin moving, especially if they find movement intimidating or scary. It can be painful and scary to move when we are shut down or feel frozen in place. These micromovements can gently facilitate bigger movements. It is also fine to remain with tiny movements.

It's up to you and your own sense of biorhythmicity, comfort, and relative safety how much you expand this space between with movement. Always, always rest amply. It is in rest that we truly integrate the new learnings and neural pathways created with new or comfortably familiar experiences. If you want to dance or stretch, allow yourself to move and add music if you wish. When your body senses it's time to pause, which might be at the end of a song or playlist, or when you feel tired, or when you just know you feel complete with this practice, transition to a pause. Take as long to let your movement recede toward stillness as you took to weave movement in. This is very important: Trauma, stress, distress, and just the hectic and hurried nature of society can force us to move in rhythms that are not our own. The reclamation of our own rhythm and sense of timing

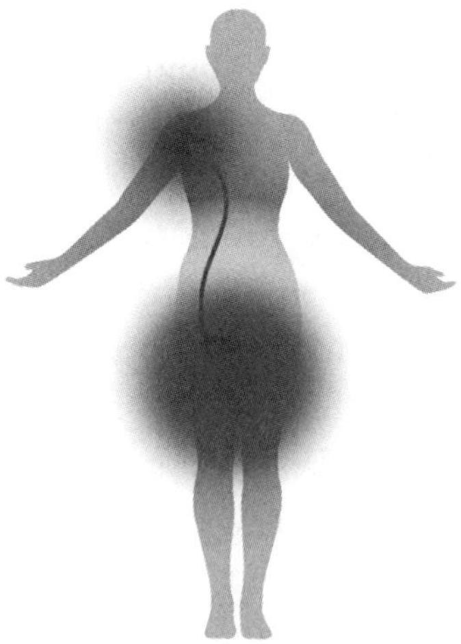

Figure 5.5 Moving the Center

is embodied justice. Timing and rhythmicity, in this framework, are secondary portals to the body and therefore to the restoration of our connection to our body.

Layer 4: Dynamic Moving Center

Once you've had time to rest adequately, or document in whatever creative way you want, there is a third and optional layer to this practice. Resume by placing your hands on your first or second centers, depending on where you left off. Sensing into your center(s) again, notice if a third center emerges. If it doesn't, you may be complete with this practice for now. This will always change, just as our center does.

If a third center emerges, repeat the same previous processes. Sense and reciprocate—offering and receiving—in both centers. Move the space in between. Continue this practice following each new center that emerges. Your hands will move from Centers 1 and 2 to 2 and 3, 3 and 4, 4 and 5, and so on. At some point, you will be a constellation of moving centers. See Figure 5.6 for how this might look and feel. Play with your constellation self however you want—move, as in Layer 3, with or without music. Moving all these centers together, whether sequentially or all at the same time, can be a fun and playful way to engage with more dynamic mobilization and movement. You might move from the spaces between the centers, as in Layer 3, or you might "hopscotch" or imaginatively move each center, sequentially or all together, in a free-form rhythmic dance. Make sure you transition slowly, in your own timing and rhythm, to pause into stillness. So often when we are guided through movement (or any) practice, we are cued to follow the facilitator's rhythm. As stated previously, reclaiming our rhythmicity helps restore embodied justice. Opportunities to begin, move through, and end a movement exploration or process in our own rhythm—be it fast, medium, or slow—and to bring movement to a pause when we are ready to can repair the moving transitions that traumatic experiences interrupt and undermine. Restoring our natural transition in movement assists the nervous system to restore transitions from rest to

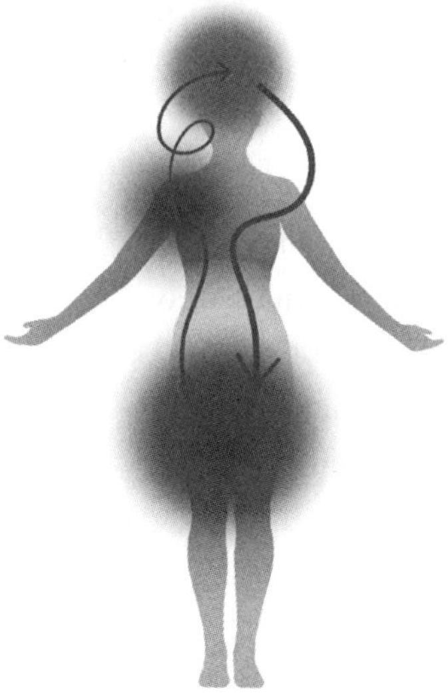

Figure 5.6 Dynamic Moving Center

activity, sleep to waking, slow to fast, and so on. Our capacity to flow smoothly and in our own way, from one movement, feeling, or thought activity to another is fueled by inner rhythmicity. Rather than just stop when you are done moving, transitioning back slowly, that is, "rewinding" the practice you are completing, helps restore our transitional capacities.

The Trilogy of Human Response

Empathy is often centered as a key trait or skill of good therapy and is emphasized in most clinical trainings and educational programs. Dr. Henry Tobey's (1999) work *Secondary Trauma and Resiliency* was my introduction to the dangers of relying solely on empathy. Tobey differentiates compassion from empathy, two terms and concepts that are often used interchangeably. Based on many years of experience in humanitarian work, I also propose a distinction between sympathy and empathy, which can get comingled. These three concepts are worthy of deconstruction in terms of their true meanings, and

Sympathy	A human response based on feeling sad about/sorry for another person's pain. ***"I feel sorry for you."***
Empathy	An interpersonal skill/human response based on identification with another person's pain. ***"I feel your pain."***
Compassion	The ability to recognize pain and suffering in another human, because we recognize and know our own pain and suffering. In this recognition we know this pain in self and other is not the same. ***"I recognize your pain because I have my own pain."***

Figure 5.7 Sympathy, Empathy, and Compassion Table

while this does not always bear out across languages, they seem quite different concepts.

Above (Figure 5.7) is a table containing Dr. Tobey's definitions of these three concepts, which I now call the Trilogy of Human Response. Take a moment to read the concepts on the left, and then read the definitions on the right. Do these definitions correspond with your understanding of the concepts? What is new for you, and what is different from how you use these terms, if anything? What's familiar?

Sympathy, which is "I feel sorry for you," has its place in human caring, but, from a human rights and social justice context, is not appropriate in psychotherapeutic or humanitarian helping contexts. Sympathy is not helpful if one is suffering due to abuse of power. Our ability to sympathize is certainly related to our ability to empathize, but sympathy alone may augment a survivor's sense of (and actual) disempowerment.

Misplaced sympathy is quite rampant in humanitarian work, which maintains many elements of colonialism (that's a subject for another book). Sympathy disempowers and is often expressed in words like "Oh, those poor [refugees, people, victims; fill in the blank]—they are really suffering. They need so much help and I can help them." Obviously, this is a broad generalization, and it occurs frequently. In an article titled "What Language Does Your Body Speak" (Gray, 2016, p. 33), therapists and humanitarian responders are invited to consider which of these three responses is their go-to when acting in a helping manner. It's a worthy question for all of us.

Empathy is often heralded as the key component to human connection. Empathy and compassion are often used interchangeably, as in "We need to practice more empathy and compassion." Empathy is perhaps the most widely cited emotion endorsed in psychotherapy. It is a human emotion that enables us to connect to another person's emotions, or feelings, and as such is widely lauded as a primary and essential tool for positive psychological, therapeutic, and healing work.

The nautilus shell spiral is once again an image that might more accurately depict the relationship between these three concepts. All three—sympathy, empathy, and compassion—are meaningful human responses to varying contexts, moments, and experiences. They are developmental in the sense that sympathy might be considered the most primary, and be in the center, with empathy being like a chamber that develops later, and compassion being the emotion or response that evolves last, from the foundation of sympathy and empathy. In this possibility, the spiraling nautilus represents both our individual lives and our personal capacity to develop as compassionate humans, and our bio-collective—all life emerging from a single center with compassion as an evolutionary trajectory that includes all of us, from the simpler life forms such as microorganisms that keep our soil fertile, to the complexity of collective human life.

There is certainly a place for sympathy. We feel sorry for the smooshed creature on the road and the family they may leave behind in the hard-to-survive natural world. Empathy, which is "I feel your pain" (or any other emotion), might also be useful for both parties, as when we can feel what another feels, be it joy, suffering, pain, or ecstasy. We can connect. Compassion is "I recognize your pain [or joy, suffering, etc.] because I know my own." Compassion is infused with contemplative nonattachment. Empathy has its risks, though, and when I read about these in Babette Rothschild's (2002, p. 2) wonderful body of work, it was another client who taught me about the risks of empathy, and further research fortified what he taught me:

MICHAEL: THE RISKS OF EMPATHY

I met with Michael to begin our initial assessment. His story is still one of the cruelest I have ever heard. I was trying to "meet him": to connect, listen well, communicate that I understood him. It was my own mother who once pointed out that I tend to physically lean forward too much when I am listening with intention. I think I was probably doing this; I know I was funneling all the empathy I could source into our nonverbal connection.

Michael suddenly stopped talking and looked at me with an expression I could not quite make sense of. Then he pounded his fist on the table next to him and said sternly, "Stop mocking me!"

I paused. I blushed a little. I could not figure out what he meant, so I simply said, "I am sorry. I do not mean to mock you."

I paused and breathed. Then I said, "Is it okay to continue?"

He said yes. And we continued.

After a few more minutes, he slammed his fist on the table with even more energy and in a raised voice said, "STOP MOCKING ME!"

I was stunned. He looked irate. I breathed a few times and then said, "I am sorry you think I am mocking you. That is not what I wish to do. Can you help me understand what I am doing that feels like mocking?"

He stared at me for several seconds and then said, "You are looking right through me, like they did. That is how they hurt me."

I had already been considering the difference between empathy and compassion, and if overreliance on empathy alone was possible, and if it might be harmful. This is what Rothschild wrote about back in 2002 in "Understanding Dangers of Empathy," and her work made sense to me intuitively. Dr. Tobey's work (1999) and Dr. Tania Singer and colleagues work (Klimecki, 2014) research all verified what my client so strongly expressed: Relying on empathy alone can be harmful to the therapist and to the client. They were among the first to differentiate these terms and to recognize the unique qualities of compassion as a more holistic means of creating interconnectivity with clients (and others), and a protective factor for therapists working with and therefore exposed to difficult histories of suffering and abuse.

I have since worked out that empathy can be exploited in service of cruelty. Central to this idea is this: Empathy, while clearly a core ingredient in compassion, is also a core ingredient in cruelty. Cruelty is not possible when we practice compassion. Therefore, the very same emotion that offers us connection to others is also a useful tool to increase another's suffering. The origins of this idea are in Anna Salter's (1995, pp. 250–251) book *Transforming Trauma*. The most sadistic perpetrators can utilize their empathic abilities to increase the suffering and pain of their victims. Consider this idea on a global level: Could the human species, if we moved beyond our current biological, physiological, psychological, and emotional/mental state of being "soft wired for empathy," enhance the possibility we inherently embody to become beings who are soft (or, perhaps even hard) wired for compassion? And if we can do this, would we more consistently relate to one another in ways that promote equanimity, especially when we are in a helping relationship? What would our embodiment and practice of compassion communicate to others? How would we see, and be seen?

Much later, in conversations with renowned meditation teachers Sharon Salzberg and Roshi Joan Halifax I found both agreed that empathy and compassion are different, and that compassion makes cruelty impossible. This is when it occurred to me that these three distinct but related responses are evolutionary and developmental, and that humans may be on a trajectory toward being hardwired for compassion.

This idea also stems from a video Jeremy Rifkin published in 2010 called "The Empathic Civilization." In this video, Rifkin promotes the idea that because humans are soft wired for empathy, a gift of our evolution, we can create a more equanimous, kind civilization. This theory offers hope, and while a good beginning to what's possible, it begs for more consideration of the limits of empathy and the place and potency of compassion as the pathway to individual, collective, and global health, equanimity, and civilization. If humans are soft-wired for empathy, as some claim mirror neuron research seems to suggest (albeit, in my understanding, not definitively), and if this is an evolutionarily emergent property of our humanity, is there a possibility that human mammals could become hardwired for empathy (i.e., born with this trait or ability intrinsically developed)? This question begs the possibility that we humans might be on an evolutionary trajectory toward being hardwired for compassion, a more highly evolved state of being that promotes responses that might be more reciprocal and kinder than empathy, because in compassion, cruelty is not possible. It seems that compassion is the human response that can contribute to a more wholistically compassionate and therefore kinder civilization. This idea broadens the work from the individual's session to the global impact of practicing compassion in every relationship (human and more than human) we have. The possibilities are profound.

In "Vagal Pathways: Portals to Compassion," Porges (2017) promotes the idea that experiencing compassion and a state of oneness may be an emergent process of higher brain functions while a ventral vagal state is maintained. He defines two bidirectional pathways: a passive pathway that functions through neuroception, and an active pathway that is implemented through voluntary activities and practices that connect, calm, energize, and promote rest such as ritual, dance, contemplative practice, and prayer. His suggestion that movement, dance, and other embodied practices are active pathways speaks volumes to all the ways working with movement and the body not only enhances trauma treatment but might also increase compassion locally (i.e., person to person) and when we consciously practice self-compassion and "ripple" this mindful practice outwards, globally. I refer to the latter as "glo-regulation," expanding on the notion that self-regulation is coregulation. Self-regulation as coregulation might foster a more global ("glo") regulation: literally creating an environment of relative safety for as many of us as possible.

We also might refer to this as eco-regulation to describe our ability to regulate with the world around us, according to our ecology, or place, which promotes our sense of belonging. The idea of eco-regulation is not new; it reflects Indigenous sources of wisdom based on our connection to the world of all things. Bioception and geoception derive from this concept. As covered in Chapter 2, Polyvagal Theory is a theory of evolution and emergence. That our ANS is a literal gift of our evolutionary ancestors, from far simpler life forms to our mammalian cousins, and is a constant dancing pathway to possibility and emergence, is an example of how we as physical bodies reflect the greater natural world. Connecting to an environment that reflects and mirrors us might offer more possibility that the environment can become as safe as can be for all.

Cultivating Self-Compassion

Kelly McGonigal (2013), in her TED talk "How to Make Stress Your Friend," shares research on self-compassion, showing that five minutes a day practicing a focused attention practice develops self-compassion. This practice is essentially the Vipassana as taught by the Buddha, so credit must go to yet another example of how ancient medicine has long promoted what science is only beginning to explain in its own language.

Development of self-compassion is essential to self-care. It is our capacity to be compassionate to ourselves that promotes self-love and self-respect. These are core to self-regulation as the basis of self-care. This is a worthy self-care practice; what better way to promote our capacity to offer our clients our experience of self-compassion in promotion of theirs? This is also a fundamental practice for client stabilization and regulation. Most clients I have worked with learn this in the context that is specifically helpful for them. That is, it's not taught as a spiritually driven meditation practice but to ameliorate symptoms and by extension, suffering. For clients who cannot relax or sleep, it's relaxation practice. For those who have a hard time concentrating or remembering and adjusting for any cognitive issues or effects of traumatic brain injury, it's a focusing practice. For those who dissociate, it's a presencing practice. The following practice is written the way it has been helpful for clients; following the description is a suggestion for using this practice to explore the Trilogy of Human Response and flex and exercise our self-compassion "muscles."

CULTIVATING SELF-COMPASSION: FOCUSED ATTENTION PRACTICE

This focused attention practice consists of three primary elements: body, breath, and mind.

Body: Buddhist and contemplative practice rely on the use of a meditation cushion to anchor the body in a relaxed, alert posture. This posture supports alignment and ease in the spine in a balanced constructive collaboration of being relaxed, just alert enough; of yielding. We should be neither efforting nor tense nor collapsed. For those without a cushion, perching on your "sitz" bones, the bony protrusions in your butt that you sit on, can have the same effect on posture. This is the body component of this practice: to sit in relaxed alertness by perching like a bird on a branch, on our sitz bones.

Breath: Breath is the heart of this practice. Our breath is composed of an inhale and an exhale. We each have our own unique rhythm of inhaling and exhaling. For the breath component of this practice, we simply watch our outbreath, or exhale, every time we do it. We don't change our breath in any way, and we inhale and exhale naturally. The quality of attention we use to notice every exhale is called "20% attention"—imagine a butterfly alighting on a flower and then lifting off, lightly and gracefully. This is the "effort" of our noticing. If we strain or try too hard, we undermine the downregulating, quieting aspect of this practice and the opportunity to quiet the mind. The breath component is to observe every exhale with the light attention of a butterfly landing on a flower, then quickly flying off.

Mind: It is natural and usual that during this practice, your mind will get busy. This is when the Trilogy of Human Response is relevant, because it's an interesting time to notice your attitude toward yourself when you are distracted by thinking and forget to observe your exhale. The practice here is to simply notice your thought, and let it go—our attention here is like how we tend to our breath, with the addition of naming it, for example, when you catch yourself thinking and not tending to your exhale, just say (aloud or in your mind) "thought." This acknowledgment allows our busy minds to accept our distraction and shift attention back to breath, without judgment, that is, with self-compassion. The mind component is: Every time you are distracted by your thoughts, notice them and interrupt them by saying "thought" aloud or in your mind. You can imagine a railroad crossing gate with the word "thoughts" on it stopping your thinking, or you can visualize a little being who summoned your attention so you hand them a raincoat or lunchbox, pat them on their head, and send them off with the acknowledgment of their name: thought.

THE TRILOGY OF HUMAN RESPONSE PRACTICE: BACK-TO-BACK, HEART-TO-HEART

Once you have a sense of this practice, here is an invitation to play with it in the context of the Trilogy of Human Response. In contemplative trainings, many teachers encourage meditators to use "witness consciousness," which means to not judge ourselves when we get distracted by thoughts (or anything else). In this practice, working in proximity with another person, you can sense the difference between practicing alone and practicing in pairs as an experiment in how your nervous system self- and coregulates when you are in proximity to another's nervous system.

Here's the scaffold:

In Part 1 of this practice, you will practice by yourself, albeit near your partner. In Part 2, you will practice back-to-back with your partner. It is up to you and your partner to decide ahead of time whether you will literally touch backs physically or just be close enough to sense the energy between your back and your partner's back.

1. Find a partner. This can be a friend, family member, willing acquaintance, even a pet who can sit still and attune

to you. You can also use an inanimate object like a big cushion, as connecting to people after interpersonal trauma can be difficult for some.

2. Sit side by side with enough space that you feel like you are alone, or solo, for Part 1. Decide now whether you and your partner will choose to touch physically, back-to-back, for Part 2, or just sit close enough to sense each other. Have everything you need to shift from sitting side by side with space between you to back-to-back, touching or in proximity, so when it's time to shift to Part 2, you can shift silently and easily. Also decide how long you wish to practice each part (suggestion is 2–5 minutes, for this exploration). Always adjust in your own body for what suits you.
3. Take a moment to shift toward physical comfort. Once you are as physically comfortable as possible, begin to practice focused attention alongside your partner, in your own "space bubble" or kinesphere. Make sure you've set the timer to go off after your agreed-upon time in Part 1.
4. As you practice individually together, notice how kind and compassionate you are to yourself when your mind distracts you by thinking. Do you feel sorry for yourself, or angry (sympathy)? Do you get lost and over-attached to your emotions about your distraction (empathy) and find it difficult to redirect your attention back to your breath? Do you compare yourself to others who might be better meditators, or do you simply allow yourself to be as human as you are—which reflects compassion?
5. After you complete your designated time in individual practice, move so that you and your partner are back-to-back as previously agreed: touching physically or not touching. When you are both settled, and as physically comfortable as possible, begin the practice again, with awareness that you are in this space with another person. Notice if it is different to practice focused attention with

another person directly in your kinesphere. Does it affect your breathing, your comfort? Do you adjust your body to support yourself and/or your partner? As you consider all the ways actively practicing with another person (or pet) affects your practice, where do these adjustments fit in the Trilogy? Do you tend to take care of yourself or your partner more? Do you merge and lose yourself, or connect and maintain yourself while sensing their presence? Your way of expressing these three emotions, responses, or states may not align with this simplistic example; sense into how you experience your response to your humanness and where your response might fit in this trilogy.

All this information is useful in our self-awareness, which informs us of the quality of attention we bring to our work with clients. As my client taught me, when we are not paying attention to our needs, we cannot be as mindfully, heartfully, and body-fully present for our clients, as they deserve. This self-awareness might also be seen as a spiral, a constantly connecting and nourishing dance of self-regulation, self-compassion, self-love, self-respect, and self-reciprocity, which are all core to self-care as a primary clinical skill. More globally, as we human beings gain meaning for our lives and offer services and teachings that are truly relevant, respectful, and in service to others, we are in service of evolution. As journeyers on the road of evolution, with unknown possibilities and potential for our own individual and collective advancement, as well as the planetary community's well-being, practices that promote compassion may serve not only our own and our clients' well-being as we work with survivors of trauma; we may also contribute to the phylogenetic enhancement of our species. Compassion as a practice and an emotional response that may benefit from our empathic connection, but that also serves to distinguish mine from yours, might promote levels of regard and respect that communicate more equanimity in our helping interactions and interventions.

Section II

Practice

This section shares the work. The chapters are organized according to the neural circuits and their primary and hybrid states and actions, and reference their blended states. Chapters are not finite: Each one is inspired by client ANS and movement patterns and their ideas, feedback, and restorative, emergent processes, community exchanges, and the practices we have cocreated over the years. Chapters are also possibility; the practices shared could move to almost any other chapter. They are fluid and adaptable. Readers are encouraged to engage with them as inquiry. Try them on in your own body and learn what they offer you for your own self-care, self-compassion, self-respect, self-love, and self-regulation. Experience your own state-shifting wisdom and notice what unhelpful patterns they can disrupt, and what new movements and patterns become possible. Be the soil that roots them in your own way of moving and then play with them and offer them to others. Figure P.2 shows the foci of these six chapters in Section II, which follow the primary (enough safety for social engagement, flow and wholeness, mobilization, immobilization) and hybrid states and actions (the continuum of freeze, noted as freeze in Figure P.2 for space, the continuum of play, the continuum of nourishment) arising from the three neural circuits: the ventral vagal circuit (VVC) , the sympathetic nervous system (SNS), and the dorsal vagal circuit (DVC). These states, except for DVC shutdown, are movement and move us. Emergent states are all the states that emerge from any variation when two or three neural circuits are recruited at the same time in immediate response or reaction to the environment. Blended and emergent states are symbolically represented by the heart in the area where all three concentric circles connect because the heart is innervated by neural fibers from all three circuits. This heart-centered space is where the DVC joins the VVC and SNS for more contemplative or sensual play, or where all three circuits are co-recruited as in appeasement or limbic dominance, Kroll's (2025) term for the unique altered state of consciousness that occurs during childbirth. She defines limbic dominance: "Limbic dominance may represent a childbirth-specific emergent state in which the nervous system flows fluidly between ventral, ventral-sympathetic, and ventral-dorsal patterns, with safety as the anchoring condition." Our capacity to move through these from the ventrally mediated sense of relative safety is flow. Integrated flow or just flow can refer to any blend of states that supports us to meet the moment we are in as resiliently as possible, in wholeness. The clinical symptoms, complaints, and issues we work with occur when this flow is fragmented by the imprint of a primary, hybrid, or blended patterned state in response to danger or life threat, in service of survival.

Figure P.2 is complicated for some of my clients. When this happens, I draw a "polyvagal sea," an image many clients understand and appreciate. I also offer a visualization to teach this material with clients and students. I draw an earthy brown

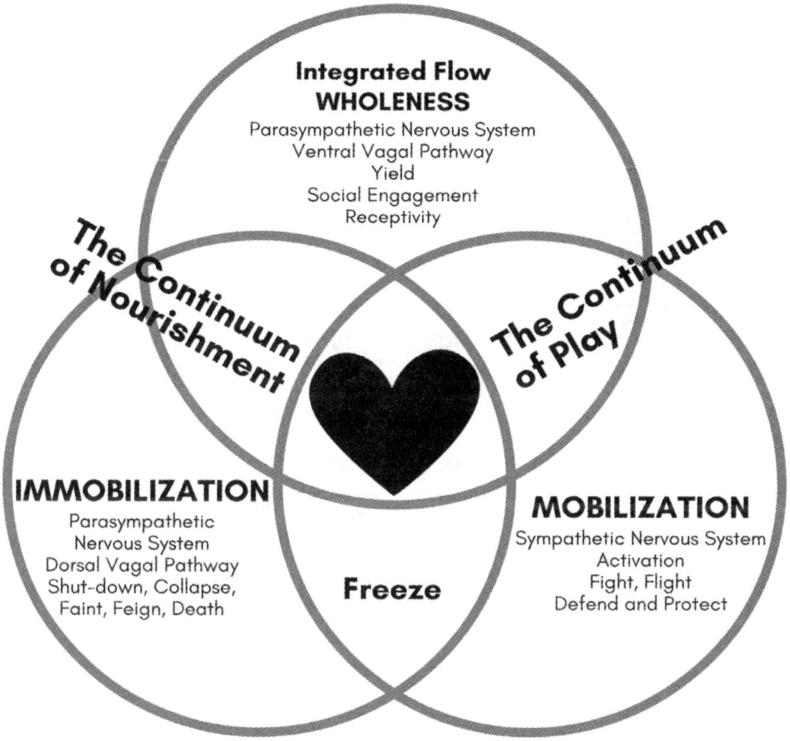

Figure P.2 Polyvagal-Informed Somatic and Dance/Movement Psychotherapy or the Neural Dance *(Credit: Sara von Koningsveld)*

ocean bed for the DVC; a swirl of blue and green colors and currents for the SNS; and an ocean surface with playful creatures, a boat, some rain, and some sunbeams changing the coloring, movement, and lighting of the surface for the VVC. We often draw the image together, adding the features of our favorite ocean or sea. The visualization practice is "riffed" off the following paragraph, adapted for the client/student and context. Feel free to read it aloud and then imagine you are there:

Take a moment to imagine your favorite sea, wherever it is. Focus on the seabed, the ocean's roots, full of rich nutrients that supply all the oceans and earth's inhabitants with much-needed ground and form, nourishment and diversity. Oscillate your attention to imagine the sea waters, the colors of these waters, the sea life there. These changes depend on where you are; the ocean, too, has culture. Appreciate the movement, the energy, the many layers of currents that literally move all the life here. The ocean, like the plant nation, is a primary source of oxygen, essential to our movement, connection, and flow. Rising up off the seabed, this diversity of breathing, nourishing, moving life is in eternal reciprocal exchange with everything above and around it—sky and earth. Imagine the ocean surface in all her expressions: Calm. Wild. Turbulent. Clear. Dynamic. Wavy. The light dancing, the whitecaps cresting, fish leaping, whales breeching, and birds diving. The ocean's surface meets the world like we do, nourished from our roots, moved by and moving the diversity that lives inside us, engaging with the world it is part of.

Whether guiding clients or students I choose words that I sense are relevant for their experience of the ocean. Just imagining the ocean can be enough, and sometimes, people enjoy reflection or creative process time, like journaling, drawing, moving, or sounding afterward.

Content warning: Section II contains client vignettes and stories. Although each vignette and story is a composite, still, through these vignettes, clients' voices are raised, with their permission and often at their request, so they are heard. Psychotherapy in all its forms works with the consequences of life's challenges, stresses, unbearable life experiences, and everything in between. We sometimes have opportunities to work from a public health and prevention perspective, but not often enough. These vignettes reference clients' abuses, not in detail, but the abuses they experience are named. Working with trauma is, by definition, context specific. We cannot promote reciprocity, respect, dignity, and belonging if we do not consider each client's unique context for exposure and suffering, restoration and liberation. Please tend to yourself and pause as needed. Thank you for reading these stories. We can never un-know what we know. In that spirit, may our witnessing here and everywhere we accompany our clients forge a path to a collective dismantling of supremacy, oppression, and violence.

CHAPTER 6

The Dorsal Vagal Circuit

SEAT OF TERROR, SEAT OF BLISS

Nature does not hurry, yet everything is accomplished.

—LAO TZU

If you've ever been on a roller coaster, or a carnival ride where you suddenly drop down from a peak height, you may have felt your stomach drop before you experience a mini "blackout." It can feel like the pit of your stomach is falling out of you, and it can have a quality of cold heat that rises up through your heart to your throat. Your mind goes completely blank and when you re-engage with your surroundings, you have a momentary gap in memory. When this happens on a ride, or in a plane that hits sudden turbulence, or even a car driving so fast over a hill with a steep decline that it is airborne for a moment and then speeds downhill too fast, the corporeal experience is similar to terror. Clients describe similar physical sensations; the difference is, they don't choose to ride the roller coaster or drive the car. They are forced into physical and psychological pain so unimaginable their body recruits the parasympathetic dorsal vagal circuit (DVC) and shuts down so that they are spared the pain they are being subjected to. Endorphins are released to increase pain tolerance and offer some somatic grace to endure the suffering. The DVC brake immediately slows the heart rate, inhibiting the ventral vagal circuit (VVC) in its tracks, completely bypassing the sympathetic nervous system's energy surge.

The first time I witnessed this, I was sitting with a young woman who had escaped a sex trafficking ring in southern New Mexico. A female client of mine was married to one of the traffickers and was trying to help several young women and protect her own life. She eventually escaped to another state. She referred the girl to me, and when we began to talk, I smelled her terror. Her breath became so shallow it was barely perceptible and smelled acrid and bitter. Her skin went pale and had a grayish cast. Her eyes fluttered involuntarily, and then her whole body jerked into a deathly stillness. Remembering, her body began to shut down again.

Working with shutdown is one of the most complex clinical skills. Working somatically, it requires enormous patience and often endless moments of witnessing, of sitting with and accompanying deep suffering.

From shutdown, the road to a more engaged presence is not a straight line. When working with survivors of trauma, the restorative process rarely follows the hierarchical evolution of the ANS. The DVC-mediated immobilization is a complete shutdown and is the most challenging clinical presentation to work with. The lack of energy and vitality is palpable. It's impossible to talk our way out of this shutdown. In the words of a client coming out of shutdown, "I cannot move. I must be still. My body is a minefield, and it terrifies me."

Immobilization in terror is a body-based, neurophysiological state (immobilization) and (in)action that sometimes dangerously slows heart rate, respiration, and other neurophysiological rhythms. Humans cannot sustain true shutdown for long because of our demand for oxygen to feed and nourish our biological and physiological functioning. The increasing popularity of Polyvagal Theory has resulted in a tendency to promote "ventral vibes" and "being in ventral," which can be problematic when working with clients who are stuck in shutdown or who repeatedly shut down in session. Privileging the ventral-governed state of safety and emergent pathway of social engagement assumes a level of safety that is mostly absent with clients who have survived human rights violations. This is why relative safety is an important concept and why it is helpful to assume a continuum of "not safe" as a starting state in new clients.

Many clinicians also assume that clients who shut down in the moment of exposure pass through the sympathetic circuit before the dorsal vagal brake immobilizes them. That's not true. Faced with the overwhelming terror of perceived life threat, human mammals can immediately bypass the SNS and shut down. When dissolution does follow the hierarchical trail to the SNS first, sympathetic activation (Chapter 8) or freeze (Chapter 7) states can emerge.

Likewise, in the restorative process it is essential to note that not only can it backfire to focus on "getting to ventral" from dorsal—we may also have to navigate ongoing states such as freeze, or emergent state-driven survival strategies such as appeasement, before we can state shift into a non-fear-based state like mobilization in the continuum of play. When working clinically with a person who is shut down, it can be difficult to help them shift into the more nourishing DVC-mediated rest and settle states that support activities like meditation, napping, and intimacy. The vulnerability of stillness can be overwhelming and spark repeated shutdown or high-activation states. One of the lessons of this work is the idea of sideways and even diagonal state shifting. Working with a client who is shut down, we may have to upregulate mobilization in fear through various "degrees" of freeze because the only way out of shutdown is movement. Once there is movement, we are no longer shut down. Movement can be scary, so we navigate moving with some fear present before we can regulate sideways or state shift to mobilization without fear, the playful actions that arise from this hybrid state. We may dance between fear and safe-as-can-be in mobilization states before we can access the ventrally mediated relative safety of social engagement, wholeness, and flow. This can take several sessions or several years. Clients can still shutdown, because it is a "default" somatic pattern induced arising from the exposure to

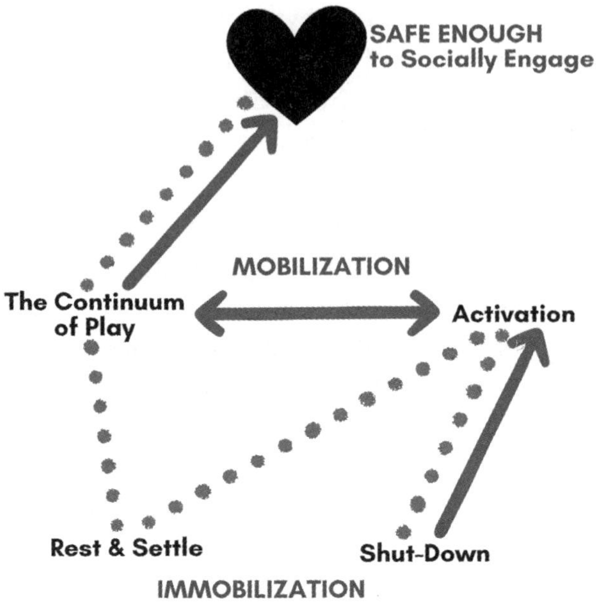

Figure 6.1 Multidirectional State Shifting

perceived life threat and ensuant trauma feedback loop. This process of moving between the states arising from the neural circuits and all the emergent states and the actions and strategies they ignite is multidirectional state shifting. States arise from the energy generated by each neural circuit, when recruited to meet a demand. This recruitment generates energy that mobilizes us toward or away from or immobilizes us to hide us. This neural dance contributes to an endless possibility of emergent states and their actions and strategies to help us survive, restore our social and relational capacities, and reengage with life.

Figure 6.1 shows the possibilities for multidirectional, multidimensional state shifting to either up, down, sideways, or diagonally regulate. The dotted and solid lines with arrows suggest two possible pathways in state shifting between primary and hybrid states that therapists and clients may navigate in the restorative process. There are myriad possible blended states along these state-shifting pathways. The process itself is much more animated than this drawing.

The Heart as State-Shifting Central

Figure 6.2 could land in many chapters of this book. It is positioned here to acknowledge the trajectory of Section II, which follows the circuits of the ANS and the primary, hybrid, and blended emergent and patterned states they initiate to champion our survival. All three neural circuits innervate the heart and influence its physiology and function, and it's the DVC's innervation at the heart, the dorsal vagal brake, that shuts us down when terror is felt by perception of life threat. Figure 6.2 is another way to creatively illustrate the multidirectional, multidimensional state-shifting pathways described in Figure 6.1 in a more ANS-inclusive way. The infinity signs represent the nonlinear, spiraling energy of the ANS as it supports us to meet the demands and invitations of the world in ways that ensure our survival and promote life-nourishing connection and engagement. The VVC is centered in the heart, placed at the center of the image to represent the vagal brake that promotes engaged, relational flow states when the environment is safe enough to support this. The horizontal line represents the continuum of relative safety. It shows how the continuums of nourishment and play arise from the heart center, VVC-mediated alignment, and the "hum" of two or all three circuits integrating in flow. The horizontal continuum represents a safe-as-can-be environment, and the vertical represents the primary state shifts that occur when faced with danger or life threat. We speed up in SNS activation mobilization and shut down in DVC immobilization. The infinity sign represents the non-static nature of this. Danger and life threats exist on a continuum of neuroception to perception. Both infinity signs spiral in and out of the lines because we truly experience a variety of primary, hybrid, and blended states depending on the perception of safety, fear, and/or terror. The solid lines represent the flow between states that is available on the continuum of relative safety, and the broken line symbolizes the fragmented nature of fear- and terror-based states.

Figure 6.3 amplifies this idea by adding more spiraling infinities that more dynamically represent hybrid and blended states. When two or

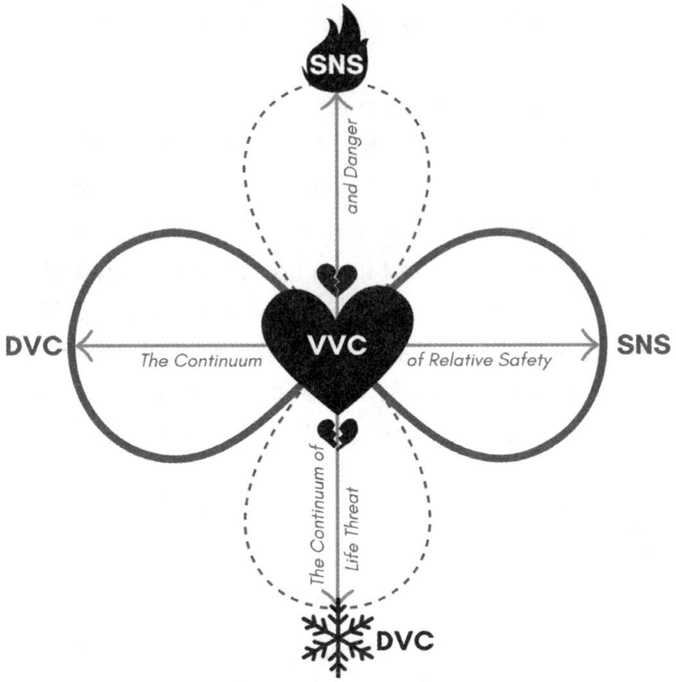

Figure 6.2 Heart-Centered State Shifting

more circuits are recruited, these petals overlap and can create myriad emergent hybrid and blended states that may not yet be named. There is much more micromobilization and micromovement at the level of the ANS than this two-dimensional figure can relay. The feeling states we experience can be subtle to intense and disorienting, and we may or may not express them outwardly.

Working With Clinical Shutdown

This case vignette describes Rachel's restorative journey. It shares highlights from work done over an 18-month period at a U.S.-based torture treatment program where we provided mental health, medical, social, and legal services. Clients were assigned to psychotherapy

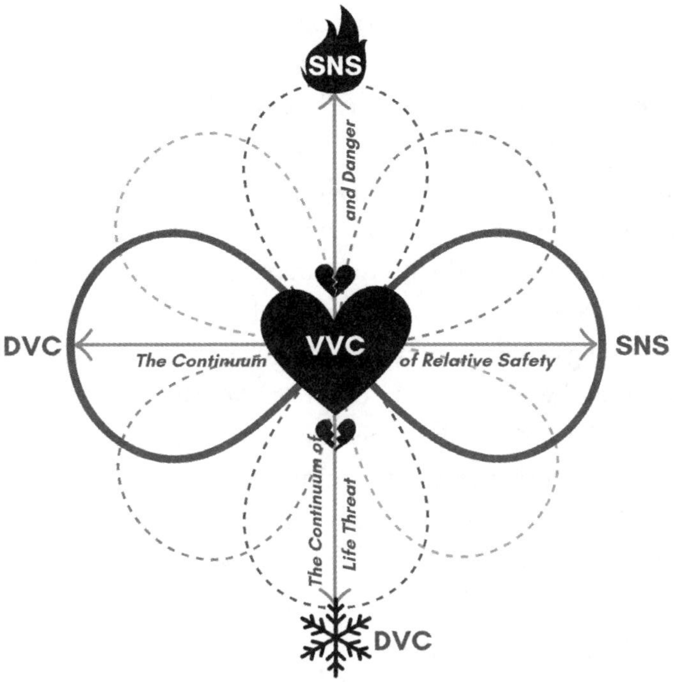

Figure 6.3 Infinity of Emergence

based on their interest and willingness, the level of severity of exposure and symptoms, and the experience and comfort level of the therapist. Another factor was the availability of therapists. Rachel presented with such intense shutdown that the intaking and assessing clinician did not feel comfortable working with her. As I was the senior clinician and clinical director, the team requested I take this case. It was truly painful to sit with the depth of shutdown and suffering Rachel exhibited. This vignette excerpts more of our work that contributes to the PVISDMP concepts of micromobilizations and reciprocal alliance. Working with Rachel illuminates how yield, micromobilizations, and micromovements offer an effective and relatively safe way to begin to move out of shutdown and shift multidirectionally through primary, hybrid, and blended states in service of the restoration of a ventrally mediated return to wholeness.

RACHEL: YIELD AND MICROMOBILIZATIONS

Rachel had lived in a prison cell designed for 10 women, and occupied by 70 women, for seven years. While incarcerated, she could only leave the cell when she was forced to do hard labor, such as moving large rocks for no reason other than sadistic cruelty. Rachel now lived with unbearable physical and psychological pain. She rarely left home, refused to go to church despite being a religious woman and former religious leader in her community, and would not take calls from her children back home. Anytime I asked her about her experiences, she shut down. Sitting before me, her eyes were vacant, her face expressionless, and her body collapsed and hypotonic.

Feeling stuck, I asked her directly if she thought I could help her. She said, "Yes—I think you can." I asked how, and she said, "Help me live with less pain."

I usually don't wish to begin with pain. I prefer to begin with something more resourced. My first client's reaction to too much movement connected to painful memories left me hesitant to begin with someone's pain. But pain is where we began. This was the first opportunity Rachel gave me to go a little deeper. I now appreciate how this initiated what was to become the concept and practice of reciprocal alliance. I recognized that from her collapsed, shut down, immobilized-in-terror state, she could only feel pain. Pain was her connection to feeling, to SNS energy, so it was also a connection to life. Anytime we talked about the origins of her pain, her long-time imprisonment, and her current suffering, she shut down. Pain brought her back. She still had scars from being stabbed in the very muscles she used for forced labor. This intentional infliction of both physical and psychological pain is how oppressors continue to control their victims long after their physical control of their victims has ended. Its core is the "design" of torture and other sadistic forms of abuse. She related her pain to the entrapment she experienced for seven years. She often referred to "the unbearable torture of being so tightly packed with other women that I could barely breathe."

For the first four weeks, this is what we did. Of the two painful areas in her body, one in her right leg and one in her right shoulder, the pain in her leg was the most intolerable. She wanted to be free of it. The only relief she knew was to rest it on a pillow. To link our work to her time at home, between sessions, I introduced a physio ball to rest her leg on. As she rested her leg on the ball, I invited her to describe any similarities to resting the same leg on a pillow at home. Physio balls instantly invite the body, or body part, to yield. Try sitting on one and notice how your sense of weight and inner state shift. Using the ball, we built on an already identified somatic resource. Witnessing, I observed increased yield in her leg, which soon began to spread to the rest of her body.

Over the next four weeks, she noticed a slight decrease in her pain. This noticing heralds a shift in attention that signals a micromobilization. She described it as "spreading out and softening," which resonated with my observation of her yield. She said, "My leg can relax a little more, and rest." About three weeks into this exploration, she used the term "ease" to describe how her leg felt. So I introduced micromobilizations, which can be conceptualized as both attentional shifts and "pre-movements," inviting her to notice what she felt inside her leg (or elsewhere in her body), under her skin, that let her know she was relaxing more. Sometimes tiny twitches were barely visible around her mouth and eyes and her breathing would suddenly shift. These were my cues to her internal attention shifting experience of micromobilization. Experiencing yield was helping Rachel begin to shift her from shutdown to a slightly more alert and present state. Rachel's yield was both a state she described as softening, which was more comfortable, and an action. Her leg became visibly relaxed and stronger. Yield is physically visible in the body and contributes to our body's prosodic flow as movement. Once there is even the slightest movement, we are no longer shut down, even if just for a moment.

Rachel began to sense the movement in her leg just a little bit. Because it was resting on a physio ball, the ball moved her leg slightly. Asking her to sense into this, she felt something other than the locked-down pain that made her terrified of moving. These very tiny movements are what are now called "micromobilizations" in PVISDMP. Micromobilizations are nervous system movements that indicate the ANS is beginning to state shift. They are the smallest streaming of sensation, attentional shifts, and flickers of movement we can perceive. They appear as pulses on the skin surface or just underneath the skin. They might be a barely perceptible quiver of the lips or an eyelid. Sometimes they are not visible; the client may describe them as physical sensations underneath the skin they perceive as movement. They can be integrated into therapy by inviting or respectfully directing a client's attention toward something new, or familiarly safe enough, in the space. Borrowing from Deb Dana, they are movement "glimmers," and they seed micromovements, which are bigger streams of energy moving that are more visible. An example is a person's leg trembling while it is stationary and not actually moving. Micromovements represent the liberation of formerly repressed sensations, emotions, and memories that begin to express in the body. The smaller and less perceptible ANS micromobilizations can initiate micromovements as they expand and seed more visible movement. When Rachel first placed her leg on the physio ball, it would initially collapse and scare her. As it relaxed, it began to tense and hurt more. Rising out of shutdown can feel scary and create a recoil of tension and vigilance. After a few sessions, as she yielded, she described tiny flickers and pulses under her skin. Eventually these became micromovements that appeared as ripples of movement in her superficial muscles, and leg twitches. Micromovements are an effective and relatively safe way for clients who are immobilized in terror to begin to shift out of shutdown and prepare for bigger movements that engage the somatic nervous system and more of the musculoskeletal system. These bigger movements increase engagement and connection to the environment. When movement begins to locomote or change our posture or when we move a whole-body part, the SNS is being recruited, and we are rising up out of dorsal. Rachel's tiny micromovements signaled renewed engagement, and together we navigated the fear that often accompanied them.

This was our work for four weeks, during which I played subtly with moving myself in space and in relationship to her—alternating between sitting closer to her and moving farther away. Beginning with the Space-Place-Pace practice, I initially sat by her side so she could see me in her periphery. She preferred this over me sitting directly in front of her. As we played with the movements in her leg, I would move myself just a little closer toward her and ask her if that was okay. When it wasn't, I moved back a bit. I also played with moving in and out of her direct gaze, soliciting her feedback so she could begin to restore her own interoceptive capacities to choose how close or far apart our bodies were. I made eye contact for a little longer and intentionally softened my sometimes overly focused gaze. She began to state shift, which I perceived through hearing her exhale longer and more frequently. She also wiggled in her chair and began to try to sit up more erectly, looking at me more directly. I sat more upright and breathed audibly, so she could sense me breathing with her. By the end of these four weeks, she still had pain, but it was less intense, and she could put more weight on her leg. She could meet my gaze for a few moments. She could sit up a little taller. These small but mighty changes signaled even more movement. We were transitioning from micromovements to bigger movements as her ANS expanded its capacity for coregulation.

Tiny mobilizations had birthed a more connected and sustained gaze, a more relaxed, alert posture and supple spine as sitting up straighter yielded into her pelvic floor and weight.

This was the beginning of a shift to larger movements,

> including dance, as part of a restorative process that took 14 months and culminated with her offering me her dance to freedom. In these 14 months we wove together traumatic memories and, eventually, life-affirming memories through movement and verbal storytelling.

This work with Rachel birthed the concept of reciprocal alliance, now core to PVISDMP. Reciprocal alliance signifies client empowerment through the sharing of power in our client-therapist relationship. It shifts the traditional idea of therapist as healer and client as healed, which can amplify the already existing power differential, to one of the cultivation of equal power through dignity, respect, and belonging. To create a sense of shared reciprocity, clients are offered more opportunities to be the experts, without burdening them. Working in multicultural contexts of any sort, therapists can learn about client cultures through our own research. Inviting clients to teach us and being enthusiastic and caring about their worldview can foster their empowerment. A simple example is disclosure: Most therapists are trained not to disclose anything personal. In many cultures, knowing more about a person's life helps establish the beginnings of trust. I have shared more than I was taught to do about the composition of my family, who my ancestors are, and so on. Movement is sometimes described as a universal language, because we all speak it and rely on it in our early development. And not assuming we know what a movement, gesture, or even facial expression means and taking time to ask the client what it means to them supports reciprocity. The once-preferred therapist neutral or poker face is another example: In a polyvagal-informed practice, a soft, kind face is more welcoming and offers cues that are more likely to be neurocepted as relatively safe. Because this relationship is situated in the context of mental or behavioral health, therapists always have power. Every place we dismantle power contributes to broader liberation.

Rachel also taught me to slow down and work small to safely reengage her ANS capacity for regulation through multiple and multidirectional pathways. As much as I wished for her to restore her full expressive capacities as quickly as possible, I honored her timing. This initial work of yielding, micromobilizations, and micromovements took almost two months. It was very slow, and I had to check my own desire to see her shift out of pain more quickly and to see more evidence of increased engagement. It took the full two months for me to feel like we actually made progress because each time she came in, she exhibited flat affect, would dissociate when we were checking in, and said she hadn't noticed any change since the prior session. Slowing down allowed Rachel to eventually reclaim her own sense of timing, which occurred about halfway through our work together. She arrived at our session exclaiming that she was "returning home to [her] body" because she had noticeably less pain and increased mobility. This restoration of personal timing is a pathway to embodied justice.

Micromobilizations and Micromovements

When micromobilizations grow to become more visible micromovements, we may notice our clients taking a deeper breath. The power of a single breath that reaches a little farther into their body merits acknowledgment and celebration. The spark that is a micromobilization, a barely perceptible movement, can become the tiny movement that tells us we are still alive. This could be an inhale that visibly travels all the way down to the sternum when previously it stopped in the throat. It can be the ability to roll a formerly immobilized and stuck shoulder back or forward a quarter of an inch (or more). This can facilitate easing into the weight of presence, being able to support oneself more in different postures, and finding connection to place, to begin the process of sensing our belonging.

One way I invite clients to find the yield that supports the DVC/VVC hybrid receptivity, which allows us to accept more external support, is to extend the weight exploration in Chapter 1 into a more extended yield practice.

YIELD PRACTICE

1. Shift to Comfort. Take a baseline of your sense of weight, sensing the points of contact between you and the surface or object you are sitting on, and sensing the support you are, or are not, receiving. Also sense into yield if you have an idea how your body does this.
2. Locate your sitz bones. See if you can perch on them like we did in the focused attention practice in Chapter 5.
3. Our exhale has an ability to downregulate or relax us. Notice the exhale part of your breath, and then intentionally use your exhale to increase the support of the chair. A creative way my clients find helpful to do this is this: Imagine that each time you exhale, your exhale is a stream of mist traveling down your body, alongside your spine. Sometimes a client will ask if they will still exhale properly, and I assure them they will. Our human bodies have been breathing for us a very long time!
4. Locate your sitz bones again and imagine they are suction cups like an octopus has (or any other image that works). As your exhale streams down your spine, see it exiting through your sitz bones, "melting" into the chair. If the concept of melting doesn't work, choose something that does—softening, pressing more, anything that works for you.
5. Pause and notice if you sense your body resting and settling into the chair more. To enhance yield, add this second action to your exhale: Widen your sitz bones on each exhale. Imagine they are spreading horizontally or laterally, which can create more space in between. This increases surface area, which promotes even more yield and receptivity to support. Do this as long as is comfortable.
6. Recheck your sense of weight and yield.

Some clients only need to do a few breaths like this, and some clients get tired or begin to get activated after just a few breaths. When that happens, we pause. Either way, whether they can only do a short practice or can do this for several minutes or several rounds, with pauses and rests in between, sensing their weight through those points of contact can remind their bodies to rest and find more support. Most clients, if not immediately, will eventually notice that they are more yielded, more able to sense their weight and support, and more present. This is a microempowerment because when we are more present we are more connected to and in our bodies.

MIRIAM: LEARNING TO REST

Rest is the counterpoint to shutdown. And it requires levels of relative safety and comfort that are not accessible in an immobilized state. Learning to rest can be pivotal to the other work of the restorative process for clients whose shutdown exhausts them. Miriam was so immobilized she collapsed for days and then, in her words, "fought" her shutdown by forcing herself to do her usual things like shopping, cooking, and so on. This state shifting up out of shutdown was fragmented and distressing. She could not sustain these levels of engagement; she would become very irritable and reactive, a common pattern for clients who experienced both mobilization and immobilization states when enduring traumatic experiences. Miriam's shutdown was alleviated only through sporadic, brief attempts at engagement that created surges of cranky activation followed by collapse.

> Miriam arrived to the United States after losing her husband and a child to the ongoing conflict and turmoil in her home country. Her other children arrived with her. She was extremely depressed. She walked, breathed, moved, and sat like she was carrying an unbearable amount of weight. I always felt heavy in her presence.

We got stuck a lot. She did not want to talk about anything—challenging and traumatic, or strengthening and life affirming—in depth. Any time I tried to engage her in remembering, processing, and/or resourcing, she would say a little about her condition and complaints, and then just stop talking. It was difficult for her to find anything helpful or hopeful in her life; she focused on pain, loss, and exhaustion and her many health issues. Often, she would "disappear"—her eyes far away, her body perfectly still, her face expressionless—and then she would change the subject. Her biggest complaint among many was about the lack of sleep. She also described a lot of pain in her legs, chest, and belly area when awake. This usually sent her back to bed, trying to sleep again. She experienced some intrusive memories and dreams during waking time and attempted sleep, and these intrusions were one of several factors contributing to her inability to sleep.

The DVC, as part of the homeostasis-restoring parasympathetic nervous system, contributes to our capacity for rest and sleep. It requires a state of relative safety and an ability to calm down and relax enough to let go into slumber. It is connected to the nourishment of experiencing union and harmony in interpersonal relationships, including with spirit, the natural world, and more-than-human friends. It is also a state that we can experience on our own, when we are safe as can be in an environment—a cozy warm bed, a hammock or comfy chair, or with a dear friend—where we can relax and let go.

In my ongoing and often frustrating work with Miriam, I often felt surprised that she showed up for our sessions. I listened a lot, checking my own rising irritation that she refused to engage in depth work, complained about the same things over and over, and kept asking me to tend to things her case manager wasn't getting to quickly enough. Her chronic immobilization interfered with her follow-through and self-care. Still, I welcomed her, listened, and occasionally offered a practice or idea to help with her tiredness, her pain, her irritability. Though she rejected almost everything, she would sometimes smile and thank me for being someone she could talk to. About six months into our work together, I started to find her sleeping or dozing on the couch in the waiting area when I went to meet her for our sessions. She would always be a little embarrassed when I woke her up, and I assured her it was okay. The third time this happened, I asked her if she was arriving earlier intentionally, and if she had any ideas why she liked to sleep on the couch. She responded that my office, and the building my office was in, were beginning to feel like a familiar and comforting place, and she felt very relaxed. She didn't mean to fall asleep; she just did.

From that day forward, we worked on sleep. I invited Miriam to rest, and even sleep, on my office couch. Her first response was, understandably, "I don't want to sleep while you are looking at me." I told her I would rest, too, and I did. I would soften my gaze while remaining seated in my chair and guide us both through some breathing practices, and she would drift off. Sometimes she actually slept part of the time. We set an alarm with my iPhone, and she chose the alarm sound each time so she could be prepared for the sound that would cue her to wake up. When the sound went off, I would guide her through micromobilizations. Sometimes I invited her to notice a couple full breaths and then return to her rest, and we would repeat this, adding more breaths each time, until she was noticing her breath for longer than she was resting. This can also be practiced as eyes open, taking in the space around us, and then returning to eyes closed. This is how we humans are meant to naturally transition from sleep or rest to waking, and restoring this biorhythmic transition regulates the ANS. This conscious, invited attentional shift is a micromobilization that begins to restore our capacity for fluid attention. Once Miriam was sensing her breath and focusing her attention on it for a more sustained interval, I invited her to let breath become movement that stirred her; that is, micromovements. She would then slowly, slowly allow movement to spread through her body as much or as little as was comfortable for her, until she could upregulate through slow SNS arousal to sit up for our check-in. Over time, Miriam slept more at night. After about three months, she was sleeping five to six hours a night with less intrusions, nightmares, or other interruptions.

Nervous systems communicate through transmissions. Coregulating in rest with Miriam helped retrain her ANS to engage calm enough states to promote sleep, and to upregulate with more ease and flow. Typical psychotherapy does not endorse a client and a therapist resting together. Sleeping, especially lying down in the horizontal dimension, a client is more vulnerable. I did not neglect this fact. Miriam did not completely lie down; we used a pile of cushions to prop her in a half sitting/half lying-down posture. I intentionally remained sitting, so I could be nonintrusive and watchful with my attention at the same time. I lowered and softened my gaze so that I was not looking at her and was still present, oscillating my attention between Miriam and my breathing. I consciously breathed with her, and I relaxed. This was an unexpected and clinically unusual process. Sleep disorders are often treated with psychiatric medication or cognitive behavioral therapy, both valid treatments. A polyvagal-informed somatic approach recognizes that the therapist's ANS offers a powerfully transmitted message that can remind clients whose patterns of immobilization only shift occasionally to fragmented activated states how to side-shift to regulate toward rest and settle.

The following practice is a more structured PVISDMP practice that I teach to promote therapists' comfort and capacity for conscious self-regulation toward calm, restful states while engaging with clients. I also teach it to clients for home play. Stillness is part of the movement continuum, and rest is a phase in that continuum. Our ability to embody and transmit this can encourage a client's ANS to recruit the DVC's inherent and ancient contribution to states of nourishing rest.

POLYVAGAL NAPS: MICROMOBILIZING THROUGH BREATH PRACTICE

Preparation: Create a nest with a yoga or exercise mat, or a sheepskin fleece and, if necessary, blanket(s) and as many supportive cushions or bolsters as needed.

1. Shift to Comfort while lying down or semi-lying down, well supported with pillows, in your nest. Take a baseline of your weight. As you sense into your weight, also notice your sense of yield and groundedness. Grounding is an energetic, not mechanical, connection to the earth. Also notice your feeling state, which reflects your inner neurophysiological state.
2. Rest. Rest, rest, rest. This brief rest is not quite a nap; it's more akin to active, restorative resting. If you're prone to falling asleep or feeling sleepy, set a timer to wake you up in 5 to 10 minutes. Increasing our capacity for very brief rests amid waking, working, playing, and engaging is an act of self-care that helps retore our natural rest/activity, sleep/wake transition.
3. While resting, close your eyes or soften your gaze, taking some breaths and inviting your muscles to relax. Play with yielding by letting as much of your body weight rest or drop into the floor as possible.
4. If you're able to stay awake, set an alarm to allow for a transition from rest to awake and reengaged. This transition should be about one third to half of your total rest time. If you have three minutes, set it for one minute. If it's five minutes, set it for one and a half minutes. If it's 15 minutes, set it for five minutes.
5. Rest until your alarm rings. When it does, begin to micromobilize by briefly focusing your attention on your breath. This quality of attention is similar to the 20% or light attention practice described in Chapter 5. Observe a few breaths with light attention and then go back to resting. Resting is doing nothing. It is just being. Not thinking about anything or focusing on anything. Initially oscillate your attention for a few moments on your breath and then come back to resting. As you practice, increase the frequency of your light attention on breath until you are watching your breath more than resting. The simple act of

placing our attention on our breath from a deep rest state is a micromobilization because attention engages the ANS and can initiate movement.

6. To shift micromobilizations into micromovements, which invites energy to move, begin to wiggle your toes and fingers. You can also blink your eyes, wiggle your nose, or do any kind of tiny movement that is comfortable for you to do. Pause periodically. Micromove, pause, and notice if the movements begin to spread, pulse, or ripple through your body. As you notice these pulses and ripples, begin to expand them. Let the movement, or the sensation below the movement, enter more and more of your body, and to the extent that is comfortable, allow the movement to grow so that your body begins to move more visibly.
7. It's important to do this practice very slowly. These smaller movements engage our tonic muscles, which support our posture. They also engage tendons and ligaments and can initiate movement in the connective tissue. The ANS begins to wake us up because anytime we move, we stimulate the nervous system. Continue this process until as much of your body is moving as possible. You might rock, pulse, or undulate.
8. Larger expressive movements can override the more intrinsic tissues that support posture and create our natural micromovements. As you slowly invite expanded, larger movement, let these movements ripple and expand until you are moving big enough to sit up. Don't sit up in your usual patterned way; follow the ripples and pulses to take you side-lying, kneeling, and so on. You may experience movements that you've seen infants do or perhaps did as an infant.
9. When you're sitting up, take a moment to settle into the earth and notice your weight and your sense of yieldedness. Notice how you feel, comparing to your baseline, and then take a moment to look around and

connect to the environment. Compare your energy level now to when you began.

Polyvagal naps may or may not be appropriate to all clinicians' way of working. If it's not something you can do or are comfortable doing, you can teach your clients. I have nesting materials such as yoga mats, cushions, bolsters, and blankets in my office and will demonstrate how to do it, acting it out just enough to be clear. I have some of the practices I teach written up for clients and, when possible, translated into their languages. Encouraging clients to practice at home amplifies the work we do with them.

MARIA: RELEARNING INTIMACY

Intimacy and the expression of love and union are emergent processes of the DVC without terror. These blissful states have seemed irretrievable and impossible for many clients. Maria was a young woman, wife, and mother who was kidnapped during a civil war and imprisoned for almost a year. There, the guards violated her multiple times a week. She and her husband longed to have another child, but she was, in her words, "cold." She barely recalled the details of what she had been through. She had shut down completely and now could not control her immobilization reaction. Maria reacted to leaving her house, often returning home after a few steps. She tried to ride a bus to our sessions but would get off and walk home when terror rose from her belly. She often lay in bed staring vacantly. She could no longer be intimate with her husband, though they adored each other.

Our work together was complex and long term. A primary focus was the restoration of her capacity for intimacy, so this vignette focuses on that work. Because she could not find safety anywhere, I asked her what she loved to do back home, what activities provided comfort, delight, ease, and so on. She loved cooking, gardening, and making things tidy. In session, we recalled how those activities felt in her body, and we made simple drawings, using colors and symbols to represent those feelings. She took the drawings home and placed them in the appropriate room in her house so she could orient to them when she cooked, gardened, or cleaned. This was a small way of creating an environment she neurocepted as safe enough. Each moment of increased ease in these rooms afforded her ANS opportunities to increase its capacity for self-regulation or, to her, "changing my feelings to feel more like me." As she became more comfortably active at home, she wanted to work on her relationship. Her partner was one of the things in her environment that could activate her not feeling safe. His approaches for intimacy were tender, slow, and heartfelt, and she could not tolerate them. This broke both their hearts.

We decided Javier could join for a few sessions. They both described their love for one another and desire for a second child. I then invited each of them to share their first memory of each other, and their memory of when they first felt love. They described the same walk home from school when they held hands, snuck off into a bush, and kissed. They giggled like children. We paused and slowed down, and I invited them to place all their attention on the feeling inside them now while they recalled holding hands and kissing. Javier instantly felt warmth throughout his body. Maria had a harder time connecting. She felt the beginnings of warmth but described a feeling of it stopping in her belly and becoming too hot. We played a little bit with Space-Place-Pace, like Rachel, but this time, their bodies shifted their relationship to each other. Maria realized there were certain angles of relating that felt more comfortable for her. Their assigned home play was to work with these spatial relationships back home, further safeguarding the home environment. Javier knew to always announce himself when entering the room Maria was in. He would verbally cue her when he was approaching her, assuring her he was on her right (preferred) side. He also stated his wish to touch, hug, or kiss her. He paused frequently for Maria to orient and settle, which enabled her to restore her sense of timing in these interactions. This work took many months, and through it, both at home and in our sessions, Maria described experiencing almost every possible neurophysiological and emotional state. She began to recognize when she shut down, froze, became activated in fear, and felt the slow creeping of warmth and connection. As we processed these states, her emotions, and how they influenced her daily life, she spent notably less time isolated and afraid and more time in her usual activities. After almost a year, they were fully intimate again.

State Shifting From DVC in Groups

For many years I cofacilitated a refugee kids' group, attended by children from many different countries. The shared experience was displacement from war. This was unusual at the time, and many of my colleagues endorsed working with only one language when doing group work. Somatic and dance/movement therapies recognize that nonverbal communication is as informative as verbal communication. Tracking our and our clients' ANS provides ample information as to individuals' neurophysiological and emotional states, as well as our own. The ANS as intervening variable and as third space is what helps create a collective nervous system. Working with a group of children, ages eight to 15 from several countries and accompanied by interpreters when necessary (many of the children learned English quickly), resulted in a veritable panoply of states.

This was an active group: we moved, danced, drummed, drew, sculpted, sang, and processed all of these activities together. When I detected state shifts in the direction of immobilization or mobilization in one or a few children, I began to adapt a simple breathing practice called sternal breathing. As we copracticed this, I noticed that it seemed to state shift the children in the direction most helpful for them. The children who were shutting down would upregulate with increased energy and movement. The children who were in sympathetic activation states might regulate sideways to more playful states or relax and calm down to a more DVC-mediated relaxed yield state. Sometimes we would have to navigate the element of fear in these state shifts that cooccurred in many bodies at the same time.

To do this, I would begin by saying "pause" so that all the children could hear me, especially if we were engaged in a noisy practice. When I simply said, "Let's breathe together," the kids knew, from prior instruction, to lie on the ground with their knees bent, or sit down comfortably, and place their hands on their sternums to begin.

STERNAL BREATHING PRACTICE

1. Shift to Comfort in the posture you choose. You can be lying down with legs extended or bent knees, sitting on the ground or in a chair, or even standing.
2. Take a baseline of your breath. Notice if it's fast or slow, shallow or deep. Notice where you sense it in your body.
3. Place your hand on your sternum (your breastbone, the heart's protective shield), and notice the natural movement of the sternum as you breathe.

An important note for clinical application: Some people will not feel movement. With freeze mobilization/immobilization states, and some highly activated or completely shutdown states, the tissue surrounding the sternum can be so hypertonic or hypotonic that movement is not palpable or visible. Assure the client that if that is occurring, that is okay for now and doesn't have to be changed. **There is no demand for change.** This ensures an honoring and recognition of the client's own timing and of their ANS pattern, championing their survival. I will often say, "When our breathing changes and gets stuck enough that we don't feel its movement, or even feel the breath itself, it's our body still protecting us. It's cheerleading [or another more culturally relevant metaphor or term] for your survival." When doing this with clients, invite them to describe any movement they find in terms of location, direction, or anything else. For example, "I feel my sternum expanding sideways." "I feel my sternum rising up and down." It's important for the client to verbalize their experience of their sternal breathing in their terms before offering an adjustment.

1. Whether or not you felt movement, begin to work with the natural rhythm and movement of your breath. For the next five or 10 (or any number of breaths, or minutes), rest your hand on your sternum while you breathe. Just let your hand rest gently on the inhale. When you exhale, press your sternum lightly, using only 5–10% of your strength. Don't overthink this—choose what's comfortable for you. If your body really appreciates a little stronger push, that's okay—that's what you need at this moment, today.
2. Continue with this simple practice, following your breath's rhythm and your sternum's movement, for a few breaths or many. Pause when you want or need to. You can pause and return to your baseline or pause for a bit and then resume. Let your body tell you when you are done.
3. Check your baseline; has your breathing changed at all? If it has, how has it changed? If not, remember—part of our body's wisdom is its steadfastness not to change until it's ready. Notice how you feel.

Sternal breathing can be practiced for 30 seconds, five minutes or much longer. When working with clients, I remind them that change is sometimes uncomfortable and brings up emotions or memories. Breath is a powerful state shifter. These are the potent moments when deeper processing work can begin. If you are practicing this on your own, pause often and stay within your range of comfort unless you feel supported and resourced enough to feel big things on your own.

This simple practice can be very effective quickly because it can elicit state shifting in the direction that regulates each person. Collectively, it can "glo-regulate" the shared space.

Harvest

Working with clients who are shut down requires patience, and an ability and willingness to slow our work down and work with a "less is more" approach. The multidirectional nature of the restorative process is far more complex and intricate than can be described here. Navigating the corridors of terror with clients can feel like crawling through a dark tunnel, seeking the possibility of light in every tiny state shift. Centering practices like micromobilizations and micromovements, which can be as tiny as inviting someone to notice one or two breaths, or to sigh loud enough that they can hear it, or to make eye contact for a second, can find those glimpses of light. Simple practices like sternal breathing that connect clients to the rise and fall of the sternum, done for even a few breathing cycles, initiate movement. It is essential to attune to our own state shifts and practice self-compassion to self-regulate so we can track clients and remain centered and present. Shutdown disrupts awareness of the body and all its functions and processes. It hinders clients' capacity for somatic awareness and their ability to describe or share what they experience. The therapist's own body may at times be the only reference point to sense client states. Working with shutdown may be one of the most compelling reasons that self-care is the most essential clinical skill for working with trauma. It affords therapists the patience and the presence to remain body-fully open and compassionate while listening to clients' suffering, processing their stories at the level of the body, and protecting ourselves from our own vicarious trauma imprint.

CHAPTER 7

The Freeze State

DORSAL RISING

> It's turning the thunder into grace,
> knowing sometimes the break in your heart
> is like the hole in the flute.
> Sometimes it's the place
> where the music comes through.
> —ANDREA GIBSON, "GOSPEL SALT," 2022

"Deer in the headlights" is a colloquial expression that vividly describes the neurophysiological hybrid state of freeze. The intense expression of fear emanating from the eyes, locked in stillness and immobile, reflects the intensity of this autonomic hybrid survival state. In 1994, while deployed to Rwanda in the aftermath of the genocide, I witnessed massive flatbed trucks filled with people returning to the country they had fled. The fixed stare of horror and fear in each pair of eyes has never left me. They fled the terror, and both the energy of flight and the lockdown of terror was etched in their eyes.

Freeze is both a hybrid state and an action, or what I refer to as an (in)action survival strategy because of the literal lack of physical movement. While the energy of the SNS swirls inside, the body is tense and still on the outside. At the most practical human level, states are what we feel. Neurophysiological states contribute to how we act, move, and express ourselves. PVISDMP distinguishes states from the survival strategies and actions commonly called behavior or behavioral strategy. Survival strategies, actions, and (in)actions arise from what we feel when facing danger, threat, or adversity. For many clients, the word "behavior" invokes ideas of being evaluated and judged, which can be disempowering and shame inducing. In freeze, the ANS recruits both DVC and SNS energy at the same time. Freeze is different from shutdown because the SNS is engaged, meaning there is energy beneath our external frozen actions.

The hybrid state of freeze is often described as the brake and accelerator being pushed at the same time. This happens because we are in activated states that are too intense to bear or have gone on so long we can no longer sustain them. For many years, before Polyvagal Theory illuminated the role of the DVC brake and ensuing immobilization in a terror state, "freeze" and "shutdown" were used interchangeably. They are not the same thing. Freeze, unlike shutdown, can also occur without fear, which is why it is also an action and a continuum. An example is the highly attentive, highly tonic focus of the sniper. The focus is so intense that they appear "frozen" in stillness. We can distinguish fear-based freeze from focus-based freeze. Clinically, we can experience freeze downregulating from the high activation intensity of SNS or as we state shift up out of DVC shutdown. As we navigate multidirectional state shifting, we may encounter both fear- and focused-based freeze on the path to mobilization without fear, or the continuum of play. Working with small movements to gently coax the SNS out from underneath the frozen exterior, grounding, which recruits dorsal rootedness, and the spine, initiator of liberated movement, inform the practices this chapter offers as pathways to more playful and relational engagement.

Navigating Freeze Through Micromovements

In Chapter 6 I described the early phase of Rachel's treatment. Micromobilizations eased the pain in her leg, enabling us to begin exploring slightly bigger micromovements. While micromobilizations are the attentional shifts and/or non-to-barely perceptible pre-movements that signal ANS shifts, micromovements are the tiny to small movements of the smaller tissue groups like connective tissue, tonic muscles, ligaments, and tendons. These are the underprivileged quiet voices of movement that trauma often represses and even silences. The following case vignette, excerpted from my work with Rachel, describes in more detail the process of transitioning from micromobilizations to micromovements.

> After Rachel found more ease and less pain in her leg, her micromobilizations became micromovements. These small pulsations in her leg began to move her leg, signaling movement out of shutdown. I encouraged her to press her leg into a physio ball ever so slightly, and release. Initially this was painful. With pauses to rest in between presses, she was able to extend and then withdraw her leg, imitating important reflexive actions (extensor thrust and flexor withdrawal) that support the ability to kick, push, and pull legs toward or away from something. I imagined the strain on her legs of being trapped in a crowded cell, the physical duress of forced labor, and the desire anyone would have to kick their abuser away.

When micromobilizations become micromovements, the sympathetic nervous system is engaged. When there's movement, it's impossible to be shut down. Navigating this terrain of fear is an essential part of the restorative process. With increasing movement, clients can experience more pain, more fear, and more uncertainty. Many of my therapist students express understandable concern when these things arise out of concern for activating the client. Doing this slowly, and with the ever-present ability to back off by either the client's or therapist's decision, overwhelming activation can be contained and even avoided. This is where timing is key: When enough respect, relative safety, and reciprocity are established, these moments can be portals to processing traumatic memories.

In Rachel's case, she began to move the ball with her leg forward and back, side to side, and then in multiple directions in circles and spirals. The small movements seemed to redistribute the pain and diffuse it so that she began to sit up more, sustain eye contact, and share more verbally. As the pain in her leg was redistributed, the muscles and fascia sometimes spasmed, causing her to cry out in pain. In these moments we paused, and I gently asked her to begin sharing about the things she had endured that had caused her legs to work so hard, to stand for unbearable long hours, and to heal from physical torture. As she shared and cried, the muscles around her face and eyes began to soften. She also expanded her movements so that it wasn't just the ball moving her, she was moving the ball and then consciously moving her leg. Simple as that may seem, it is profound when it arises after shutdown. After about four weeks, Rachel wanted to work on her right shoulder, where she still felt extreme pain. Both her shoulder and her thigh were scarred from her torture. Her right shoulder had such intense pain that she literally described it as "frozen in terror."

We began her shoulder work with micromovements. I asked her to connect her shoulder to her shoulder blade with the tiniest movements possible. This was intuitive. Observing the tension in the back side of her shoulder and the collapse forward, I imagined a little compression in the back and opening in the front might ease the frozen terror. She was barely able to squeeze her shoulder and the base of her scapula together. She described feeling intense fear under the frozenness, as if this was the actual physical location of a freeze. Neurophysiological and feeling states can coinhabit areas of the body as psychic pain.

When I asked Rachel what would help her liberate this frozen area, she said she wasn't sure and felt like "I need to push on something until it explodes." This was one of the strongest statements she had ever made. We tried pushing into a wall, physio balls, and other objects. It hurt too much. Feeling a bit stuck myself, I asked her if she had an idea what was in there that needed to explode. Her response: "My struggle."

I suggested that perhaps she needed to experience the struggle that was in there, and to my surprise, she began to share her struggle. For several sessions she described in some detail what it took for her to survive her seven years of detention in a tiny, cramped cell. Her story was, and is, one of the most tragic I have heard. Periodically, I invited her to pause, move her legs in familiar micromovements, and to keep tracking her shoulder. All the while I tracked both our ANSs and managed to intervene when she began to shut down again. Her muscles would lose tone quite quickly, her eyes would appear to lose their shine, and her gaze would go blank. Her breathing became very slow and shallow. I learned to detect a shift in my ANS as this was happening: I began to activate, experiencing tingly sensations in my belly, increased heart rate, and quickened breath. It was uncomfortable. To intervene, I would gently say her name and invite her to press her legs into the always handy physio ball, make eye contact, and breathe with me.

One day, she arrived and announced she wanted to move her arm. She said she needed "pressure" to move it. Looking around my office, I grabbed a physiotherapy stretch band with medium tension and attached it to a doorknob. Sitting her away from the door so that she could both tense and slacken the band, I invited her to increase and decrease the band's length between herself and the door. I encouraged her to vary her intensity and sometimes changed the tension of the band. She would often tighten up her face and make intense gasping and grunting sounds when the tension was increased.

There are many ways to use these simple movements and actions to process somatically held trauma memories; intensifying the movement is one of them. We can invite clients to make their movements bigger or smaller, focus them in a smaller area of the body or generalize them to include more of their body, increase or decrease speed, and/or create a contrasting movement. For more on this approach, readers are encouraged to check out Christine Caldwell's Moving Cycle approach, in her books *Getting Our Bodies Back* (1996), *Bodyfulness* (2018), and *Conscious Moving* (2024). This is one of the ways she developed what she calls "movement tags," which are unconscious, pre-conscious, or subconscious movements, usually repetitive, that clients display when discussing anything with a charge. They often link to a repressed memory and/or the neurophysiological roots, that is, the somatic imprint of the memory. Her 2024 book covers this work in depth. With Rachel, increasing the intensity of conscious movements we created, called "potent gestures," opened the door for us to process her traumatic memories in both the verbal and nonverbal, explicit and implicit domains. Potent gestures are gestures that arise organically in our work, or that we cocreate with clients, and they can occur when talking about both intense trauma and powerful memories rooted in our resilience.

> Increasing band tension and encouraging her to use more strength to stretch and release the band over time allowed us to keep moving farther away from the door. Using metaphor to diversify both tension and intensity, I asked her to consider that she was also moving farther away, each day, from these memories and from the way her government captors treated her. Some of the gestures we explored were squeezing fruit to juice it, squeezing a ball (we actually practiced with a small squishy ball like those used in yoga, Pilates, or physical therapy) and pushing something away with so much energy it required squeezing all the muscles as tightly as possible. This metaphor- and gesture-inspired exploration increased her range of movement and engaged more of her arm and eventually shoulder and shoulder blade in the movement. At about eight weeks into this, she began to push and pull more, with great effort and tension. She often pulled so strongly I thought she would break the band. The micromovements we

began with became potent gestures, inspired by her need to move her arm with pressure. With Rachel, I suggested the gesture she explored because she couldn't think of any. This is common with shutdown clients. With some clients, the gestures may emerge from them, based on a memory or something they want to change. Often clients and I cocreate the gesture out of strong content, such as the loss of a beloved person or their anger at their perpetrator. Rachel's struggle gesture became a movement sequence that included more of her arm, shoulder, head, and face. She gathered every muscle in her face tightly, held the band at its tensest point for what seemed like several minutes, and then let it go with a loud groan-like sound. Growing the movement slowly and amplifying it from a simple gesture to a potent gesture to a movement sequence enabled Rachel to shift the freeze in her shoulder and shoulder blade, right at the site of her traumatic wounding, and tolerate SNS energy and activation that initiated bigger and more movement, which scared her before.

Rachel described, with unusual emotion, that this felt like breaking through the struggle and moving out of it. Because of her initially immobilized state, she often showed little or no emotion. In this instance, she began to move her arm more, and the movement traveled into her entire arm, shoulder, and upper torso. Her movement both intensified and sped up. Her muscles were clearly tensing and squeezing with a lot of energy. At one point she gasped loudly, dropped the band, and began to cry. Just before she did this, I observed her simultaneously upregulate from freeze to activation and sideways-regulate in and out of slightly more playful states. It resembled competitive play, a state of mobilization without fear that can have periodic infusions of activation. The intensity of competition can oscillate between feeling like fear and feeling like dominance, strength, ecstasy, and power. Throughout her process, SNS activation appeared as brief to sustained surges accompanied by increased facial micromovements. Her face twisted and contorted in what appeared to me as rage, fear, focus, and power. This exploration offered Rachel an opportunity to begin to regulate her nervous system through several pathways of state shifting. We welcomed and invited these experiences even though at times they felt scary to her. As she began to express and describe this fear to me, she was engaging in a coregulated relationship that eventually became playful.

One of the practices that helps clients shift from freeze utilizes a physio ball, like Rachel and I had. Physio balls naturally promote yield, and the feedback from the yielding surface balances and regulates the ANS. Here is a simple way to do this.

PRACTICE: PHYSIO BALL YIELD EXPLORATION

1. Place a physio ball next to a chair. If you are not used to a physio ball, having a saucer to place it in can be helpful. Sit in the chair.
2. Take a moment to practice Shifting to Comfort and then take a baseline of your weight. When you have a sense of your weight, notice your sense of yield, if this is becoming (or already is) familiar to you.
3. Notice what it feels like to sit in a chair. Notice how relaxed or settled your body is. Notice how your spine feels. Does it feel strong, relaxed, free, tight? If you have pain, notice the location and intensity of the pain. Yielding can decrease pain, though it doesn't always.
4. Move to sitting on the ball. Notice if there are any shifts in any of the above. Because physio balls promote yield, we can notice a sense of release, letting go, softening, or other words you choose. We can notice more ease in our spine. We can also notice more tension and rigidity in our bodies. Sometimes changes feel worse. This is an indication of where we have work to do.
5. Only spend as much time on the ball as is comfortable. They take getting used to initially as they can feel less stable than a chair. Over time, physio balls promote our own stability

by softening fascial tissue and increasing the strength of our core muscle groups and balancing and correcting the dynamic tonic and phasic muscle engagement necessary for both core strength and spinal fluidity.

6. Go back to the chair and compare your sense of weight and yield now with your baseline. Notice what's changed, if anything. As always, there is no demand for change.
7. Go back and forth between chair and ball, spending more time on the ball. This contrast in posture and movement can promote vagal tone. The sacrum will naturally move through sacral neutral if you spend enough time on the ball and fascial layers will soften which increases receptivity and signals increased internal ease.
8. Once you are comfortable on the ball, begin to explore another contrast. Play first with moving the ball. Notice how you move. Circles? Spirals? Wiggles? Play with bigger and smaller movements.
9. Now let the ball move you. Rest on the ball and sense the movement that this softer, yielding surface invites. This engages the fascia. Pausing like this invites awareness of micromobilizations and micromovements. The feedback from the gentle give of the ball to our bodies can promote yielded receptivity. Moving the ball engages larger muscle groups and larger circular movements, which are reparative for the nervous system. Our bodies naturally move in circles, spirals, and infinity shapes. A defining feature of trauma is a loss of fluidity or flow in movement. It can literally become visibly fragmented, because movement is always shaped by our neurophysiological states.
10. Play with this back and forth until you feel connected to the ball. When you are no longer working hard to sit on the ball and can settle into it, and feel relaxed, alert, and settled, you have found a yield.
11. It's not uncommon to fall off the ball, especially when

people are using it the first few times. That's why I recommend having a saucer to place it in. The ball will still move, and it will also be more stable. Clients can also explore moving between the ball in a saucer and the ball without the saucer. When some of my clients have fallen off, it's offered a moment of playful levity. Since I always sit on a ball as well, I am always willing to fall off the ball with them. Engaging with the practices we invite clients to do cultivates reciprocity.

The Pain of Freeze

I tailor this physio ball exploration for each of my client's needs. We spend a session or many sessions practicing going between chair and ball. We may move to the ball immediately and abandon the chair. We may need a saucer under the ball one time or many. We may play with moving from chair to ball, back and forth, for a few sessions or months. It can appear simple, and I have had clients and students say, "It's not a big deal to sit on that ball," and then fall off. The complexity and multilayered experience of the neural feedback from the give of the ball offers profound sensory input that can quickly shift neurophysiological states and requires us to track our moving center. This can add powerful ground when processing traumatic memories and re-associating with our strength and resilience.

I used this practice with a client whose main complaint was also unbearable pain. In many ways, pain can be considered an absence of yield, and psychic pain is, from my observation, akin to freeze. Psychic pain is pain that has no physical or medical etiology, and it is very common in (and not limited to) survivors of human rights abuse like torture, child abuse, and oppression. Psychic pain commonly contributes to freeze as state and (in)action. Movement can become stiff and fragmented and lack the flow that is visible in ventrally mediated states. In PVISDMP, this is referred to as an absence of movement prosody affecting our body prosody. Vocal prosody is one of Dr. Porges's "markers of engagement" (personal communication, May 13, 2010). The simplest way to describe vocal prosody is the lyrical movement of our voice, as in a mother's lullaby. This is directly linked to the social nervous system, cranial nerve pairs 5, 7, 9, 10 (the vagus nerve), and 11, that are part of the ventral vagal complex. Cranial nerves 9 and 10 mediate vocalizations. When we feel safe enough, our voice has more range. Fear can make it more monotonic, and terror can silence it. If you can recall listening to someone who is afraid or terrified, you will likely remember a lack of prosody. Similarly, our movement can lose its prosodic flow, which is the actual sequencing of energy through our body. Because this energy becomes interrupted and truncated in fear and terror, our movements physically express the internal experience of the freeze state. We can see this in the speed, quality, and location of movement. In the VVC-mediated flow state of wholeness and social engagement, we tend to move more fluidly in whatever way is natural for us.

With clients who express pain, whether it's physical or psychic, and with students, I use the image of a glacier in water as a metaphor for pain. When we are in pain, we lose the ability to flow, like water. Stiffness, tension, and inflammation can make us freeze like the iceberg. Pain is paradoxical in this way: Movement is often beneficial (though not always), and we feel like we cannot move because it can sharpen or worsen the pain. This contributes to feelings that are fear-based and can be overwhelming. So we remain tensely still. From a somatic and movement perspective, finding the yield that supports the area in pain can help release some of the holding that contributes to pain. The affected tissue can become rigid and hard over time, and when we move, we must use a lot of effort. The absence of yield can also look like a physical collapse and becoming physically numb. Either expression of a lack of yield causes imbalances in the tissue, indicated by polarities of overly rigid and/or overly flaccid tone. Yield is the perfect balance of soft and relaxed, awake and toned.

One way to practice this is, whenever you experience pain, take a moment to identify an area of your body that is near the painful part but doesn't hurt, Is it tense or collapsed and flaccid? Often the body areas around pain work hard or collapse, which is an absence of yield. Now see if there is any part of your body that isn't painful and feels like it is yielding, Visualize the yielded area spreading around and into the areas in pain or out of balance. See if this changes the pain. This can be abstract for those of us not familiar with working with yielding or those of us who are less somatically inclined. Most of my clients are not accustomed to focusing on a yielded area of the body. The physio ball work is a pathway to yield when the body cannot find it. The following case illustrates this and is the origin of this physio ball yield practice.

AHMED: PAIN AS FREEZE

Ahmed was a 28-year-old male who arrived in the United States with his mother and two younger siblings. His father died in the protracted war in a Middle Eastern country. His mother, Mary, was my client, and her sessions consistently focused on her concerns for her eldest and all the ways he had changed since escaping from their perpetrators. I tried to redirect her to the reason she had come to see me—her overwhelm with U.S. culture and grief at losing her husband. I understood enough about her culture and religion to know that her role as mother was important to her. Therefore, my suggestion that she not discuss her worries about her son in therapy could be a cultural imposition. From a typical psychotherapeutic perspective, it might be common to try to redirect the client to her work rather than her son's work. Because she came from a more collective culture that centered family as core to sense of self, I knew I could not separate her suffering from her son's.

After learning as much as I could about her perspective and her role as mother, Mary and I agreed it would be beneficial for him to see me. She convinced him by telling him I worked "with the body and movement" and could help his pain.

When I began working with Ahmed, I only knew that he was his mom's biggest worry. Because he was the eldest, it was expected that he would step in as the patriarch of the family. His mother complained that he was not carrying out the duties of the elder male. He was supposed to pick his siblings up from school but often forgot. He had begun smoking and drinking beer, forbidden in his religion. In Mary's view, he was not role modeling the way a male in charge of the household should. He had been a master carpet weaver and in high demand, and refused to find a job doing this, despite numerous offers and the family's financial needs. I also knew he had no interest in mental health and experienced a lot of pain from his torture. This background is core to the work that Ahmed and I did and to my understanding of the relationship between the freeze state, pain, and yield.

During the first few sessions, I learned that he lived with intense, sharp pain in his spine that froze him. He described it as stiff and immobile but with a lot of heat and intense sensation underneath. This pain was partially due to broken vertebrae and, as he shared later, partially due to being captive and experiencing not only his own abuse but being forced to watch his mother being tortured. The intense rage he felt while being immobilized into helplessness by those who held him down and kept him in captivity for almost a year had manifested as psychic pain. In the human body, strong emotions that are forcibly repressed can create pain that feels very sharp and icy and has a lot of energy and movement below the frozen surface. In other words, clients can look shut down but have hypertonic muscles, intense surges of energy, and great tension.

As with Rachel, pain was not where I would have wanted to begin our work, and because he would only talk about the pain and only agreed to work with pain, we began there. Importantly, we consulted his physician before initiating movement work. Uncertain what to do with a client who was sitting stiffly on a chair and who moved robotically, I asked him if there was any place in his body that had less pain. There was not. He was in pain everywhere, with the sharpest point being his spine near the physical injury. This became our primary portal, and a pathway to his deeper connection with his interoception, which he had disconnected from to endure his own torture.

I invited him to settle more into the chair using the yield practice (Chapter 6) by inviting him to use his exhale to "melt" his sitz bones into the chair. It didn't work. Feeling stuck, I widened my attention to the space we were in and saw a physio ball. That's when the Physio Ball Yield Exploration Practice was born.

As I guided him from chair to ball and back and then on the ball, moving it and being moved, I did as he did. When on a chair, I was on a chair. When he was on a ball, I was too. I also moved the ball and invited him to be moved as I did this at the same time. Because of the way he embodied the freeze state, immobilized and mobilized at the same time, and in pain, I worked with a practice I call Kyros time. Kyros time is different from the chronological (Kronos) time most human societies now live in. It's not linear. It is more like the pace of dreams and altered states that are core to many healing ceremonies. Altering time and space orientation is how healing occurs in ritual spaces common in more communal societies and cultures. This slowing down at the correct moment in therapy can match the DVC's slow, grounded energy that contributes to our capacity to slow down, rest, settle, and find nourishment. It can also match the energetic frequency of immobilized shutdown states and meet clients where they are at, although this must be timed appropriately. When it is, it can be less confronting than trying to promote a client's state shift upward from immobility to mobility.

Slowing down required many pauses. When I detected an increase in Ahmed's activation, expressed as jerky movements, almost falling off the ball, or appearing disconnected from the movement of the ball, I would simply say, "Let's begin to pause by slowing our movements down." In Kyros time, it's essential to use fewer words and to carefully time any verbal input. This relies on our clinical intuition, another rationale for self-regulation as fundamental to a relationship that promotes reciprocal alliance through the restorative process. Our capacity to tend to and listen to our own interoceptive voice, to what we sense inside, can offer cues as to what our clients are experiencing. This interoceptive wisdom is part of our clinical intuition, a felt sense of knowing we are all born with.

I cued him with phrases like, "That's it. Great," "Let's slow down just a little more," "Just checking if there is anything you are noticing that you'd like to share," and "We can pause again if you want to rest, or we can speed up if your body might like that." The goal is to slow the movements and sense of time down, as slow as the client can tolerate, so they experience an alteration in their neurophysiological and emotional state. This is an advanced clinical skill that relies as much on clinical intuition as it does on training.

When it was time to finish, I said, "Keep slowing down until we are almost still. Get as still as is comfortable and let's just rest in this pause. Now, tell me what you are noticing: what sensations, what feelings, what you are thinking. Has anything changed in your pain levels?" Slowing down to check in with what's occurring in the body, and with any changes to the pain, allows for more present-moment awareness. It can also refine our ability to oscillate attention between our inner landscape, our client, and the external environment. This helps repair the disruption to our quality of attention caused by the traumatic exposure.

Initially he could slow down very quickly, which is common. Many of us are well trained to stop the minute we hear the person guiding or teaching us say anything akin to "stop." It takes time to untrain our bodies from these deeply held socioceptive patterns and rhythms. Learning to transition rhythms, movement, and any process slowly and honor one's own sense of timing is reparative. I believe this restores the ANS's ability to state shift more fluidly, in service of nervous system and emotional regulation that supports re-association and repatterning. This restores flow in our physical movement, emotional expression, cognitive processing, and presence.

The physio ball yield process combined with Kyros time was key to a shift in our work. Eventually, we could address the source of his pain. He began to reassociate his psychic pain with the horror of watching his mother's abuse and with his inability to save his father, who had been disappeared by his abusers. The yield-promoting nature of the ball work elicited helpful resource memories from his past that were buried under the anguish of his recent abuse. At his request, we amplified this work with music he loved from his country. He began to remember favorite musicians who sang "flowy" and "circular" music, and I invited him to share what he loved about the music. I also invited him to bring music in, as he had a few favorite songs recorded on tapes. Listening to music he loved from back home, he began remembering his favorite poets, and he asked if he could bring their poems in to share with me. Eventually each session began with a reading from one of his favorite writers or poets and almost dance-like movement explorations with the balls. He arrived one day excited, a shift in the quality of his SNS from activation to playful. He recalled a story about a flute that was made from a tree branch that was hollowed out after being cut off its tree. The beauty of the flute's music was due to its mourning the loss of its core. He found this metaphor meaningful to his experience, and he likened his "broken" spine to the flute. His discovery through this poem and the metaphor of the hollowed-out flute catalyzed a significant shift in our work. He began to share his experiences of being held captive and was able to link his current issues with his mother and family to his history of abuse and to the loss of his father. He reflected on his inability to step into his culturally designated role as the male leader and role model in his family.

We processed the actual memory of physical torture that created his spinal injury and pain, and we also co-identified that he was depressed, suffered from PTSD, and had survivor guilt because he did not protect his mother from their perpetrators. He recalled how excruciating it was during his physical abuse to suppress his screams while enduring so much pain. We co-identified that this was the intense energy—a silenced scream—he felt underneath his frozen-feeling exterior. He attributed the sluggishness and pain that made his body feel stiff and frozen on the outside to the helplessness and overwhelm he experienced being forced to witness his mother's abuse. For the first time, he shared aloud that his heart felt heavy and broken because he had let his father down by not protecting his mother. The imprint of this complex suffering became the ripple of helplessness that became his inability to show up as the male leader in his family. This was his freeze.

Ongoing somatic and movement work combined with verbal processing and frequent returns to the ball to reregulate his ANS were instrumental in his return to work and to assuming his proper role in family and community. He graduated from therapy much more integrated into his new life. He had a full-time job at a carpet store where he was very well respected, and he loved his work again. He gave up smoking and reduced his drinking, although he had acquired a taste for a cold beer and still allowed himself to occasionally enjoy one. He centered his responsibility to his family, transported his younger siblings to and from school each day, and described feeling "whole," with "still a small hollow in my center that will never be fixed, but I can stand it now." He still experienced some physical pain; it did not overwhelm him or, as he said, "make me stuck." He developed an ability to regulate himself through various practices we explored together, and a few he created while practicing our physio ball yield practice at home.

Fluid Spine was his favorite practice, or "exercise" as he named it. He described it as "helping to move my feelings in the direction they need to go." He could now consciously state shift from freeze to feeling more "centered," in his words. The idea of the hollowed center that transformed a tree branch to a flute became a guidepost for him. The metaphor helped him accept and make meaning of his experience. He likened the hollow in his center to the loss of his father and his inability to protect his mother,

> although one of the things Ahmed shared in our verbal processing was that he had orchestrated their escape with the help of a cousin. We reflected on this through several sessions, and he was able to recognize his courage in protecting his mother by helping both of them escape.

Throughout our process, attention to his spine was core because this was where we began and where the worst pain was. It was his spine that poetically transformed into the flute. The reduction in and ability to manage pain is only part of why this is important work. The spine, as stated previously, is one of the body's pathways of interoception. Eighty percent of the sensory information transmitted to the brain via the vagus nerve, also an interoceptive pathway, is afferent—it travels upward, from the DVC and enteric or gut brain, the area of our gut bio-intelligence, deep intuition, and the ancient DVC pathway to resting, settling, and nourishment. The spinal cord is also a bidirectional pathway, and its pathways of interoception (lamina 1 spinothalamic pathway for pain, temperature, and crude touch and the medial lemniscus for proprioception, touch, and vibration) (Hindi, 2012, p. 3) connects to the entire body through multiple nerve pathways. Integrating the spine into therapy is a powerful way to integrate a polyvagal-informed somatic approach. No matter what our training is, working with the spine, we are working with movement. Our spine is the origin place of our movement. Even simple spinal stretches initiate movement. That the sympathetic nervous system originates in the spinal cord and branches out like many rivering pathways to target organs is an evolutionary stamp from when movement became lifesaving. Spine is both core support, positioned behind our body's midline, and the generator and initiator of our more complex movement, developmentally and phylogenetically. Working with simple practices like Fluid Spine can begin and support the state-shifting process from immobilization to mobilization. Opening this pathway to our inner wisdom and voice and initiator of our natural and original movement helps restore our capacity for moving in the world.

FLUID SPINE PRACTICE

This practice is best done the first time seated on a chair. With time and increased familiarity on a physio ball, you can also do it there. It's harder to do seated on the floor.

1. Sit on a chair that allows your feet to touch the ground. It can be helpful for the chair to have a straight back to provide both feedback and support to your outer spine.
2. Shift to Comfort.
3. Take a baseline of your spine. Notice things like areas that have pain, tension, or compression, and areas that feel open, free, at ease, and pain-free.

Part 1

1. When you are ready to begin, on your next inhale gently contract the following three muscle groups: your buttocks, your abductors (the outer side of your thighs), and your hamstrings. This contraction should only be with 10–20% of your strength. If you contract with a lot of strength, you can over-effort with your muscles. A 10% contraction will engage the fascial layers of your connective tissue, which is containing and connecting and often helps calm us. If you contract closer to 20% of your strength, you will engage your voluntary muscles (think big red muscles like quadriceps, hamstrings), which can invite mobilization, movement, and increased energy.
2. When you exhale, release this muscle contraction and press your feet into the floor. Do this as many times as feels right. Most of my clients start with three to five repetitions and build up to a minute or so of doing this. As you do this, notice the wave of movement that this contract-and-release with breath initiates. It might be tiny, or you may feel a little movement. If you don't sense or feel it, that's okay. Just notice if an area of your spine responds to

this. Usually, Part 1 travels to the sacrum and lower spine. Depending on our muscle tone and patterns it may travel elsewhere, and that's fine. You are still engaging your spine.

3. Pause. Rest. Check your spine against your baseline again.

Part 2

1. Repeat the same muscle contraction group on the inhalation. This time, on the exhalation, press your butt into the chair. Notice what movement wave, whether tiny or large, is initiated and where it travels to. Or notice what part of your spine moves a little, if one does. It usually travels to the lower and mid spine.
2. Rest and check in with your spine again. See if anything has shifted there.

Part 3

1. Rest your hands on your upper thighs, halfway between your knees and the fold between your thighs and your hips on your quadricep muscles. Now, we work with the upper body and spine. On your inhalation, gently contract the muscles of your upper back by squeezing your scapulas together, gently, and on the exhalation, press your hands into your upper thighs. After a few contract/release and press sequences, pause to notice where the movement wave response travels in your spine. Usually this "wave" travels to the upper spine.
2. Rest, repeat baseline. Rest invites integration and the establishment of any new neural pathways the movement exploration initiated.

Part 4

1. Now practice Parts 1, 2, and 3 at the same time. Do everything at once.
   a. On the inhalation, contract your buttocks, abductors, hamstrings, and scapula.

   b. On the exhalation, release the muscle contractions and press your feet into the earth, butt into the chair, and hands into the flesh of your upper thighs.
3. You may experience a sense of wave-like movement in your spine. It can be tiny micromovements, or your spine and back may even undulate. This is the spine's natural movement. The restoration of the spine's natural fluidity is a physical expression of resilience.
4. If it feels comfortable to take this into larger movement, begin to rock forward on the inhalation and rock back on the exhalation, amplifying the spinal wave. You can flow and rock up to standing and then take a walk and compare to your walking baseline.
5. Sit back down, rest a moment, and check in with your spine. Notice if anything has changed.

Fluid Spine and Grounding to Earth (see below) are potent somatic regulation practices for many reasons. Both combine muscle contraction with breath (respiration) practices, which increases oxygenation. Our ANS developed as it is in our mammalian bodies because our human evolution increased our complexity. This complexity requires increased oxygen. Any movement of the sacrum—tiny, gentle, or more dynamic—can promote vagal tone. When we move our sacrum subtly, or dynamically as many sacred and traditional dance forms do, we move through the still point of sacral neutral. Because the pelvic floor is fascia rich, sacral and pelvic floor movements can soften fascia, which becomes dense and hardened from the autonomic imprints of traumatic exposure. There is a bidirectional feedback loop between fascia and the ANS, so tense, painful fascia also signals defensive and fear-based states. Fascia is both a marker and a mediator of physiological resilience (Porges, 2025).

Using the spinal wave to rise up off the chair is a posture change. Posture changes as simple as sitting to standing, standing to sitting, or taking a brief walk are helpful in therapy and generally easy for any therapist to use. When we change posture, baroreceptors (blood pressure receptors) will signal our brain and ANS, and our vagal tone will increase or decrease, depending on the beginning and ending posture, as well as the moving transition between postures. This is why movement is such a powerful and immediate state shifter and ANS regulator. Dr. Porges's term for our capacity to restore vagal tone is "vagal efficiency." Vagal efficiency means that if our vagal tone is reduced due to an environmental demand, we can increase it to recalibrate efficiently and fluidly. All the PVISDMP practices in this book are opportunities to restore vagal efficiency.

Grounding

Grounding is another helpful practice to use with clients in freeze states because it utilizes our connection to earth to root activation and to inspire gentle or smaller movement in a contained, structured practice. Structured practices can be easier for survivors to tolerate than more spontaneous free-flowing practices. Grounding is an emergent process of the primary portal of weight. Yield, and our sense of place and belonging, are also emergent processes of weight. Grounding can recruit the DVC's ability to promote immobilization without terror states, including slowed-down states of bliss, rest, settling, rest and digestion, and receptivity. It also invites gentle mobilizations and micromovements. Grounding to Earth, formerly called "polyvagal-informed grounding," promotes sacral neutral because pressing into the earth with our heels only invites the sacrum into that position. If we press with the whole foot, it tends to invite sacral extension, which is helpful for those who sit for long hours, which keeps the sacrum flexed. Sacral extension can stretch and soften the fascial layers of connective tissue surrounding the sacrum and can also initiate energy and mobilization. These movement responses will not be the same for everybody, but this is the spine's movement tendency.

GROUNDING TO EARTH PRACTICE

This practice is optimally done standing. If that is not possible, it can be done sitting.

1. Shift to Comfort.
2. Take a baseline of your sense of weight and yield. When you have a sense of your weight, sense how grounded (connected to the earth) you are.
3. As in Fluid Spine, inhale and gently (10–20% of your strength) contract the same three muscle groups: buttocks/glutes, abductors, and hamstrings. Exhale and release. While releasing, press just your heels (not your whole foot) into the earth. You do not need to lift your toes or upper foot up.
4. Repeat this for as long as is comfortable.
5. Pause, rest, integrate. Check your baseline sense of weight and groundedness.

Harvest

The practices in this chapter intentionally integrate the wisdom of Polyvagal Theory. Because the freeze state is a hybrid of immobilization and mobilization, it can look like a frozen collapse, or it can appear as rigidity and tension, or everything in between, in a body's movement, attitudes, facial expressions, and emotions and actions. The stuckness of energy that wants to move in ways that were repressed, truncated, or interrupted can cause psychic pain. Pain, a common expression of freeze in survivors of relational, interpersonal, and intentional traumatic exposure, is a call to attend to energy that's just waiting to move. From freeze, working with any movement engenders every possible direction in state shifting; up, down, sideways, and diagonal. Freeze can also create a narrative of being stuck. It is a painful somatic dichotomy that longs to move toward relief, relative safety, and connection and doesn't know how. Working on a movement continuum from micro to dynamic, from tiny ANS signals to potent gestures and moving sequences, can elicit SNS energy to find pathways and possibilities out of stuck places. Incorporating awareness of the spine creates another pathway. Grounding practices and practices that recruit the DVC's origins in ancient earthiness can channel SNS energy in ways that both harness it and liberate it so that we begin to find the flow to move out of fear and closer to wholeness.

CHAPTER 8

Sympathetic Overdrive

This body is yours. No one can ever take it from you, if only you will accept yourself, claim it again—your arms, your spine, your ribs, the small of your back. It's all yours. All this bounty, all this beauty, all this strength and grace is yours.

—JEAN HEGLAND, 1996, *INTO THE FOREST*

If you have ever known, dreamed of, or imagined the sensation of running unencumbered, you have met your sympathetic nervous system (SNS). In this instance, it's being co-recruited with your ventral vagal circuit (VVC). The VVC vagal brake is perhaps released enough to allow the swiftness of flight so that your feet skim the earth while you breathe fully and feel your accelerated heartbeat like dancing lightning. You might have a panoramic vision of the world you're running though: You can see the vast field of flowers or expanse of the big blue ocean you are running toward. The associated feeling of freedom and playfulness allows you to feel connected to your environment and whoever you are sharing it with, human or more than human.

If you've ever run in fear, you'll also know speediness, albeit likely a jerkier, tighter, more intense acceleration accompanied by feelings of fear. Your heart's rapid beat might feel uncomfortable, and its thumping might sound ominous. Your breath is faster and comes in spurts that can feel strained and make it feel more difficult to breathe. Your vision may be more focused and a bit blotchy as you run away from something, or, if you must head toward something to fight, you may see color and a small sliver of your surroundings with intense focus. You may only see the danger. This is also the surge of SNS energy, propelling you to defend or protect yourself from the danger that fuels and feeds the fear you feel.

It's an interesting inquiry to consider if the SNS ever operates by itself. Sandwiched between the elder parasympathetic dorsal vagal circuit (DVC) and the newer parasympathetic VVC (cheekily referred to as a "vagal sandwich"), it fires up and initiates a cascade of biohormonal and neurophysiological actions that give us energy, focus, and strength. This is when the vagal brake is removed. The vagal brake is the ventral nerve fiber that innervates the sinoatrial node of the heart, inhibiting the SNS from allowing the surge of energy it potentiates when necessary for survival. As the VVC releases its SNS inhibition, and our heart rate, respiration, and blood pressure increase, this is helpful for mobilization in fear's fight-or-flight state. The dorsal vagal brake can induce the sudden slowing of neurophysiological function and states via heart rate, respiration, blood pressure, muscle tonicity, and more. What does this brake do when the VVC releases its inhibitory effect on the heart and the SNS exerts its influence?

In my clinical observation, the SNS can create strong surges of energy that may override any slowing down the DVC might otherwise contribute to. This is based on observation, not scientific research. The clinical presentation or actions associated with this surge are intense. One can see the energy surging through the body, resulting in extreme hypervigilance for brief periods of time; an inability to settle at all; a frantic sleeplessness that causes a person to be wired, unfocused, and edgy all day, to the point of exhaustion with sleep remaining impossible. It can be challenging to sit with these clients. Like the metaphor of "walking on eggshells," it can feel like sitting on shards of glass.

MO THE WARRIOR

One such client came to the torture treatment program where I worked at the recommendation of his attorney. Mo had failed his first asylum attempt and was trying again. The attorney thought therapy and an asylum evaluation would help him. When I sat down with Mo, I learned that he was a decorated sniper back home and that he had been captured and held by the military from a warring country.

> As part of his torture, Mo was driven while hooded to villages inside the borders of his home country and forced to shoot women and children, at gunpoint. His wife and children had fled to another country in Central Asia, and all he could dream about was being reunited with them. He loved his family, his country, and God above all else. He expressed remorse at what he did but did not visibly demonstrate it. He remained very stiff, defended, and tight when stating that he was sorry for what he did. He knew if he refused to kill his countrypeople, he would be shot. All that mattered to him was to be reunited with his family.
>
> Mo had heard of cognitive behavioral therapy (CBT) and wanted to explore that approach. He imagined it could "change his brain" so he didn't have as many negative thoughts. He was afraid of never seeing his family again, of something bad happening to them, which, given that he was targeted in his home country and wasn't entirely assured of his safety where his family was living, was understandable. These thoughts plagued him day and night. He said he would sometimes "disappear" in them, and while I did not initially observe dissociative states when we worked together, I could imagine how he would dissociate at home or work.

Dissociation is often associated with shutdown and freeze. It can also occur with highly activated states because of the intensity of the feeling states arising from the neurophysiological energy produced by hormones like norepinephrine and cortisol accelerating our bodies. It is a qualitatively different out-of-body experience than dissociation arising from shutdown and freeze. I have observed clients appearing sped up and absent at the same time.

> He often described himself as wanting to live but not certain he was worthy of living. He was very conflicted about this. His family was everything to him, and he wanted to be together with them anywhere. His first choice was the United States, and he had already decided he would meet them where they were hiding if he was not awarded asylum, despite the risks. He also questioned his worthiness of family and love, because of the things he was forced to do to stay alive during his capture. One of the cruelest forms of human rights abuse is forcing someone to perpetrate violence on another person. This happens in many, many forms of systemic, interpersonal, oppressive, and institutional abuse.
>
> I recruited a colleague to do the CBT work I was not then trained to do, and I accompanied her in the sessions. We made progress in terms of his ability to connect his sense of doom to his past, forced actions (killing fellow countrypeople), and to a belief that he would be punished for what he did. It was very difficult for him to connect to and name the emotions he was feeling about all of this, and he struggled and resisted connecting his beliefs to his body. When my colleague and I agreed we had gone as far as we could with CBT, I resumed working with him somatically.
>
> One of the things I learned about him during his CBT sessions was that he was both a judo and a yoga practitioner. He loved both, and I asked him if he would be willing to integrate yoga into our work, thinking that would be the most efficient way to support him to connect more to his emotions and his body. He enthusiastically said yes and at the same time jumped off his chair, declaring he would demonstrate how well he did a handstand. Then he did the handstand with such intense sympathetic energy that one of his heels put a hole in my wall. He

sat down, beaming, and I simply said, "You clearly have a lot of physical strength. Perhaps we can use that in our work together."

We began to integrate yoga into our sessions in a variety of ways. I would ask him questions about his experiences of being held captive and of his current asylum-seeking process and about his family back home and his hopes for the future. We would periodically pause, and I would invite him to teach me one of his favorite yoga poses. Over time we began reciprocally sharing the teacher role and took turns deciding which asana we would practice together. Some of these Asanas morphed into potent gestures.

At one point when he was speaking about his sniping abilities, he described his formerly very high rank in his country's military and shared, with palpable pride, how highly respected he was for these abilities. I asked him directly if he was proud of this, and he began to say yes and then paused. His body suddenly became very rigid and tense, and I could see activation building. The charge was intense. In an angry voice that I had not yet heard, he began to speak with more detail about what he was forced to do. As he continued speaking, he became more agitated and angrier. I experienced a surge of heat deep in my core, so I paused us, as was our agreement, and asked if we could do some active yoga to move his anger. He quickly became very tense and angry and got up and left the session. I was stunned and had no idea if he would return the next week. He did.

I began the session by asking him what he recalled about storming out of our session. He said he remembered feeling angry and like he had to leave. I then asked him if he could tell me more specifically what he remembered feeling in that moment. He was able to name anger and rage toward those who captured him and forced him to use the very art and skill he was proud of and respected for, a skill he believed a true soldier and master should only use for "the right reason."

When I asked him if we could cease talking and just leave a moment for him to feel what he was feeling, he didn't say anything, and then suddenly, he got up and began to do the

Mountain pose, albeit with so much tension I could sense that more postural change and movement might be helpful. I invited him to do the Warrior pose, both 1 and 2, transitioning back and forth to relieve some his tension and invite the captive energy to move and to become movement. He did this speedily so I joined him, and I both witnessed and interoceptively sensed effort in his muscles. He began to breathe very heavily. I saw pulsing beneath the surface of his skin, which I sensed as micromobilizations "on steroids." I asked him if he could notice his breath and his heartbeat; he said they were speeding up, his heart was "loud," and to me, he appeared to be getting angrier. Knowing that interrupting sympathetic activation by promoting calming down and relaxing frequently backfires, I knew I needed to meet his energy where it was at. I asked him if we could bring some breath into his pose. His first response was, "That won't help me. I'm already breathing. I have a lot of energy to move." This was his typical response to any invitation that he perceived was me asking him to sense and feel something deep inside of himself.

I then reframed it and said, "I would like to support you with breath from outside. As I observe you and sense the energy between us as I do my warrior poses, I feel like I need some structure, something to hold all that energy. Does that sound familiar to you?" He agreed and allowed me to use some props that he could push against or press against to create a feedback loop from the outside to the inside, using the three dimensions of his breath, described below.

We continued to transition between Warrior 1 and onto Warrior 2 slowly. It was not easy for him to move slowly, which is why I added a physical way of working with breath. Because breath can be activating, being physical with breath, that is, beginning with movement of the physical body and then adding breath, can increase relative safety and make it comfortable enough to engage with breath work to eventually slow down. Bringing awareness to breath brings awareness to sensation, and this can overwhelm clients who are not yet resourced and regulated enough and/or whose bodies still feel overwhelmed with uncomfortable sensation.

The following description of the three dimensions of breath practice is one way to work with breath dimensionality. As Chapter 1 details, all our breaths and all our movements are dimensional and are built on three foundational dimensions: horizontal (side to side), vertical (up/down), and sagittal (forward/back). Amplifying these three dimensions individually, even though they collaborate to shape and move us together, is useful to help clients understand where they may be holding their breath. Breath shapes movement: It can both constrict and expand it. Connecting breath to movement and movement to breath helps restore movement prosody.

We took turns guiding each other through Warrior 1 and 2. As we did this, I invited Mo to play with pushing his hands and feet into a wall (real or imagined) and then reach. He pushed to reach with a lot of effort and, often, strain. All his reaches began with tightening his muscles and straining his shoulders or hips. The dissipation of the energy sequence was visible by the time it reached his hands and feet. I could literally see the energy stuck in his body, unable to extend through his limbs to support his posture.

That's when I began to work with the three dimensions of breath. Looking back, I did so rather crudely, and this is what contributed to the cocreation, with Mo, of three different ways to explore these three dimensions of breath and movement described below (semivertically or sitting to explore structure and function), in Chapter 9 (standing and moving), and Chapter 11 (lying in horizontally and sensing). For the horizontal dimension, I invited him to hold two books of the same size and weight against the side of his body (left and right outer ribcage, just under his armpits). When he cued me verbally that it was okay, I took over holding the books there, and he resumed the pose. I invited him to press or push the books away from his body on the inhale and let them follow his ribs as they dropped back toward his body. Doing this, he was able to unstick some of the energy closer to his core and move it to the end points of his hands and feet. This sideways state shift from activation to a less fearless focus in the direction of more grounded, playful movement increased his sense of yield, or what he referred to as "strong calm and focus."

To enhance his awareness of the vertical sense of self and sense of place dimension of his breath, we used a squishy PVC ball on top of his head to push up against. He insisted on a book at first, and I noticed that he retained the quality of effort and strain trying to push a book up. The soft squishy ball helped him find the subtle quality of pushing his head with his whole spine versus just his neck and shoulders, which invites the yield beneath the push. Once he found more ease and flow in this vertical dimension, I asked him to imagine his tailbone reaching to the ground while his head reached rather than pushed the ball up. This increased the flow of energy in his spine, and he was able to extend his back and arms and feel grounded in his legs.

For the sagittal/front-and-back moving and relational dimension, we used the ball on his sternum, and he inhaled it away from himself and let it rest back in toward his back body on the exhale, and with his permission, I pressed another ball into his spine, behind the sternum. This awareness of the expansion that is possible between front and back body was the most profound for him. He remembered feeling some of the pride he felt when serving in his country's army. We worked with the embodied feeling of this pride to begin connecting to his emotions. This work became the portal that allowed us to do much deeper work with internalized shame, intense fear, and immobilizing terror rooted in the reality of never seeing his family again. What followed is beyond the scope of this book: We spent another five months connecting those feelings to what he had been forced to do, how he perceived his countrypeople and family might see him, how he saw himself, and why all this instigated the fear he felt straining his body, mind, movement, and spirit.

The Three Dimensions of Breath

This Three Dimensions of Breath practice has three components that arose from the work I did with Mo. I first taught it in Indonesia after the tsunami of 2004, and it became an integrated part of a psychological first aid training and manual there as a stabilization practice. It now has three distinct parts, described as follows, that pay homage to the developmental and evolutionary nature of these three dimensions.

SENSING DIMENSIONALITY IN BREATH

Sensing our dimensionality internally relates to our earliest horizontal dimension. When I teach this, I invite students to lie down in the horizontal dimension, which is the first dimension we explore in infancy—a time when we are primarily sensorial. The vulnerability of lying down is rarely appropriate for my clients, and while I have had clients willing to play with this, it is usually after learning Structure and Function (#2), that is, out of developmental order. Sensing the internal experience of breath can be scary and triggering for many survivors, especially those who experienced intimate forms of exposure where they were painfully aware of their own breathing or the sound of the perpetrators. Because breath increases internal awareness and sensation, it is important to work toward our capacity to sense our internal experience of breath, and the timing of when to do this depends on the client's ability to self- and co-regulate. This is described in Chapter 11.

STRUCTURE AND FUNCTION

This is what I most commonly use with clients, as it can be done easily in a chair, semivertically, where they often feel the relatively safest. When I teach, I usually begin with this, even though it's out of order developmentally, because it tends to be the least confrontational and most accessible way to begin to connect to our breath's dimensionality. The description for this follows below. This approach is helpful for channeling surges of activation into more structured movement actions that help "sideways regulate" the energy to mobilization in more playful, less defensive states.

MOVING AND BREATHING

This is done standing up and moving (sagittal), and many of my clients enjoy taking breath into movement. It's a powerful way to teach the essential connection between breath and movement, and it can be done in two directions: Breath can inspire, ignite, and choreograph movement, or, when breath is challenging or scary, we can begin with movement and then add breath. This is described in Chapter 9.

Structure and Function

"Structure and Function" describe the structures, that is, areas of the body where it is generally most accessible to palpate or feel each dimension of breath individually (structure). Function refers to sensing with our hands what each dimension does (widen, lengthen, expand forward to back).

Sit as comfortably as possible on a chair and practice Shifting to Comfort.

1. When you are comfortable enough, take a baseline of your breath. An effective way to do this is to notice the comparative length of your inhale and exhale. Human breath is usually composed of a relatively similar length of inhalation and exhalation. Many experiences in life can change and repattern this, as traumatic experiences almost always do. As you begin exploring each dimension, pay attention to which dimension is easier, more fluid, and which is harder or less familiar. You may notice differences in your capacity to feel these dimensions within each dimension, that is, one side of the ribcage might expand more than the other.
2. Begin by tracking the horizontal dimension of breath. The easiest way to palpate this is to place your hands on the

side of your ribcage, that is, the side of your body just under your armpits. Notice how much each side widens to expand side to side on your inhale. On the exhale, your ribs will rest back into your body. The action is on the inhale. Do this as many times as is comfortable and then let it go. Rest and integrate. Check your breath now, comparing to your baseline. You can bring playful mobilization into this practice by moving your hands along the side of your body to see where else breath reaches.

3. To palpate the vertical or lengthening dimension of breath, place a hand on the top of your head or on your occipital ridge. Place another hand at the base of your spine, somewhere on the sacrum or tailbone. Notice the lengthening of your spine on the inhale, and the return on the exhale. Each time we inhale, our body has the potential to lengthen. Notice if it's easier to feel on the upper or lower end of your spine. If you want to play, you can move your hands up and down your spine or the front of your body if that's easier to reach.
4. To palpate the sagittal, place one hand on your sternum, as instructed in Chapter 6. And if possible, place your other hand on the area of your back/spine that's behind your sternum. This time, you are paying attention to how your sternum rises into your hand on your inhale while your back rises into the hand there. As always, the exhale is a return to neutral or resting place. I often use the image of a fireplace bellows or blowing up and releasing air in a balloon to help clients sense this dimension.

When you have completed palpating and feeling each of the three dimensions of breath, take a pause to rest and integrate. Then check the relative length of your inhale and exhale again. Notice if there is a change, and if there is, whether it's comfortable or not. As always, there is no demand for change.

This practice intentionally invites noticing and does not instruct you to change the breath, as many practices, such as deep belly breathing and diaphragmatic breathing, do. Because breath increases awareness of internal sensation, it can increase the sympathetic activation surge because it can invoke scary feelings inside. This sometimes creates panic-like responses when someone is manipulated or pushed to change too soon.

While seemingly subtle, breath is profound. It is our life force: the wave we ride in and out, Spirit. It is a veil between worlds in many sacred traditions. This practice utilizes the potential each one of us has for full dimensional breathing in a way that supports safe-as-can-be containment. It also organizes breath to help regulate out of highly charged states, and it can be used in individual therapy, group, and even communal settings.

This breath work can be taught as a practice and can stoke conversation or psychosocial education about breath, movement, the ANS, and dimensionality in group settings. I have taught parents and caregivers to do this with their children, as it is also a useful assessment. For example, noting where breath does not "fill out" in the horizontal dimension is useful information that can indicate a physical injury and tight muscles or scar tissue or even a place where ongoing traumatic imprints and ensuant patterns can physically change the movement of breath. Because this dimension corresponds with the early developmental tasks of learning safety and trust, challenges in this dimension can offer portals for inquiry and therapeutic work. With younger kids and teens, I often use this approach in a playful way to support a transition from elevated levels of activation to more playful mobilized energy. In these instances, I don't ask or suggest any changes in the tempo, rhythm, or any aspect of their breath. I just invite them to touch the areas where each dimension is most easily felt and to feel the movement of their breath. Connecting to the movement reduces the intensity of the charge by redirecting attention from inner experiences to something more external. Using props, as I did with Mo, can promote a shift in attention to the external, outside the body, and introduce the possibility of support.

Group and Community Work

Thus far, this book has shared case vignettes that highlight examples from mostly individual therapy (many of these individual cases do include family, couple, and group work not described in detail). There is a lot to say about group and community work.

I facilitated a children's group at a refugee mental health/torture treatment program for six years. It began as a traditional therapeutic group for children: 10 weeks, cofacilitated, two hours weekly at the same time and day. Participation in the group was based on the shared theme of displacement. All the children had fled war and migrated to the United States as refugees. I invited children from all the different countries we served, and the age range was 8–14.

This is not a usual approach to group therapy, and colleagues reminded me of this. Many of them criticized the group format and structure and insisted the group should only include children from the same country, speaking the same language, and have a narrower age range. I understood their rationale for this, and we were a small program with 1.5 therapists and a smaller community of refugees. I also believed that the children's shared experience of war was a powerful connection and knew our creative arts and movement-based curriculum could work with multiple language interpretation at once. The children, parents, and donors loved the group so much that at the children's request, we continued it weekly for six years, continuing our renegade approach based on the community's wishes.

Two of the children, a brother and sister, came from a country in West Africa long embroiled in the diamond wars. Both were referred to the group by their teachers: the boy, Leo, who was older, because he was having "angry outbursts" and getting in fights at school, and the girl, Tatiana, because she appeared isolated and depressed. They both were interactive and friendly with the other children in the group and became animated and playful with all the kids. One morning, Leo arrived without his sister. He seemed very tense. I had heard some things about the situation at home from a volunteer working with them but didn't know much other than that their mother was very isolated and rarely came out of her room when the volunteer visited. I met with the husband several times, both to enroll his kids in the group and because he was considering therapy. He became too busy for the latter, but in one of our meetings, he had disclosed the guilt he felt at being away when rebels attacked their village. His wife was raped while the children hid under her bed. Knowing this haunted me, and as he swore me to secrecy, I never mentioned it when speaking with teachers or the volunteer. I held out hope he would return to therapy.

THE STRANGER

We were doing our usual movement warm-up. We stood in a circle, and I let the kids pick music. Leo chose Papa Wemba's "Sala Keba," and we began moving together, quite lyrically. Music influences the quality, shape, tempo, and intensity of our movement; it reflects and can affect our inner rhythms, moods, emotions, and movements. This is how movement tells stories. Whether it's stiff, fluid, fragmented, staccato, slow, or smooth, it is that way because of what we sense and feel inside.

Every week, the group decided which child would select warm-up music for the next group. This was a leadership, dignity, and reciprocity opportunity, allowing for a child to influence the environment that would entrain us all together through music, rhythm, movement, and dance. In a typical dance/movement therapy way, I followed the kids' movements, verbally acknowledging shifts in movement style, speed, and shapes.

The warm-up began with easy swaying movements that were growing faster. In what I experienced as a flash, the intensity shifted, and suddenly it was not congruent with the lyrical, melodic, bouncy music. There was an increasing force and fierceness in the kids' movements, and I realized it was emanating from Leo. His eyes were wide open, staring but not seeming to look at anything. He was moving more stiffly; his muscles were tight, his facial expression frozen in a wide-eyed stare. The quivering heat in my belly signaled fear. I continued to follow, and as the children followed his lead, I felt like I might lose control of the group. The children were riding a wave of sympathetic charge that was beginning to feel like anger. In the most inviting and permissive voice I could summon, I said to Leo, "Leo, it looks like you are focused on something. Can you tell us what it is?"

After a pause, he yelled, "The stranger!" and began to punch the air in multiple directions in a frantic, untethered way. His energy level was so elevated he appeared to almost levitate with each wild punch.

I asked him where the stranger was and he said, "I don't know." I then asked, "Would it help if you could find him?", knowing that could go either way. In what I sensed was a replay of what he had experienced auditorily, but not visibly, when his mother was attacked, my intuition told me that visibility might offer some containment to this highly charged activation that seemed to literally fly out of his body.

He nodded and said, "He's in the middle," so I said, "Okay, the stranger is in the middle. What do you want us to do?"

He replied, "Punch him!" This was a "sticky" moment for me. We were on a neurophysiological precipice. I understood his desire and need to complete an incomplete, "strangled" impulse to defend and protect his mother.

I also knew that this would be activating and scary for some of the children. So I said, "Can we punch as part of our dance together?" to redirect the sympathetic charge toward a more connected, mobilized collective state. It was not just his ANS; it was our collective ANS that was elevating.

Living in war and conflict-affected areas requires a unique ANS adaptability. This may seem counterintuitive, as the emergent states of survival often become the imprints that pattern posttraumatic stress disorder, moral injury, and other symptoms and conditions associated with exposure to violence and horror. In recent years these conditions are recognized not as pathologies but rather as adaptations to survival, ongoing until the ANS neurocepts an increase in relative safety. This can take time. The context of exposure will influence the emergent states anyone experiences. Whether one is a combat soldier, a civilian fleeing persecution, a mother protecting children or a child left alone, or part of a rebel militia is all context, i.e., the "how we meet the world" in moments of extreme exposure. In all contexts I have worked with, from veterans and active-duty military to refugees who fled war, as well as my own ANS experience of working and living in active war zones and low intensity conflicts, elevated vigilance is survival-serving. And it's exhausting. Working with many communities affected by war, I have observed that the collective nervous systems of shared experience can ameliorate the exhaustion because one becomes part of a collective nervous system united in action. In an environment of exposure, the collective shared mobilization to defend and protect can reduce the individual burden which decreases individual intensity. We are not alone. This is true in group therapy as well: Sharing intense vigilance and mobilization can contribute to a sense of collective strength and power that promotes state-shifting from defensive, protective mobilized activation to mobilization somewhere along the continuum of play. Isolation is perhaps the most heartbreaking ongoing experience of the survivor of trauma because it perpetuates feelings survivors have of being "crazy" and misunderstood, which in turn perpetuates the silence of being alone. We may have to navigate clients' uncomfortably intense emotions and horrific recollections and images to state shift. Movement and moving together is a potent pathway to alchemize fear to expressive mobilization.

> Leo was still punching, and I knew that the dissociative nature of this type of activation did not often lend itself to rapid state shifting. I went with what was happening and offered cues such as, "Which direction are we punching? How strong are we punching?" and "Can we punch all together?" to bring the punch movement together in a unified, cohesive rhythm. This collective entrainment can promote collective coregulation through state shifting, and in this instance, I was facilitating a "sideways" state

shift from sympathetic activation to mobilized continuum of play, the subject of Chapter 9.

Leo responded quite violently, "Kill the stranger!" He repeated this, and several of the kids joined in what was becoming a chant.

Knowing that Leo deserved to express his emotions, and that I needed to protect the group, I allowed this to continue for about 30 seconds, and then I said, "Sometimes there are other ways to treat a stranger. Who has an idea?"

One of the younger kids yelled, "Let's make him float," and so we shifted our collective movements, which I verbally cued to bring us together, to lifting the stranger up and tossing them into the air.

Another child suggested, "Hide the stranger," and we went around the circle inviting each child to put the stranger somewhere out of sight. Each child would break away and tuck the stranger under a table, in a drawer, and so on, while we clapped, and then rejoin our now very entrained movement.

As we did this, our movements continued to synchronize, and then the music changed to a more rhythmic, funky song with a strong 4/4 bass beat. I noted this aloud and asked, "Who wants to change our movement to match this new rhythm?" One of the older kids offered a strong stomp, which is what I was hoping for. Strong rhythms and movements can entrain and contain activation quite quickly.

We began to center our movements in our feet and legs, marching, stomping, and stepping on earth. One of the children then said, "Hey, we should punch again to go with our feet," which brought us full circle movement-wise. We added punching-like movements, and as the movements became stronger and more synchronized, the collective ANS began to naturally slow and downregulate. The random strikes at an invisible perpetrator in the middle of our circle became coordinated movements that punched up, down, in, out, and in as many directions as the kids suggested. I cued the direction changes with words like, "Okay,

> which way do we need to punch?" I also cued the intensity and rhythm of the punches by saying, "Are we punching hard or soft, fast or slow?" These simple cues create an opportunity to coordinate and become a unified force supporting Leo in his expression of rage and anger. As the stomping and punching slowed, and as the kids became more tired, I changed the music back to the original flowing song. Our stomps became steps, and our punches became circles and arcs. We repeated the song twice, and it took that time to shift the energy of the punching from a hard, staccato, high-energy punch to a more flowing, bouncing, almost wave-like collective movement that the stranger exited on. He was pushed down a river, never to be seen again. This felt like completion.

I did invite Leo to check in with me after the session, and he really didn't want to talk. He simply said, "I feel better." At one point earlier in my work I may have pushed him to share more; I respected his family's silence around what had happened to his mother. There were strong cultural norms around rape; they came from a community where a woman being raped was usually a reason to expel her from the community. Suspending judgment is an enormous practice in human rights psychotherapy. Because the ANS operates below the stories, this is one way Polyvagal Theory upholds a humanitarian ethos; be they individual, collective, or cultural stories. I understood the family, especially the father, felt deep guilt about what had happened and had chosen to flee their home so he would not be pressured to abandon his wife. His love for her was deep.

I updated Leo's father and reinvited him and the kids for individual therapy. He said he would think about it. Though they never engaged, the father did come in for a few "meetings," and I used this time to acknowledge and witness the experience his family had, his love for and commitment to protecting his wife, and recommended the children receive school counseling, which they did. Our program offered consultation to school counselors to support them in their work with our young refugee community.

Rhythm as Connection and Unity

Everything is rhythm because everything moves. Seasonal cycles, the day/night cycle, the ebb and flow of tide are all rhythmic. Rhythm is a primary organizer for all life. Human development can be seen as sequential rhythms, from the softly syncopated floppiness of early scooting to the strong, more defined pushes that emerge in tiny bodies learning to stand up. Chapter 10 covers rhythm in more depth as it focuses on PVISDMP's core rhythmicity practices. Rhythm, initially expressed in punches and stomps, was what shifted this children's group dance/movement circle from rapidly elevating in sympathetic activation to a more unified, cohesive collective field, organized by rhythm.

Stomping

Stomping is a common rhythmic movement that most of us do, especially when we are children. It can be easily integrated into somatic work. Stomping primarily relies on large voluntary muscles like the glutes and quadriceps, so it can increase energy and mobilize. It can also meet high-activation energy and organize and contain it because of its inherent rhythmicity and engagement with the neuromuscular and musculoskeletal systems, which integrates both branches of the peripheral nervous system. Stomping has additional benefits, like increasing bone destiny, especially when it's done on a natural surface (e.g., not a concrete sidewalk).

Stomping arose naturally in this children's group because we were up and moving. This isn't always the case. Depending on the context a therapist is working in, stomping can be incorporated with sitting or standing. Other forms of ambulation like marching, "walking strong," pushing feet off the earth, and even bouncing or jumping can be used if stomping seems too strong or is not accessible to a person due to injury, disability, or shyness. Shifting posture from sitting to standing will shift vagal tone, initially lowering it as our blood pressure increases. Once we adjust and are comfortable in the new posture, the VVC restores vagal tone by inhibiting the sympathetic circuit, recruited when we begin to move. This promotes vagal efficiency.

Some clients and therapists might find it awkward to stomp. Here are some ways to facilitate this important rhythmic movement that efficiently contains activation in individual and group settings.

INDIVIDUAL WORK

Activated clients often want to, and/or benefit from, moving their legs to channel the activation of mobilization in fear. They can engage in a continuum of stomps, from slow softer stomps, which are essentially strong pushes, to full-force dynamic moving stomps. Grounding to Earth can do this. One way to invite stomping while sitting fits into the ever-growing plethora of bilateral stimulation methods and techniques that many therapists use. When a client begins to become activated:

1. Invite them to begin stomping (or marching or jumping if that's more acceptable to them) individually and sequentially, that is, left to right or right to left, rhythmically. Once they have achieved an even rhythm (I stomp with them and count if they are having a hard time keeping a steady rhythm), invite clients to begin to touch the knee that is raised with the opposite hand. It's a bit like hand-knee patty-cake with oneself. This regulates the nervous system and grounds and contains the sympathetic charge. Stomping becomes more than a simple movement; it's a moving form of bilateral stimulation, long known to regulate the ANS because it shifts the ANS from sympathetic to parasympathetic dominance. Because both hemispheres of the brain are engaged, emotions are regulated, and our cognitive, emotional, and intuitive capacities are integrated.
2. If clients are willing to stand up, they can stomp in place and then do the same thing, knee to hand or elbow.
3. I always stomp with them. Establishing reciprocal alliance is rooted in therapists' willingness to accompany the client

in any somatic and movement practice we invite them to do. Some clients are quite keen to move about the space and can be invited to alternate stomping, walking, marching, or skipping—any form of ambulating—and notice what they feel and how their feelings change as they alternate ambulations. I move through the space with them, witnessing and accompanying.

4. For clients for whom mobility is an issue, or who are shy or unwilling or unable for any reason to stomp, I invite them to "slow stomp." Slow stomping is an effective way to encourage clients to begin to practice and play with more energetic movements, as a portal to playful mobilization. Many clients find it less confrontative. I offer clients a physio ball and place it in front of their feet with a chair or wall behind so they can slowly stomp, offering verbal cues such as to press, push, or stomp the ball "like stretchy chewy gum." Or "like kneading dough."

Press, push, and stomp are also a continuum. Pressing is gentler than pushing and is a preparation for push. Push has the same relationship to stomp. Engaging any movement practice in a continuum of varying efforts is similar to beginning with micromobilizations and micromovements before larger movements. It can ease clients into movement in a way that is less scary and confronting. The incoherent, frantic, intense quality of too much energy is contained by more vigorous stomping, or any rhythmic movement. As the case vignette describes, stomping was quite natural for this group of children, preteens, and teens. Generally, this is true of younger clients individually and in groups, and especially in groups. Groups will often naturally entrain toward staccato, stomping, pushing, and powerful movement when energy rises. Any simple verbal cue such as "I see [person's name] is moving their legs really strongly, stomping on the floor" can begin to move a group of energetic people into a uniformly rhythmic movement that regulates the collective nervous system.

Community Work: Haiti

One of the most compelling examples of a collective sympathetic activation occurred when I was working with children living on the streets of Haiti. This is a complex context at the intersection of humanitarian work, Haiti's unique history, and a large community of children who find themselves without homes due to this complex intersectionality of history, colonization, oppression, suffering, and resilience. Each aspect of this complexity would merit an entire chapter or book. For the purposes of using somatics and movement to work with activation that is a necessary survival strategy being expressed in daily actions, this chapter shares only the broad basic context and a favorite practice that helped the children take the edge off their highly activated states and shift into states that supported more collaborative engagement.

I first met a community of young men, ages 6–16, living on the streets of Port-au-Prince when I was in Haiti studying dance in 1999, not long after the embargo years. I returned and lived in a home with these young men, eating with them, hanging out with them, joining them in school, and contributing to their classes, as well as supporting a dance troupe they had formed to bring more emotionality to their performances, and offering dance/movement therapy when requested. Haiti became my second home and a spiritual home, and I also worked with other programs assisting and supporting children who, for myriad reasons secondary to Haiti's complex societal issues and challenges, lived in peer groups on the streets rather than with their families. At the risk of sounding like a generalization, Haiti, often depicted as a place of tragedy and violence, is a place of some of the most extreme adversity and resilience I have ever experienced. To understand the depth of this, I recommend Paul Farmer's book *The Uses of Haiti* (1994), Jean Casimir's *The Haitians: A Decolonial History* (2020), and Elizabeth Abbott's *Haiti: A Modern History* (2011) for each book's insightful alternative perspectives on this island nation.

Somatic and movement therapies are not usually highlighted in humanitarian work. Complex humanitarian emergencies and disaster response are very complicated, bureaucratic, long-term situations that necessarily focus on rescue first, and then recovery, while trying to ensure basic needs. Child-friendly spaces and recreational or psychosocial activities are the most commonplace processes for psychological support. I worked with children from my first trip in 1998 and subsequent trips through 2012, with a variety of programs from residential to day programs, in Cité Soleil, central Port-au-Prince, Cap-Haïtien, and elsewhere through earthquakes, hurricanes, low-intensity conflicts, the embargo years, and gang violence. The children I lived, ate, worked, and played with endured daily struggles trying to maintain hygiene, feed themselves however they could, and stay dry in the rainy season and cool in the dry season. It's a heartbreaking environment with constant cues of rejection, isolation, and separation. Naturally, the children need to maintain a level of vigilance to protect themselves and often to defend themselves from law enforcement, other gangs, and people who feel threatened by them.

The appropriateness of trauma therapy and trauma work is an ongoing discourse in the humanitarian field. After many years working in this space, it is clear to me that this is not the time to process trauma, and that psychosocial education about the adaptive survival strategies the human body offers us is most helpful. When survivors learn about the ANS and that even the uncomfortable ways they feel signal that their nervous systems are "championing their survival," they often describe it as "liberating" knowledge. These young men live in environments that are not welcoming, and often truly dangerous and life threatening. Their understanding that their reactions are their own body feeling "enough strength to protect and defend themselves when necessary" helped them understand that their "bodies were their strength" and the source of their power to lift themselves up when the society around them pushed them down. This became a motto for one group of men, many of whom participated in gangs while on the streets, whom I worked with for over 10 years with periodic visits. I trained the staff, and any work I did with the kids was attended by all staff so the work could continue beyond my stays there.

We used a variety of group processes (as well as individual therapies, when needed) to support these young men to navigate their lives.

Drumming and dancing, including learning their own cultural rhythms and dances; playful and competitive games that offered challenging and collaborative leadership opportunities; and both very structured and semistructured movement-based practices became very popular learning and community-building time for these young men. Their absolute favorite was a simple still-to-moving practice called Slow Flow. This was a bit surprising, as it is a more meditative and contemplative practice of slow, fluid movement in service of restoring transition in movement sequences to repair the neural pathways. Anytime we gathered, the boys would shout "Slow Flow!" and giggle with a youthfulness that I wished they could experience more consistently and spontaneously in their everyday lives. I learned, after several trips, that they practiced it on their own, and some of the boys even taught it to others so they could "expand into their power."

SLOW FLOW PRACTICE

To prepare for Slow Flow, have fluid, groovy, juicy, flowing music cued up. It can be mellow or upbeat, depending on the direction you hope to state shift toward. Slow Flow is beneficial in several ways. It stretches and flexes the spine, that primary pathway of interoception. Any practice that engages the spine in slow movements fortifies our interoceptive capacities. In Haiti the boys took turns selecting music, and inviting clients to do this ensures music that is culturally referenced. Slow Flow can help clients connect to their proprioceptive capacities and to their bodies moving in space. Proprioception is always disrupted by trauma. If we think of proprioception as our own internal GPS, it's perhaps easy to conceive how the imprint of traumatic experience in our body alters it. Slow Flow is also a restorative, regulating five-minute transition practice between sessions and, depending on the music used, can calm, energize, and/or center us.

1. Standing or sitting, get as physically comfortable as you can.
2. Take a baseline of your spine. Notice how comfortable

it is, for example, does it feel flexible, tight, painful, free? Also notice how you feel, reflect on your neurophysiological state.

3. Locate the bottom of your spine, which is the tip of your tailbone.
4. Begin tracing tiny, tiny circles in either direction with the tip of your tailbone. For some clients, using a metaphor—such as a spoon that is stirring batter or soup, a calligraphy pen that is writing, a paint brush painting, and so on—can help initiate this tiny micromovement. The physical movement is barely visible.
5. Slowly, begin to add more of the spine to the movement. Once the tip of the tailbone is circling, add the rest of the tailbone. Then add the sacrum. Then slowly add each vertebra of the spine, until your whole spine is creating circles. When your entire spine is circling, your body may begin moving in slow, circular shapes that expand and contract. This is an example of micromovements becoming movement.
6. Move for as long as is comfortable, and add music if you want, and then when your body cues you it's done, slowly, slowly, begin to bring the movement to a pause. Rewind and reverse the practice, bringing any moving areas of your body to a pause until only your spine is moving. Then pause the spinal movements beginning from the top of the spine, vertebra by vertebra, until only the tip of the tailbone is moving, In other words, reversing the direction of how we began this practice to include the entire body into slow circular movement.
7. Once paused, rest and integrate and compare your spine and how you feel now to your baseline.

If clients can enjoy or want to engage with more dynamic movement or dance, they can begin to locomote their moving, dancing body through the space, exploring the environment around them. This can be therapist-guided or left open-ended for the client to do with light verbal cueing such as, "Now that your whole spine is circling, can you add your shoulders? Your neck? Your head?" "Now that your whole body is moving, can you begin moving your body through the room?" I often invite them to imagine they are sending circular and spiraling ripples out into the space, and to notice what ripples or waves come back. This is a way to integrate socioception and culturoception into this moving practice. If every moving body considered the ripples we send out to the world and endeavored to affect the environment with ripples of kindness and compassion, we might discover that kinder, more compassionate ripples return to us.

For some clients, moving just the spine is enough. They may prefer to do it sitting. For others it may be enough to stay seated and draw tailbone or tailbone and sacrum circles, spirals, and infinity shapes into the chair. If clients cannot find their tailbones, they can initiate this fluid movement from their sacrum or even their lumbar spine. No matter how big or small, quiet or dynamically they move, rewinding this moving practice in reverse direction as slowly and mindfully as they began ,until they return to stillness, is important. These transitions are reparative to the nervous system, and help restore the prosodic flow of our bodies energy and movement.

Adding music can amplify the expressivity of this practice and can also offer bigger movement to contain the sympathetic activation. I always encourage clients to choose music using cues like "slow and flowy," "fluid," "groovy," and so on. They can also choose music based on how they feel and what they prefer to move to. I will choose the music if they don't want to or cannot.

Adding shapes—such as circles becoming spirals and infinity signs—as the spine is "joining" the movement or when the whole body is moving can also change the quality, pace, and expressivity of the movement, which will amplify and complexify state shifting. This can be done with varying degrees of structure depending on the therapist's style and relationship to using movement.

Always complete the practice by pausing, resting and integrating. Compare to baseline.

Harvest

The SNS moves us. It is a pathway, an initiation, and a transition. Emergent between the two branches of the parasympathetic nervous system on the phylogenetic trail, it is the bridge between shutdown and social engagement. When breath, rhythmic movement, and structured and creative movement practices are integrated into any psychotherapy, it amplifies the potency of the work, and play, we engage in. Both this and the previous chapter offer ways to integrate the spine, our body's prime mover and birthplace of the SNS, into individual and group psychotherapy, and even communal work. Our spines are a living map of the evolutionary journey that our human mammalian experience emerged from. Our upright spine centers us and is central to how we orient to ourselves, the environment, and our communities. To mobilize is to invoke movement as lifeguard, liberator, and ally. While the charge of sympathetic activation can be overwhelming, it is also the energy that activates connection and collective movement. Working with groups and communities who share themes of suffering, marginalization, and loss, harnessing the collective energy of movement can foster a collective whole. Strong shared rhythmic movements are a powerful way to channel feelings of overwhelm so they become action and, when necessary, the uprising from shutdown, or being kept down by repressive and oppressive forces. It's the sympathetic nervous system that inspires us to rise.

CHAPTER 9

The Continuum of Play

OUR NEURAL PLAYGROUND

Play is the mediator of the invisible and visible.
—DORA M. KALFF, 1991, *INTRODUCTION TO SANDPLAY THERAPY*

Play and playfulness are often considered a domain of childhood. For all of us humans, no matter what our age, play is a biological imperative. It is as essential for human mammals as it is for all animals. I was introduced to this idea in graduate school and immediately recognized that somatic, dance, and movement therapy, because of its centering of movement in a variety of forms and expressions, naturally includes play in therapy.

Play is a "mobilization without fear" hybrid state of the sympathetic nervous system (SNS) and ventral vagal circuit (VVC). Play is also an action. Play is something we do; it is a noun and a verb. Playfulness reflects the hybrid state that arises from a surge of sympathetic energy. Because the VVC is also contributing to how we feel, this sympathetically inspired state uplifts, upraises, motivates, energizes, and moves us in a broad continuum of ways.

Working with movement naturally invites play into psychotherapy. While many somatic approaches center somatic awareness and may engage with some movement, having a variety of movement-based practices that honor the continuum of the body's movements makes playful states more accessible to therapy. The continuum of movement described in Chapters 6 and 7, from micromobilizations and micromovements to larger, visible movement, is one such practice. Breath made audible is sound, and sound and movement exist on a continuum. Movement is why we can hear a hummingbird's wings. Breath inspires and manifests in movement, and dance is the creative expression of movement—yet another movement continuum. Breath, sound, and movement, be they subtle breathing practices, structured grounding practices, simple somatic practices, or more expressive moving processes like dance—all have the potential to connect clients to playful engagement.

One of my most memorable moments occurred when a client I worked with at a torture treatment center complained about how all the therapists he had worked with previously wanted to hear his stories over and over "and put them under a magnifying glass." He said, "As if I am going to forget the horrible things that happened to me. That's impossible. I wish I could, and I never will." I explained that it was essential to revisit and process some (not all) of his memories of trauma so he could be less captive to the memories and their ANS imprints. I then asked him what he hoped for in our work together. He looked me in the eyes and held my gaze before responding, "Remind me about joy. Remind me how to dance and sing. Remind me what color looks like, and what flowers smell like. Remind me where life begins again."

Play does this. This SNS-VVC hybrid action can include other humans, or not. We can play alone, as children often do when engaging with developmentally appropriate toys or exploring. We can play with making sounds or singing or dancing along with music. We can also play with sunlight and shade in trees by letting our eyes follow the light and shadow dance and maybe dancing with it. Floating in ocean waves is a form of natural play, and animals can be playmates too. Pets are often willing to fetch a ball or tug on a rope. Wild animals can offer playful moments. Imagine a favorite forest or sea creature doing something that is delightful to watch. That's play too. When we are engaged in more passive, sensual or contemplative play, it's plausible that DVC is also contributing to a sense of being calm, grounded, rested, and supported in play.

MAHMOUD: THE MILITARY CONTRACTOR

In 2018, Mahmoud, a young man from the Middle East, who had been a contractor for the US military helping to protect our troops in the war, was referred to me. He had lived for many years in another Middle Eastern country, where his son was tragically killed. Following his son's death, his wife returned to their home country with their only other child, a daughter, and Mahmoud came to the United States alone, broken and isolated. He oscillated between two states in the continuum of freeze: immobilized freeze, when he spoke about his family or the past, and an edgy, vigilant, frozen-like, stuck mobilization state when he spoke about his life now.

I sensed this latter state as trying to play, a stifled reach from an effortful push that had no yield supporting it. It was clear he wanted to be social and begin again, and he said as much. His body prosody and posture were stiff. His eyes reached mine with effort: When he looked at me, he looked like he was straining to see something beyond me. His vocal prosody was also muted, and I often had to ask him to repeat things because his voice dropped so low. It was difficult to connect with him.

In our second session, Mahmoud talked about his frustration at not meeting people. He worked out at gyms, shopped in malls, and dragged himself (he described it as being "harder and harder to do") to as many public places as he could, hoping to connect with people. These forays made him feel lonelier. He shared examples of how he tried to connect, like asking a cashier questions and chatting at the gym. People were nonresponsive and disinterested. It confused him, and it broke his heart. As I was listening to him describe this, and observing him, I noticed that his face showed no emotion. It was less expressive than a neutral poker face. His voice had a low pitch, monotonic rhythm, and quiet quality. I asked him, "Do you think your face shows what you feel and what you want to express?"

He instantly said, "No. I know it doesn't. My face feels stiff." His raw disclosure surprised me because we were in the very beginning of our work together.

I asked if he would be willing to work on his facial expressions and their connection to his emotions. We were just beginning to work with various movement therapy props to promote balance, stimulate bilateral movement, and regulate his nervous system. We used tuning boards (similar to a balance board, but more cushioned so the movement provides feedback to the spine), and he eagerly asked to learn as much as possible about his ANS. He read books I recommended and quickly understood that his face reflected his heart, and the nerve pathways of his face were connected to the parts of his ANS that regulate his social and relational capacities.

I asked him if he would make faces with me. He looked at me quizzically and asked me to explain. So, I made faces, moving and gesturing with my facial muscles in fairly ridiculous and unusual ways. He laughed and said, "No way." He was too self-conscious to do something silly with his therapist. I asked if he would make faces in a mirror, and he said he felt like he would look stupid and feel stupid, and he already experienced feeling inadequate. I then asked if there was anything he listened to; a sound or piece of music that made him feel emotional in ways that he could express on his face. We discussed smiles and frowns as universal expressions, and he said, "Yes. I love listening to birds sing." He left that day with the following home play assignment: Sit in his favorite chair in front of a large picture window and watch birds. Listening to them sing, he would let his face "play the music" of their song. He agreed to this. He seemed excited for the task.

We checked in over the next several weeks about this daily practice. Because he felt more "life" in his face, and less facial tension, particularly around his ears where his muscles were often painfully tight, he did practice consistently. After a month, his face began to show more expressivity. His gaze was less strained and more contactful. This was the beginning of four years of hard work that culminated in his getting a job, marrying, and having a child. Through our work, he always wanted to understand the rationale for the movement and somatic processes we did. He began to speak about his feelings and actions through a polyvagal ANS lens. His face-making home play evolved into us making faces together, and his eventual family made faces at the dinner table to playfully coregulate while conourishing together. He taught his wife and young son the things he was learning, and she attended two sessions to ask her own questions about regulation and coregulation of their ANS, and how Mahmoud's emotions affected his actions. She had always been concerned about his flat voice and expression, which she associated with depression.

Face making is a great way to exercise the neural pathways of the VVC and the social nervous system. Nerves are tissue, and while they don't need to be toned in the same ways muscles do, they must benefit from neural exercises and movement to support their role in transmitting sensory information bidirectionally. When facial muscles are hypertonic and tense, or hypotonic and sluggish, the nerve pathways can be affected, and the reduction in our natural facial expressivity affects our feelings, our own emotions, and our expression of emotions. It also affects how others see and respond to us.

PRACTICE: FACE DANCE

Face dancing is a practice that immediately engages the VVC. It can be done alone, with or without a mirror, with a friend or partner, in a group, or as Mahmoud did, in response to birds or any more-than-human ally.

To prepare, practice these four smiles:

1. Smile with your mouth.
2. Do an upside-down smile with your mouth (for this purpose, it's not a frown).
3. Smile with your eyes (i.e., lift up the corners of your eyes).
4. Do an upside-down smile with your eyes, which is not a frown. Curl the corners of your eyes downward.
5. To face dance, begin to play with these small micromovements of the face, and connect the dots.

I usually coach clients with invitations like this:

1. "Can you make a small smile with your mouth and at the same time do an upside-down smile with your eyes? Now, can you imagine the left corner of your eye is dancing with the right corner of your mouth?" "Can you imagine the right corner of your eye dancing with the left corner of your mouth?" Another way to say this is, "Can the left corner of your eye send energy or movement to the right corner of your mouth?" The verbal cues can be any descriptive invitation that promotes movement in the striated muscles of the face.
2. Next I might suggest, "Now try smiling with your eyes and mouth at the same time. Can you connect the dots between each of these four corners by moving the muscles [or space] between them?"
3. Finally, I will lead the client: "Begin to let these four shapes move your whole face while you keep connecting the dots. Your face is dancing!"

This practice engages the VVC pathways and helps liberate any tension in the striated muscles of the face. It also can be "refreshingly silly," as one client put it, and help clients (and therapists) feel a little more levity and playfulness. In Mahmoud's case, he was stuck in a freeze state when he recalled the past, and this freeze interfered with his felt ability to fully express himself and to interact with others. His initially stiff face dance helped him oscillate from the unsatisfactorily truncated play state into a fuller continuum of play states.

The continuum of play is emergent and represents the varying degrees or levels to which each circuit—the SNS and the VVC—dynamically input their energies in service of play. This is constantly changing, like clouds moving in a sky. This all depends on the needs of this developmental and psychological biological imperative. Play can have a role in establishing territory, winning a game, intimate pleasure, or just having fun. Each circuit will input less or more. In slower forms of play, such as sensual foreplay or relaxing play (e.g., free movement in an ocean or lake or dangling one's feet in a cool stream), the DVC is also involved.

The sympathetic activation that invites play can be expressed through many actions. It can be sensual, dramatic, silly, erotic, joyful, lyrical, competitive, and quiet. Dogs play to establish dominance. Sports are competitive play; the teamwork is relational and social, and there is often an edge in the style of play due to the desire to win. Team sports are both collaborative and competitive, so the SNS is constantly contributing energy to connect with others on the same team, presumably with the same goals and intentions, and also to effectively outrun or guard a competitor. For clients like Mahmoud who struggle to move towards connection and are on the edge of being playful or describe that trying to connect with others requires effort, titrating play with a small neural exercise like a face dance is a solid beginning to recruit the VVC/SNS partnership for just the right amount of play.

Playing with Breath

Breath and movement are inextricably linked. They fire, fuel, and restore flow to one another. Breath can equally limit and constrain our movement or expand it. And like the ANS, breath and movement have a bidirectional relationship. Melissa, the women's rights activist who requested that I incorporate yoga into our work to focus on her garnering the courage to leave her home, take walks, exercise, dance, and rejoin the world, initially did yoga mechanically. She struggled to connect the poses to feelings, and then to connect her feelings to her interoception—inner sensation, her felt sense experience. Integrating movement with breath was the key to her ability to sense into the inner experience of yoga-inspired movements so she could integrate emergent feelings of relative safety, calm, focus, courage, and more to her daily life.

I offered each asana we explored in response to what she wished to work on, such as relaxing when home alone or focusing when preparing a meal or cleaning. Early in therapy she was frustrated that the changes she desired—to feel safer traveling farther away from her home, to participate in exercise classes, go shopping, and go out with her family—weren't happening fast enough. She led a women's movement in her home country and was self-admittedly "impatient for change." It was when we dimensionalized her movement with breath that she noticed the emotions associated with her movement, both in my office and when she practiced at home. That's also when she began to connect with her inner interoceptive experience more.

Dimensionalizing Chair to Sky

Breath is fundamental to movement and life, and it can be an intimate experience because it takes us deep inside our body. Having learned from clients to work cautiously with breath, especially early in treatment, I learned to adjust and adapt many of the common breath-based practices like deep belly or diaphragmatic breaths. While those are all helpful practices, if they are implemented before a client's capacity for self-regulation is restored, they can activate uncomfortable emotions and potentially kindle retraumatization. When sensing one's breath or connecting to the interior experience of breath is dysregulating for someone, it can be helpful to begin with movement and then add breath. Though breath often initiates movement, in polyvagal and resilience-informed somatic therapies, the restoration of breath and movement's synergistic relationship is what helps restore our VVC-mediated flow in our body and movement prosody.

I invited Melissa to explore the three dimensions of breath as Structure and Function (Chapter 4) with each pose. For example, when we were doing the "stretching from chair to sky" shape, we began with the vertical dimension, which is where I most commonly begin. The reasons for this are core to the creative, intuitive, and improvisational spirit required to be truly resilience informed and survivor centered. Beginning in the vertical dimension with SNS-mediated movement is out of order, developmentally speaking. Vertical is in between horizontal and sagittal. Our human and movement development is hierarchical and spirals at the same time, creating a feedback loop. The vertical dimension follows the horizontal dimension, where we explore space and rest-and-settle actions cradled in the nourishing aspects of the DVC developmentally, and prior to the sagittal dimension, where we explore reaching and relationship in a more VVC-mediated space. Because the vertical dimension pertains to the SNS as our initiator of movement, and our ability to push toward a sense of boundaried self in our socio-ecological frame, it is often relatively safer to begin there. Being comfortable in the horizontal dimension requires a sense of relative safety and trust, the primary learning actions of the earliest developmental phase, which takes time to develop in therapy. Likewise, to move and engage with others with enough safety and agency to promote reciprocity requires the crossroads foundation of the horizontal and vertical dimensions. Beginning movement in the middle, the in-between space, can offer clients opportunities to shift states in an ever-expanding and connecting spiral feedback loop between rest and relationship.

MOVING THE THREE DIMENSIONS OF BREATH PRACTICE

I invited Melissa to breathe in and sense the elongation of the vertical dimension and action that naturally occurs with inhalation. When she began her stretch, we practiced that several times. When that felt comfortable in her body, we explored using the exhale beat to settle more deeply into the resting forward part of her body pose. When she was comfortable with that, we combined them until her breath and movement felt fluid and connected to her. Then we began inviting more free-form, flowing movement into this two-part pose. Doing this helps transitions in movement, which ultimately can support transitions in life. When both movement and life situations occur with more yield, there can be more ease and grace. This level of comfort signaled an integration of early developmental actions that were affected by her traumatic exposures. It also increased her capacity for self-regulation. This was pivotal for her, for both movement and play to expand from "too afraid to leave home" to driving herself and a friend to "NIA" (Neuromuscular Integrative Action) class—and every movement process we explored in between.

Here's a simple way to build on Structure and Function to align movement and breath:

1. Stand (or sit, if preferred or necessary) and Shift to Comfort.
2. Take a baseline of your breath. Notice the comparative length of your inhale and exhale to connect with your breathing pattern today.
3. Starting with the horizontal dimension, practice Structure and Function. You can also begin with the Sensing Breath Dimensionality practice covered in Chapter 11.
4. Once you sense the physical movement of your horizontal dimension, either as structure or sensing, release your hands and see how this horizontal dimension moves you. Another way to say that is: How does the horizontal dimension choreograph your movement? Begin to move that choreography. Notice which body parts instantly start moving. Does this movement stay in those body parts or spread to other body parts? Are there any areas of your body that are not moving? If it feels okay, invite those nonmoving body parts to begin moving. If that's not comfortable, just stick with the areas of your body that are already moving.

5. With kids, I say something simpler like, "Can you make a horizontal or widening movement? What does it look like? What body part are you moving? What's not moving? What does this movement remind you of?" This invites amplifying or spreading the movement. Kids can answer with animals, colors, superhero figures, or any metaphorical, symbolic, or literal image and they can be invited to move like any of these.
6. Remind clients they can move as much or little, big or small, as they want to. This can be a several-second, structured movement practice, or it can last many minutes of a flowing dance. Adding music enhances the latter option.
7. Bring this movement exploration to a pause. Rest. Integrate. Check your breath now compared to your baseline.

Repeat this with the two remaining dimensions (vertical and sagittal).

After completing all three dimensions, do all three at the same time. This is a great time to add music and turn it into a dance if that's comfortable for the client (or therapist). This is also a wonderful self-compassion and self-care practice.

Bread, Salt, and Heart

"Bread, Salt, and Heart" is a phrase with deep cultural meaning in Kosovo. It means that no matter what's going on, and no matter how hard times are, any person who comes to the door will be welcomed with bread, salt, and heart. I learned this from a Kosovar women's group I cofacilitated with a fellow DMT as the war there was ending. A DMT-enthusiastic case manager for a local refugee resettlement agency was resettling a large group of women, some with families and some arriving solo, who had survived the war of 1998–1999. She requested that my colleague and I offer a DMT group for them. This is our experience.

We eagerly planned the group to take place over 10 weeks, and methodically and carefully we cocreated the curriculum based on our work at the survivors' center. Most therapeutic groups are eight weeks; because we worked with interpreters, we added two sessions to make up for interpretation time. When the women arrived for the first group, we gathered and explained our mission, goals, ideas, and plans. We were met with silence and unwaveringly unexpressive, immobilized faces. After a long pause, we asked again if anyone wanted to ask or offer anything before we got started. One of the women quietly said, "We only dance when we are happy. We are not happy."

That was a wake-up call. Our enthusiastic colleague had assumed DMT would be welcome, based on her own appreciation of the work. We had certainly planned to introduce dance and even movement slowly, knowing that timing is core to how clients receive any somatic or movement practice. We had not expected this.

We pivoted and worked with what the women wanted, what was culturally appropriate for them—storytelling. They told us that because they were new to each other, and to us, each one had to tell their story. Because they were very recently displaced, it wasn't their life story, it was their trauma story, the horrors and injustices of war. All of them were painful to listen to. All of them merited deep listening and witness. It was excruciating. The emotional charge was intense, and at times I bumped up against my own training about the need to titrate trauma content to increase regulation capacities.

I felt my own body working hard to stay out of sympathetic activation. In their storytelling they shared details of things they had witnessed: violence to loved ones, explosions, deaths, and mutilations. This was content that I don't usually push for, especially early on. I will always listen to such details when clients want to share their past horrors, but I rarely ask for them. This collective sharing of their painful stories of displacement, violence, and loss seemed to be a culturally referenced way for them to find shared experience to connect them, distressing as it was. I have experienced this in other communal situations where war, violence, and oppression are the connecting thread of experience, and this is why the concepts of culturoception and socioception are so important. The tendency to immediately privilege safety when an individual, group, or community is united through a shared theme of human rights violations can be perceived as dismissive and disrespectful. It's important to remember that our clients are survivors. A key question for all we clinicians who choose to engage with, witness, and confront the immense cruelty and suffering in this world is: when my instinct is to avoid hearing painful, terrible stories to protect my client, which one of us in this moment am I protecting? This is difficult, uncomfortable work and sometimes, therapists are understandably more avoidant than clients. As often as we might shift to comfort to remain present in this work, we are also tasked with sitting in big discomfort in the face of the cruel injustices we are confronting.

This went on for weeks. Around week 5, we learned the meaning of "bread, salt, and heart" after doing a communal sand tray process. Each woman contributed to a large group-cocreated symbol in the middle of the sand tray and also had a section of the tray to create their own symbolic three-dimensional image. Many of them recreated their homes, and this is how we came to learn about this custom of welcoming others. The saying arises from a deeply held cultural belief that even if one has nothing, a loaf of bread with a little salt and welcoming hearts can ease any distressed traveler into our home. It was clear that this was an ethos of their culture. As we asked to learn more, Tatiana, our group's elder, grew very quiet, and her eyes teared up as she looked at the home created in the sand. After a few moments, she raised her arms and said, "I am tired. I need to move." And she began to stretch.

Recognizing a rare moment to introduce movement, I said, "What a great idea. My body wants to move too. How about if we all stretch?" Within moments, a room full of twenty-plus women ranging from ages 18 to 80 were stretching. Stretching is a universal form of movement. I have never met a person who doesn't stretch. Grabbing this opportunity, I invited the women into a circle and suggested we do a "group stretch." Tatiana, who initiated this, was also the one who opened every group by lighting a candle next to our altar of bread, salt, and a heart-shaped stone. I invited her to show us her favorite morning stretch. This invitation usually invokes movement quickly. I always invite people not to overthink it but to sense it, to imagine just waking up and feeling their first stretch. I then invited Tatiana to create a simple one- or two-gesture stretch sequence to share. As she did, I invited others to follow. I then invited us to send it around our circle, very similar to the telephone game.

I cued the women to observe Tatiana's stretch and then imitate it, doing it "exactly like her." I reminded them, as the stretch went around the circle, to remember how they saw her move while they stretched because the farther away each person was from Tatiana, the more she had to rely on the person next to her to learn the movements. I reminded them to wait for the prior person to finish, to keep from speeding up and to allow everyone an opportunity for full leadership and expression. When we completed one circle of sharing, I cued them to return the stretch by sending it in the opposite direction. It always began and ended with Tatiana. Each time we sent the stretch back around the circle in an opposite direction, I cued them, "Speed it up, superfast. Come on, faster, faster, faster! Do it just like Tatiana does it while you speed up." I used descriptive words, the tone and tempo of my voice and gesturing with my body to initiate faster movement. Then I would change the pace, speaking very slowly and dropping my tone: "Now let's slow it down. Really, r-e-a-l-l-y-, r—e—a—l—l—y s——l——o——w." while alternating my vocal and movement/body prosody. We played with rhythm, which invokes playfulness, as well as different textures, shapes, and movement contours, which naturally state shift how we feel. These playful state-shifts aid in re-establishing restorative neural feedback loops. Inviting the women to notice if and how the way they felt changed, we also offered descriptive observations of how the collective nervous system was changing. Levity, warmth, and playfulness infused the space. It's an engaging and playful way to mimic the mirroring we hopefully received in our childhood, and/or to repair it if we didn't receive it. It welcomes a whole continuum of play into somatic movement.

Mirroring is an essential human exchange in early childhood development. We learn to move and express our bodies by being mirrored, and it is also how we know we are seen by others. From a somatic perspective, mirroring can promote shared body states, which in turn can foster empathy, which feeds our need and ability to see and be seen, feel and be felt.

Attunement is also an essential developmental action and an important way to witness in work with survivors. To turn this into attunement practice, I invited another woman, Jana, to share her simple (simple is essential to avoid movements that are too complicated and can overwhelm or induce shame) stretch with these cues: "Now let's do Jana's stretch. This time we are going to send her stretch all the way around in our unique way. Jana will pass it to Jillian, who passes it to Mimi, who passes it to Ariana, and so on. Take time to 'receive' the stretch that begins with Jana, feel it in your body, and then make your own stretch and pass it on. We'll still be doing Jana's stretch, in our own unique way. We're sharing our movement, like a gift." Using the same rhythm cues to speed up and slow down, or make it "bigger and bigger" or "smaller all the way to tiny," the women shaped a shared movement sequence that seemed to tell its own collective story. In this way, we became a river of moving prosody and a collectively prosodic body.

Afterward we talked about what each circle of sharing felt like, what they saw, and what it reminded them of. This practice cultivates empathy when a movement or shape is imitated and fosters attunement when movements are seen and shared with each person's unique style. Attunement cultivates compassion because it is a recognition of the source of something we simultaneously share and have our own individual experience of. Developmentally, attunement comes later than mirroring, so we are also honoring our personal development in shared movement, which is reparative and restorative. This practice became a weekly ritual, and at the request of a younger group member in our last group, we added their cultural music to what became our dance.

Stretching to Play

Stretching is a common and universally known way to move. It can be used in individual, group, and community work. The basic scaffold of this structured to open-ended play-inducing practice is as follows.

Individual: Stretching can be used when a client expresses the need to move, either/both of you feel stuck, or your own body cues you that movement would support the process you are in. Invite the client to pause and stretch. They can be invited to do:

1. A favorite stretch
2. A favorite morning (or evening or any time of day) stretch
3. Any number of personal stretches: juicy, calming, relaxing, stress-relieving

When we therapists sense a need to move our bodies, we may be sensing what's helpful for our clients as well, through our ANS cotransmissions. This helps clients befriend their ANS. Stretching is posture change, which promotes vagal efficiency. The greater range of movement and prosodic movement a client can learn to express, while maintaining connection with themselves and others, the more each posture change promotes vagal tone and efficiency. This is covered more in Chapter 10.

Stretching can be very structured, for example, we can lead our clients through a counted stretch, such as stretching to one side with the same side arm arched over the head and counting to 5 or 10, depending on their tolerance for exploring new movements or revisiting familiar movements. Expanding and changing movement, that is, increasing the movement repertoire, is considered a path to increasing expressivity in DMT. As simple as this may seem, movement can elicit memories through the activation of physical sensations and ensuing emotional memory recall. These can be painful memories we process with clients, and more benign memories that can re-associate to clients' resources and resilience. The latter can "birth" powerful potent gestures.

Mirroring and attuning with our clients can increase ease in service of relative safety and promote connection and reciprocity. Checking in about how feelings change is helpful for clients to understand how movement supports their own regulation and is an effective therapeutic restorative practice. Clients can easily practice stretching at home and even document their changing responses in terms of physical (e.g., pain, tension), emotional (i.e., changes in how they feel), cognitive (such as focus and attention), problem solving, and whatever specific issues are being addressed.

The case vignette from the Kosovar women's group describes how to use stretching with groups. It can be helpful when energy needs to move, to promote collective vagal tone and efficiency through exploring different shapes, and to promote and teach state shifting. This can also promote connection and vitality and increase social and relational capacities, build community, and allow participants to share experiences of healing and restoration. It offers leadership opportunities for group members when they get to share a stretch, especially when invited to facilitate the passing of the stretch around the circle. For groups that meet regularly, a different group member can be invited to share a stretch as a movement warm-up, an ice breaker, or as a state-shifting regulation practice when needed.

Pandiculation: Nature's Stretching

Pandiculation is another form of stretching that I call natural or animal stretching. It is more complex and holistic than the usual stretching, which, while helpful for ease in the larger muscle groups of our physical body, does not usually engage as fully with the connective tissue and the nervous system. Because pandiculation does, it fosters emotional and psychological ease as well. Pandiculation entered somatics with practitioners like Tomas Hanna, who noted decreases in physical pain and tension, and improvements in posture when patients were assisted to make targeted (i.e., a specific area of the body, often as small as a hand or finger) concentric contraction (shortening the space between the original and attachments) followed by eccentric release (lengthening the same muscles slowly) while they were still resisting or "under a load." The resistance is provided by the practitioner's weight or a prop, which requires the person to lengthen the muscle and release the contraction very, very slowly. This intentional form of pandiculation builds on the wisdom of natural pandiculation, which is the involuntary stretching of the soft tissues.

I call it animal stretching because it is often seen in our fellow mammals. Think of a cat doing one of their long, luscious stretches that seems to go on forever and includes their whole body. They seem to be suspended in time when they do this. It looks like a whole-body yawn. Yawning is a special type of pandiculation that affects the muscles of the mouth, respiratory system, and upper spine, the terrain of the VVC and SNS (Baenninger, 1997, p. 199).

When pandiculation occurs naturally, as it does in the transitions between sleep and waking up, it engages the entire myofascial system (voluntary muscles plus connective tissue), which resets the central nervous system to respond to stimuli in the environment. Because we know that the myofascial system connects us, that is, links multiple body parts, we know that pandiculation can preserve the connective integrative role the myofascial system plays. It also sends biofeedback to our entire nervous system about the level of tension in our muscles, which helps reduce muscular tension and increase more pleasurable or satisfying feelings. The pandicular contract-and-release rhythm resets the gamma loop, a feedback loop in our nervous system that helps regulate muscle tone and posture. This also gives us more control of our voluntary muscles, which helps restore the fluid movement that expresses our inner neurophysiological state. This is a direct pathway to the wholeness the VVC offers us.

Another way to think of this is that our inner environment and climate feel comfortable enough that we increase our sense of relative safety and move more authentically and freely in the world. This is an important embodied reflection and expression of who we are, which also means the VVC brake is restored, and the newer branch of the parasympathetic nervous system can resume its governance role.

Pandiculation is adaptable to the therapy setting. I first began integrating it as home play when working with Miriam (Chapter 6), noting that when we began the micromovements to transition her from the rest practice in my office, she would catch herself waking up slowly and suddenly startle herself awake. It was as if she was embarrassed to be seen doing the most minimal pandiculations. She always interrupted the movements with a startle and sat up quickly. I taught her about the importance of this natural stretching and invited her to allow it to happen when she woke up at home whether from a nap or sleep. If she started to move too quickly, I encouraged her to pause and remind herself to pandiculate with progressive pandiculation, described below.

Eventually, she discovered the joys of recumbent or more commonly nicknamed "pancake" pandiculation, named for our upward facing "flat" lying down shape, when she shared how pausing to notice the first thing she saw waking up and following that with natural stretching reset her "first moods for the day." This is the home play I give many clients to relearn and reintegrate. She was rediscovering curiosity, and this decreased her previously sour worldview.

Playful pandiculation is another version of pandiculation I often use when working with children individually or alone. It arose organically out of Slow Flow with the young men in Haiti and was often how the children in the kids' group described in Chapter 8 shifted from sternal breathing on the floor to standing again. All these forms of pandiculation are also wonderful therapist self-care practices.

PRACTICE: PANCAKE PANDICULATION

This form of natural stretching can be done when first awakening, to remind our bodies of something we all likely did in childhood, and to retrain our ANS to do it again.

1. When you first awaken and are still lying down, focus on the very first thing you notice: sunlight, a bird chirping, a painting or flower or color in your room. Whatever it is, observe its movement for a few moments without being distracted by anything else.
2. Then begin to follow its movement with your eyes. If it's a sound, you can imagine following it with your ears as eyes. Then slowly, in the style of micromobilizations and micromovements, begin to invite your whole body to follow in slow, stretchy movements.
3. Practice reaching for it, pushing against it, contracting and releasing—all variations with your limbs. Then add in your tailbone, head, and any other body parts you can creatively add. Eventually you can let go of following this and allow the movement to continue, folding your breath in, until you feel complete and come to a pause. Take a moment to notice how you feel before getting up.

PRACTICE: PROGRESSIVE PANDICULATION

There are several ways to do progressive pandiculation. You can begin at the bottom of your body (feet) and work your way up. You can begin at the top of your body (head) and work your way down. Or you can begin at the outer (skin) layers of your body and work your way into your bones. For this description, we will begin at the feet:

1. Take a moment to Shift to Comfort in whatever shape you are in. This can be done sitting, standing, or lying down.
2. Take a moment to notice your muscle tension. Notice what areas of your body feel tight, constricted, or painful. You can also take a weight baseline.
3. Inhaling, contract the muscles of your feet. Exhaling, let them go.
4. Inhaling, contract the muscles of your feet and your calves and lower legs (below your knees). Exhaling, let this go.

5. Inhaling, contract your feet plus your lower legs plus your knees; exhaling, let this go.
6. Continue this, body part by body part, bottom to top until your whole body contracts on the inhale and releases on the exhale. You are increasing oxygen saturation and preparing to pandiculate.
7. When your whole body is contracting, repeat this 2–10 times, exaggerating contractions to make them more and more intense. If this is uncomfortable, pause and resume the last, most comfortable, level of contraction.
8. On your last big whole-body muscle contraction, let the wave of energy and movement organically become your pandiculation. Let the wave move your body, and allow your body to follow along. Continue with pauses as needed until you feel done. Periodically inhale and squeeze your body as tightly as is tolerable, and release another wave of pandiculating, whole-body yawning movement. Allow it to end naturally.
9. Notice your weight and your muscle tension now.
10. If you do this standing up, and want to continue even more playfully, you can add music and invite groovier pandiculation. Music also enhances dimensionality in movement.

PRACTICE: PLAYFUL PANDICULATION

This is one of my favorite forms of pandiculation for self-care. Children often respond enthusiastically to it.

1. Take a moment to Shift to Comfort in whatever shape you are in. This can be done sitting, standing, or lying down.
2. Take a moment to notice your muscle tension. Notice what areas of your body feel tight, constricted, or painful. You can also take a weight baseline.
3. Choose an animal (a pet or a wild creature you can see out

your window or in a picture book or photo) and observe it for a moment.

4. Find your breath and notice the flow of your breath, that is, how and where it is moving, as if watching a river.
5. Then, watching or imagining how this animal moves, begin to move like it. In order to turn this animal imitation into natural stretching, it's important to connect your breath with your movement. What this means is to move at the rhythm of your breath. Invite gentle contractions on the inhale and release on the exhale, as in progressive pandiculation. To enhance playfulness, you can reverse this.
6. Expand this playful practice, learning from animal wisdom, our evolutionary ancestors, until you feel complete. Compare weight and muscle tension to your baseline.

Harvest

Play has not historically been a domain of psychotherapy. The integration of somatic therapies and body-based regulation practices has been helpful for making therapy more dynamic and playful. Movement on its continuum from still to subtle to slow and structured to the movement end of the spectrum—dynamic, expressive, mobilizing, and energizing—invites the entire range of somatic expression that fuels human engagement and relationship. Play and playfulness are the catalysts for this engagement. One of the first principles of PVISDMP that emerged in 2003 was that rest and settle and play were both states and actions that were essential to make body-based therapies inclusive of the whole person, neurophysiologically to spiritually. Psychotherapy, especially somatic therapies in human rights and trauma contexts, is a necessarily serious commitment between two or more people to navigate intense fear and immense suffering together. The potential for harm and retraumatization is real and is often what impedes therapists' creative, intuitive instincts. Our ethical guidelines offer clear wisdom-informed parameters for maintaining clarity in this relationship where we hold the power and therefore the responsibility to create an environment that offers consistent cues of relative safety and belonging. Initially, colleagues dismissed the inclusion of play as "not taking survivors' history seriously enough" or "avoidance of the trauma content."

My clients have consistently and repeatedly requested levity, movement, beauty, and human connection in ways that are dimensional and engaging, because that's who they are. They may not show it as freely as they once did, or they may have had few opportunities in a lifetime of oppression to express it. Nonetheless, it's there. It's the subtle but powerful hum of the ANS as an inner guide and an extension to the outer world, branching far beyond our skin, mirroring and attuning to everything around us, human and more than human, seen and unseen. It's the humming of everything that lives, and this is what we all long to be part of and connect to. One client who arrived in the United States as a refugee and lamented how the term "refugee" had become a label that seemed to define her existence experienced such immense relief when we practiced progressive pandiculation that she described feeling who she truly was, from the inside out, and not being limited by the adversities that made her seek refuge here. I hear this from many survivors: "survivor," "immigrant," "refugee," "victim," and "trauma" all become the scarlet letter that they feel is how society sees them. This is especially and painfully true when the "scarlet letter" is skin color, ethnicity, religion, dress, sexuality, gender, disability, or any of the many unique expressions of humanity that are targeted by a normative-obsessed society. Therapeutic somatic movements that bravely navigate embodied ways of seeing and being seen in reciprocity will naturally include play because play, whether as small as the vibration of energy particles or as huge as the sweeping plunge of a giant wave, is the portal to a humming ANS. Play is how we develop strength, establish territories and boundaries, burn off steam, physically vent, and state shift neurophysiologically and bio-hormonally to meet the world as the wholeness we are.

CHAPTER 10

Ventrosity

THE RHYTHM OF RECIPROCITY

Sometimes our light goes out but is blown into flame
by another human being. Each of us owes deepest
thanks to those who have rekindled this light.
—ALBERT SCHWEITZER, 1949,
MEMOIRS OF CHILDHOOD AND YOUTH

The ventral vagal circuit (VVC), also referred to as the social nervous system, might be thought of as the most celebrated circuit of the three circuits of the autonomic nervous system (ANS). As the most recently evolved part of the vagus nerve, it is part of the parasympathetic branch of the ANS that influences our facial expressions, vocal prosody, gaze, and head posture. It also plays a key role in regulating digestion, heart rate, respiration, and other autonomic functions. In this framework, these influences naturally affect the flow of our body and movement prosody, which reflects our quality of attention and our presence. How we see and are seen is through our faces; this, along with nonverbal elements of how we express ourselves in posture and movement, communicates our openness and availability for connection.

The VVC is often referred to with colloquial phrases like "ventral vibes," "going ventral," and "activating the ventral." This summarization of this uniquely mammalian branch of the vagus nerve and circuitry of many neural fibers minimizes its crucial heart-centered role in our internal rhythmicity and diversity. This highly mylineated heart-to-face pathway that inhibits the SNS in our heart is rooted in a time in our evolution when being together, connection, and community became essential for survival. This makes it core to reciprocity and as guardian, steward, and firekeeper of the mother beat of our heart.

The Ventral Vagal Circuit

When hearing anyone encourage or promote "being ventral," I often pose the question: "When we make ventral safety the preferred state, who are we marginalizing?" The VVC is the newest in the evolutionary hierarchy, and it doesn't operate alone. We cannot be solely ventral. The VVC evolved as part of the parasympathetic nervous system as did the DVC, and while it is a different parasympathetic circuit, they collaborate to cocreate the ever-shifting tides of emergent and patterned autonomic states.

There is a reciprocity in their relationship. The VVC can be conceptualized as being buoyed by the ocean of the DVC. It rises and floats off its groundedness and rootedness. The SNS is the space in between, a space that initiates movement. This relationship can be expressed as an infinity sign; a feedback loop epitomizes the idea of an eternal return. Figure 6.2 is inspired by the heart as the neural hub of this feedback loop. Because all three circuits innervate it, and the VVC inhibits the SNS and the DVC when we are safe enough for connection, it is both the initiator of regulating and dysregulating, conscious and subconscious, state shifts and the place we return to, to reregulate. The VVC governs and conducts. When we are ventral, the VVC is mediating our movements through its inhibition of the other circuits' influence on our neurophysiology. We must feel enough relative safety to sense ourselves, to be present, and to move volitionally in flow. It's the unfettered flow of energy that keeps our nervous system humming. A Yolngu teacher (S. Nulpinditj, personal communication, 2018) calls vagal tone, the scientific measure of social engagement, "aligning the stars." This alignment is what supports our capacity for attunement for self and others and the space around us that endows the yielded (DVC) receptivity (VVC) with the ability to move (SNS) in flow (VVC governance).

Vagal tone is measured indirectly through heart rate variability, the intervals between heartbeats. It is also measured by respiratory sinus arrhythmia, the naturally occurring flow between heart rate and respiration, that is, when breathing slows or quickens, as does the heart rate. Vagal efficiency is our ability to restore vagal tone when we lose it momentarily, for example, when we change posture and stand up quickly, increasing our blood pressure. These movements can be understood as a dance, a rhythmic play between heart and respiration, between heartbeats and between tiny disequilibrating moments when we go off center and then return to center. This is why the idea of the moving center in Chapter 5 is so fundamental to state shifting for regulation. Many ancient rituals and ceremonies honor shifting or falling off center as core to restoring balance and center. Possession and trance states are a decentering to recenter in a more integrated and self-reciprocal way.

In a polyvagal-informed context, when we are in the ventrally mediated state of feeling safe enough to be socially engaged, our heart rate has variability. In the sympathetically mediated mobilization state, we experience increased heart rate with decreased heart rate variability. In DVC immobilized states, our heart rate decreases, as does our variability. Another way to express this is that we lose our polyrhythmicity and become more monorhythmic, which does not support our biologically and neurophysiologically human complexity.

Reciprocal Alliance

"Reciprocal alliance," the alternative term to "therapeutic relationship," upholds the idea of equilibrium through equity in the relationships between therapist and client. The therapist, clinician, or practitioner always has power. We are being paid to provide expertise-based services to our clients, and this generates power. In traditional forms of psychotherapy, therapists commonly interpret clients' thoughts, feelings, and behaviors. This action holds big power. Reciprocal alliance is the willingness and commitment and practice of using the therapy space to promote the client's empowerment not as only client-centric, but as a reflection and expression of the ever-shifting client-therapist relationship. This is what cultivates true reciprocity. Porges and Gellar define therapeutic presence as inclusive and even based on compassion: "Mindfulness can perhaps be described as an ability to embody, reflect and demonstrate one's own state of compassion. Presence can perhaps be described or understood as an outcome of consistent mindfulness practice by the therapist" (Geller & Porges, 2014).

This proposed definition of presence pertains to reciprocity because reciprocity is an emergent process and outcome of the shared experience of compassion. Compassion, as demonstrated through mindful bodyfulness, and as necessary for presence, is a "core ingredient" for being safe enough to promote the trust that underlies reciprocal relationship between therapist and client. They feed each other.

Figure 10.1 shows the spiraling relationship of these human responses and how each contributes to the growth and presence of the

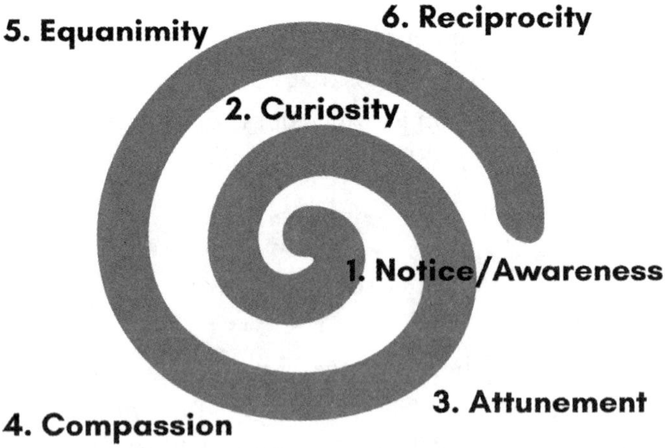

Figure 10.1 The Reciprocity Spiral

next. This is a spiral that is always looping in and out of itself, like neural feedback loops in an eternal return. This spiral is relational, and it is also a rhythm, and much more dimensional than this two-dimensional illustration. We notice, and if this promotes curiosity about what we notice, we have increased capacity to attune. Attuning is a form of noticing and an expression of compassion; we see and connect to another and can reflect this back without losing our personal integrity, that is, compassionate nonattachment. Compassion promotes equanimity. Noticing our equanimity helps us promote reciprocity in relationship. Spiraling back to noticing and being aware with curiosity, we continue to spiral in and out of these elements of our humanity. This is a rhythm like the ongoing rhythms of life: night and day, sun and moon, the tides, the wind, the sea, currents, life, and death. Core rhythmicity in PVISDMP honors the wisdom of rhythm as the fundamental movement of life. The process of establishing and cocreating reciprocal alliance is a spiraling, relational rhythm.

Cultivating Ventral in Clinical Work

When the ventral appears in clinical work, it is often a tiny presence. It isn't usually (if ever) a fully integrated expression of instant wholeness. It's the micromobilizations and micromovements that appear, like a glimmer in the eyes, a slightly deeper breath, a miniscule yield into a chair. It can also appear when clients who are patterned to regulate another's nervous system recognize their tendency to appease and placate in current situations and relationships, or begin to appease their therapists in session. One of the things Jeremiah and I worked on in our mock job interviews was his pattern of appeasement that he traced back to being imprisoned, and to navigating checkpoints where he witnessed mass killings, and now, resettling in a very white community. When he spoke of this, I reflected posture shifts I observed in him that appeared to me as if his core was shrinking. His posture would collapse in a way that was minimally visible physically. It was an energetic shift that looked like air releasing from a balloon, slowly. I'd invite him to Shift to Comfort and engage his muscles and breath in the same contract and release as Grounding to Sky. When he noticed his spine lifting, I coached him to press and then push into the back of the chair, with increasing strength. This somatic work was accompanied by deep processing of the shame he felt when he "forgot himself and others" to survive. His ability to placate and appease perpetrators in many instances resulted in him being the sole survivor. He recognized this as a pattern arising out of fear and insecurity whenever he felt overpowered.

Examples of practices that invite the VVC into its governance or mediation role are both the culmination of work with clients that navigated through many multidirectional state-shifting pathways and as another possibility for relationship for those conditioned to regulate others' ANS at the cost of their own.

RACHEL'S DANCE TO FREEDOM

Rachel's creation and sharing of her dance to freedom was a tender navigation of relative safety in our relationship, moving at the speed of the trust developing between us. It also developed a larger pool of gestures related to both her suffering and her resilience, which culminated in her self-choreographed dance. (It's impossible to describe it in detail; the dance can be seen in my ADTA talk: https://www.youtube.com/watch?v=guAkQYcMKxQ.) In Chapter 6, I describe the work with her leg and her shoulder thatresulted in her ability to share more emotions and personal history. When we completed that phase of very movement-based yield-promoting work, we were ready to shift. And I wasn't entirely sure how because she still would not share much of her story.

> Rachel arrived at my office one day with a visible increase in levity and bounce, a more upright posture, and a light in her eyes I'd not seen before. She stepped into my office after walking up

two flights of stairs previously difficult for her with increased ease and announced, “I am coming home to my body.” I asked her what she meant, and she said she was beginning to feel like her former self and wanted “to get all the way better.” She requested repeating the movement-based observation we did when we first met. At that time, I invited her to opt in to a series of very simple assessment movements based on breath and movement. Rachel struggled with them. She could barely lift her arm above her head vertically or bend it sideways horizontally. As she began to feel better, she began practicing the movements and wanted to show me how freely she could move now. At that time, she self-described as “lost” and “no longer myself.” This retracted sense of self is common among survivors I've worked with who relied on appeasing strategies to survive the cruelty of their perpetrators.

We reviewed the movements, and she asked me to film her, so she could watch herself. This self-reciprocal moment was profound for her. Being a mirror for herself—both the observed and the observer—she witnessed herself in real time, present day. She sat quietly for a while, and then said, “I can move forward.”

This was the end of the session, and I still felt stuck about where to go next time. After peer consultation from a colleague trained in brief solution-focused therapy, I decided to ask Rachel a version of the “miracle question.” With a history as grave as hers, I didn't want to be dismissive of the load she carried in the form of terror-instigated neural patterning and the weight of suffering. Her ANS and body movements were heavily patterned by immobilization. Moving forward felt hard to both of us.

Our work had been somatically focused, and she had not shared much of her history. While her body and movement narratives clearly communicated suffering, physical and psychological abuse, the absence of details about what happened and her shut-down patterning when sharing any past history contributed to my feeling stuck with her. Whenever I asked about her pre-detention or detention history, she still drifted away. Her pattern of complete shutdown decreased, and she began dissociating and would become silent, eyes vacant and body collapsed, but still able to look at me and respond verbally. I could sometimes coax her back by inviting her to practice the yield practice with the sitz bones, or contract and release her muscles as in an adaptation of Grounding to Earth and Sky (shared next) until she could track objects in the room. Sometimes, I had to be patient and wait for her to return on her own.

Riffing off her revelation that she was coming home to her body, and modeling after the idea of the miracle question, I asked what it would take for her to be home in her body. She took her time to answer with four words.

"Patience. Struggle. Time. Striving." I asked her to describe what it would look like, and she didn't respond. I offered her an opportunity to draw or move, and she chose drawing. She drew a circle with smooth brown inside and said, "This is me, my smooth brown skin, when I am whole and beautiful" (Figure 10.2).

Figure 10.2 Being Whole

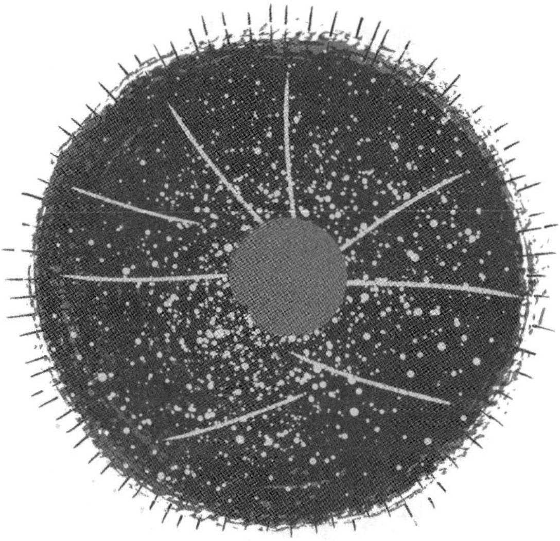

Figure 10.3 Scar

I asked her to draw herself now, and she drew her scar, which she described as "an ugly scar" (Figure 10.3).

I then asked her to draw the steps in between, and she made the drawing in Figure 10.4, which became the steps to her wholeness and to being home.

The work we did from here followed the steps to wholeness. In each session, Rachel would place her scar in the same place, in the middle of the therapy room. She would then place her "wholeness" drawing (Figure 10.2) in the past, behind the scar, at one end of the room, always in the same place. She stood there momentarily, "remembering herself." This was one of the ways we somatically explored the concept of patience. I encouraged her to remain there as long as she wanted to. She would then pick the drawing up and put it in front of the scar, as far away as she felt her sense of wholeness to be. In one of our conversations, she realized that she was familiar with being whole in the past. She used the same drawing to acknowledge both her past as whole and her future dream as returning to wholeness.

Over the course of eight months, we progressed sequentially,

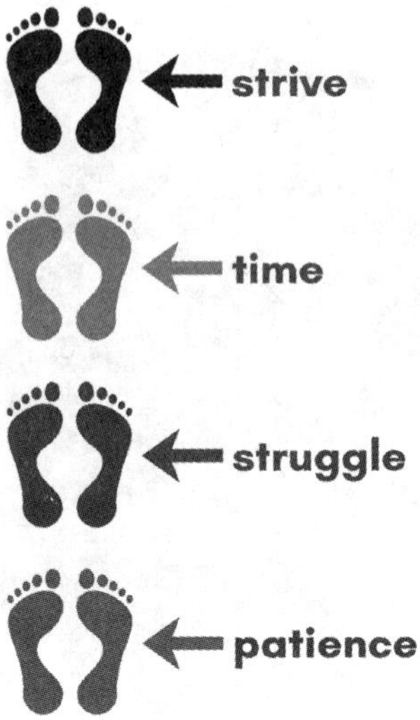

Figure 10.4 Steps to Wholeness

when Rachel decided she was ready, from one step to another. She made larger individual drawings of each step that she could easily stand on. Our practice for each exploration was this:

1. Stand on the step. Sense the energy, movement, and rhythm of this step through your feet. How does this step move you closer to wholeness? Notice what you sense in your body and what feelings emerge. Share them with me, if you wish.
2. Notice any movements that arise—simple gestures, movement sequences. Sounds, songs, and humming are welcome too.
3. Sense the rhythm of your song, sounds, movements. Is it fast or slow? Is there a song or rhythm you know that belongs with this step?
4. Share any images, memories, thoughts, feelings, people, places that come up for you.

We began with her first step, Patience, and did not move to Struggle until she was ready. In Patience she often returned to the chair we had done our prior work in and rested or closed her eyes and prayed. This was significant because when she first came to me, she had abandoned churchgoing and "only prayed alone." I frequently reminded her that when she prayed in session, she was not praying alone. Her gesture for Patience became bowed head and hands together in prayer position followed by a slow movement to raise her head up, "to see before me," and then rest her hands. There was no sound, only silence.

Struggle recapitulated the work we had done with stretch bands. She would tighten and squeeze her muscles and often release big gasping exhales. This became a strong, stomping rhythm stepped with her feet, sometimes very intensely as if she wanted to put a hole in the ground with her step. It was often arrhythmic as she tensed and released with intensity. The gesture that emerged was a clenching of her fists at her side, and then slowly raising them up. Her arms remained very close to her body and very tight. A second gesture of rising from a squat in a tight, strained rhythm, sometimes almost losing balance with very tense legs, then collapsing and then tensing again, became a movement sequence of "rising up from struggle."

Our time together involved a fair amount of conversation and eventually, very intense verbal and non-verbal processing of her memories of horror and violation. This is when Rachel began to reflect on her time in prison, what had transpired before, and stories of her time as a potato farmer. She had been forced to feed the militia when they camped on her farm, and she had been captured and imprisoned because the government accused her of aiding rebels. She spoke of the seven years she spent imprisoned, her feelings of humiliation, the horrible things she witnessed, and ways she had to placate her captors to survive. For the first time, she began to pause and take time to express her emotions. I sensed that her increasing physical capacity to move, literally, to squat down and stand up, to raise an arm that she couldn't even get above her head before, was expanding her capacity to feel herself. This is when the idea of state shifting the ANS became very real for me. I observed energy and emotional shifts just as I observed ecstatic state shifts in ceremony. It was palpable.

Her state shifting was initially "bumpy"; she could suddenly become distant or sad and crying, or tense and almost angry. Over time, the flow between states began returning, which informed this framework's concept of flow as ventral and state shifting for regulation as fundamental to the work. She was shifting from subconscious state shifts arising from her internalized terror and dysregulated ANS to being able to consciously state shift as she remembered her pre-torture life and touched into her embodied resilience. Core rhythmicity was born of this work.

Rachel taught me that identifying, hearing, and when possible, moving and expressing the rhythms she sensed for each of these steps influenced her biorhythmicity in a helpful way. The rhythm for time was more fluid than struggle. She discovered her rhythm when she took her first deep breath. Terror had limited her breath to very shallow inhalations that seemed to just touch the top of her sternum. One day, as we spoke about how she tracked time while imprisoned—she waited each day for a tiny light to appear on the concrete wall, a light only possible because of a crack somewhere in her cell that let a little light in around the same time each afternoon—she took a bigger inhalation than I had seen before. She let this breath out slowly and smoothly. She looked at me with a spark in her eyes and said, "I just breathed."

This moment taught me of the potency and power of pausing, which is a worthy polyvagal-informed practice because pausing helps the ANS reset (see Potent Pausing in Chapter 11). Rachel showed me how to acknowledge the tiniest shifts in movement and the powerful connection between breath and movement. The rhythm for time became a slow, hymn-like hum, and eventually, Rachel decided to teach me one of her favorite hymns, which we would sing together. Her gestures quickly became a moving sequence that integrated the lifting of her arms from struggle, albeit more slowly and without muscle tension. She would raise her arms and look skyward and then let her arms gently swing around her. She also began bouncing her legs a bit, easing the stiffness with which she usually stood and walked.

When we got to the fourth stage, Striving, she arrived with a Bible and exclaimed, "My story is Job's story." I asked her to explain, and she talked about God's love for Job despite his illness and his purpose in life despite being disfigured. She realized that this was true for her, too. This was a pivotal moment. She expressed "finding herself" and being less lost. At this point, she wanted us to sing together while standing and move with some of the gestures with her favorite hymn. The Striving stage became a socially engaged exploration of this song in movement and laughter as I clumsily tried to learn the song, sang off tune, and often moved more speedily than she did.

These exchanges with Rachel seeded reciprocal alliance. Rachel's natural pace taught me how to slow down to her rhythm to move with her. The day she arrived with her Bible and read me the parable of Job's body, she paused when she was done reading, looked at me, and simply said, "Thank you," while making one of our time gestures, extending her arms in front of her chest and opening them in a horizontal arc, like a "resting rainbow." The resting rainbow image became a metaphor and potent gesture during her long struggle to return to wholeness.

The next time Rachel came to see me, she told me she wanted to show me her dance to freedom and asked me to observe. She began by squatting in the almost frog-like posture she spent the most time in while in the prison cell. It was neither comfortable nor sustainable; she had to squat to keep as much of her body as possible off the filthy floor. She described the filth as "the stench of death." She recalled being held up by the sheer number of other women's bodies around her all squatting similarly to avoid the floor. The dance consisted of many of the symbolic gestures, movement sequences, and songs we had explored in our work together, storytelling through movement. The dance ended with her in as upright a posture as I had ever seen her, head tilted back, eyes starward, arms uplifted in a gesture she described as "liberation." When she finished, she said, "I know you can remember that in your body. And it's up to you to share my story with others. I am whole again."

We met for several more months, and then she only came in on an as needed basis because she was busy with her church group and worked part time in a nursing home to "take care of others as I have been taken care of." This is how coregulation can seed "glo" (global) regulation and promote equanimity and reciprocity.

Rachel still had pain and stiffness and sometimes was stooped after a day of physical work. She still missed her home, and—despite her courageous participation in church group, other social functions there, and part-time work—she still felt alone and cried in her room at times. And, she felt whole. Wholeness is not about recovery and "getting it all back." It's the restorative process that gives us back as much a sense of belonging as possible, adapting and flexible to our new circumstances and home.

GROUNDING TO SKY PRACTICE

Rachel's struggle gesture catalyzed this practice called Grounding to Sky. Grounding to Sky is a counterpart to Grounding to Earth. Grounding practices almost always promote connecting energetically to the earth. We can equally connect or "ground" to the spaciousness of sky energy. This includes the space around us, the cosmos, and the stars and planets. This practice engages the striated muscles of the face and neck, as well as the upper back, shoulders, and arms. It can gently open the heart area, just enough to be courageously vulnerable. It directly targets the VVC, heart, and upper chest, thereby encouraging oxygenation through combining contract and release with breathing and relaxing the muscles of the upper body. Grounding to Sky is helpful in conjunction with Grounding to Earth. Doing both together in either order can open the interoceptive pathway of the spine.

A little preparation information: When we begin the practice, three breaths is one set. It's recommended not to do more than three sets as the muscles begin to effort after that. This practice can be done standing or sitting. Choose which posture is most comfortable for you now.

1. Practice Shifting to Comfort.
2. Take a baseline of the muscle tension in your face (where striated muscles are innervated by the VVC), neck, shoulders, and chest, the whole area of your VVC. Ask yourself if you have the weight of the world on your shoulders (today or any day).
3. Clasp your hands together and place them above your head, as in Figure 10.5.
4. Set #1 = Three Breaths:
    a. Inhale and exhale three times. On the inhale, just inhale while standing in this shape. On each exhale, pull your hands as if you are going to pull them apart, but don't. You are creating a squeeze in your arm and upper chest and back muscles and practicing pulling and grasping.
    b. On the third exhale, pull a bit harder, release your hands, and let your arms float down. Notice what it

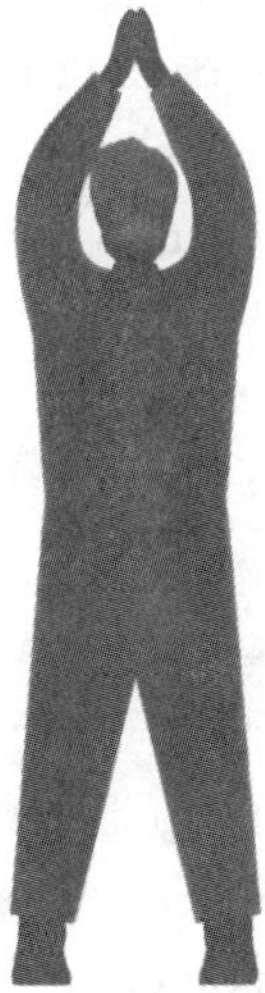

Figure 10.5 Grounding to Sky

feels like to let go. Notice if there is any change in your facial, neck, upper back, shoulder, and chest muscles.

5. Repeat up to two more times, no more than three sets (nine breaths) total.

Potent Gestures

Cocreating gestures with our clients helps root the stories, thoughts, and emotions in the body. I call these "potent gestures" because they reflect conscious reassociations of body and mind, present action and past memory.

Our bodies hold and tell our stories in many nonverbal ways. We may be aware of why we tap our foot incessantly or have a tight shoulder that is painful to move. Or we may not. When we are not, these are movement tags, as defined in Christine Caldwell's (2024) "Moving Cycle" work. Working with them helps reassociate dissociated, uncensorious somatic imprints. When they become conscious, they can become potent gestures that can reflect and express that about which we cannot speak. It can also be a symbolic movement to root into the internal experience, the physical sensation, of an experience. I often invite clients to use potent gestures we create to self-regulate between sessions, as we reengage the VVC and increase their capacity for social and relational capacity. This is what Rachel and I did, using her steps to wholeness as a pathway. Gestures were also core to the work I did with Mo.

MO: REACHING TOWARD LOVE

Integrating yoga into Mo's work was the first step in ANS regulation and body awareness for a very cognitively oriented person. As we progressed through our favorite asanas, taking turns as teacher and student, Mo shared more of his story. His poses initially began with great tension effort, and he moved with strong, yieldless pushes. His grasps truncated his reach and made pulling movements tense. These began to ease as we wove the dimensionality of breath into our movement work. The easing in movement opened him up, and he shared more of his history before capture and the cruelty he experienced while captive.

Shortly after his angry visit to my office, he arrived for a session highly activated in a fight mode. I'd seen his energy level amped up in sympathetic activation before; I had never seen him express this level of anger. His speech was sharper and more staccato than usual. He could not settle and pushed back when I invited him to use some of the practices we were accustomed to using. When I asked him what he was upset about, he told me someone had tried to steal gas from the gas station where he worked, and he ran out and cut off their ponytail. He said this with a sense of pride. It was as if he was bragging about what he did to defend the gas station he managed. He went on for some time, saying disparaging remarks about the individual whose hair he had cut off.

As he spoke, I sensed and realized in my bones that Mo's anger was self-directed. I was witnessing his own self-loathing. When he paused, I observed him in silence. Pausing to witness allows our ANS, heart, and full-bodied presence to tend to the third space, the space between ourselves, others, and the environment. It's the alchemy that makes each professional therapeutic pairing and each session unique. Before my mind understood what my body intuitively knew, I said, "I know you want me to hate you, as much as you hate yourself." Pause. "I am not going to do that. I never will. I will always choose to respect you. I will always choose love."

Mo sat very still and seemed to consider this. Then he excused himself politely and left. I did not know if I would see him again after this second quick departure from our session. He missed the next session but arrived promptly for his session the following week. My comment, unorthodox and clinically rogue as it may have been, had, in his words, "cracked my heart open." He spoke more openly about his intense shame for what he had done. He spoke about his constant prayers for those he had injured and killed. He hated his captors and recognized that his anger at the person who stole gas, occasional frustration with me and my "probing questions," and the dark way he viewed the world most of the time was because he was always "revved up angry" in a sympathetic activation state. He accepted his own anger at what had happened to him and what he had been forced to do.

He spoke of his intense love for his family, and I learned that one of the things he and his wife cherished was plant life. They were avid gardeners, and he missed that shared passion deeply. On a tight budget, he purchased one plant that he described as "the only love inside my home here." From this time forward, plants became a symbol for his love of family. As he willingly shared more of his torture history, his pre-capture family life, and his struggles in the United States, we incorporated plants in my office into our work. When he was straining to reach or extend himself in an asana, we put a plant in front of the reach so he could reach from what he felt in his heart. In this way, the asanas became gestures as he began to associate them with meaningful things from his past life: his warriorship and the respect his country had for his military service and skill; his love for his home, the house and gardens, his children and wife, and more. I encouraged him to practice these "shapes" as both asanas/poses and potent gestures while at home to help quiet his busy mind and calm his anxiety, anger, and activated ANS.

The detail of our work is beyond the scope of this chapter, and as we wove the threads of trauma, resilience, love, remorse, shame, and anger together, I learned that a bow was his most sacred and important gesture. He had begun remembering the relevance and meaning of bows as a soldier and as a judo practitioner. I asked if we might bow at the end of our practice times, and he said no—bows were reserved only for those who earned them, and he was no longer worthy. He did not believe he could offer a bow to anyone, especially himself, until he had atoned for what he had done.

We met a few more times, and I testified at Mo's asylum hearing. His petition failed, and this was his second failure. After that, he showed up for a scheduled session. He walked in with his plant and placed it between our chairs. He gestured the quiet sign, finger in front of his mouth. I started to ask about the plant, and he did it again. He said, "Please let me speak. Please listen to me." He then said he was returning to the country his family was in. I tried to speak again, knowing his risk. He shook his head again and repeated the quiet gesture. I had done this to him many times when his busy mind interfered with our somatic work. He continued to speak about his decision and said he would be returning there soon. He said this was our last session. I felt tears welling up and wanted to speak but did not, respecting Mo's request that I listen. He told me to take good care of his plant, and then he bowed to me, slowly and with intention. Saying only "Thank you," he left my office.

His bow was his final communication to me. While we had not practiced it together, we had referenced it as a gesture he would work to do again in the future. It was his embodied symbol of his history, his pride, his love, and our work. A simple gesture can hold tremendous meaning and can signal the relative safety and trust that is the strong foundation of reciprocity in human relationship.

Core Rhythmicity

Being human is being polyrhythmic. Our bodies are movement and, as movement, we are a constantly expanding and contracting, opening and closing, shifting and pausing flow of rhythms. Rhythm is a potent way to integrate Polyvagal Theory wisdom into movement-based therapies. Rhythm is truly universal: Everything pulsates, undulates, and beats with rhythm. Our ongoing interactions with the world around us are rhythm. We offer and receive. We speak and listen. We input and output. We push into and pull away. It's all rhythm. Research going back as far as 1920 demonstrates how perception of auditory rhythm affects our kinesthetic sense and motor response (Berrol, 1992, p. 25). In the 1970s, research demonstrated that the tempo of external rhythms heard have direct influence on internal neurophysiological rhythms (Berrol, 1992, p. 25). These neurophysiological rhythms are our biorhythms, and three of them are considered core rhythmicity in this framework: respiration, heart rate, and vascular feedback.

Polyrhythms are complex rhythms because two or more contrasting rhythms are playing at the same time. In music, dance, and nature, the polyrhythmicity we hear mirrors our inner landscape. From a PVISDMP perspective, this is perhaps one of the most revolutionary ways scientific theory and movement-centric somatic therapies are connected. Rhythm is a direct portal to meaningful movement, especially in multicultural contexts with the vast sociocultural, socio-spiritual, socio-geographical, and social influences on self-identity and belonging.

We keep moving because of the complex co-occurrence of our bio rhythms, the three core biorhythms being heartbeat, breath, and vascular feedback loops, a biological mechanism that helps maintain blood pressure and blood flow. Rhythmic movement is generated by this polyrhythmic biology and also our culture. Culture informs what we accept as relatively safe and pleasing music, sounds, and rhythm—this is part of culturoception. Cultural influence phrases movement in personally meaningful and satisfactory ways. Culturally relevant rhythms, gestures, movements, and movement sequences can promote health, wholeness, well-being, flow, and relative safety. From a more recent polyvagal perspective, externally stimulated and interoceptively inspired rhythmic movement that feels safe enough can stimulate our biological feedback loops and restore core rhythmicity. Fear, terror, and resultant traumatization can disrupt the flow of biological and culturally informed movement. Clients have taught me about centering spirit, faith, and mystery as meaningful and important influences on how they move through life, understand their suffering, and heal. The inclusion of one's faith is an acknowledgment of the power of Spirit, God, Creator, and Universal Love to their sense of belonging. For most of my clients, their survival was inextricably linked to their faith and their belief in something bigger than human life, the mystery. Mystery is below, as root, wisdom, and ground, and above, for those whose sense of self includes a strong connection to a broader, more-than-earthly sense of Spirit.

Seen from a trauma perspective, the natural fluidity or movement we each have as a birthright—on a continuum from stillness and breath to dynamic movement including dance—is disrupted if someone is neurophysiologically and adaptively dysregulated. Immobilization in terror and mobilization in fear both interfere with the VVC conducted flow of energy for movement. Restored, a person may once again feel liberated enough to move in phrases that are biologically and culturally meaningful.

Any of the practices in this book are helpful for recruiting the VVC-mediated flow states that help us restore our natural movement as part of restoring our sense of belonging. Breath, as the initiator of movement, is helpful. Any practice that involves longer or slower breathing, when the timing is right, can induce calm. Shorter and faster breaths can be stimulating and mobilizing. Using simple movement practices such as Moving the Three Dimensions of Breath, Slow Flow, or using music that clients identify as calming or energizing can also provide portals for the body to relax to slower beats or energize to faster beats. This is also where vocal prosody is useful to promote movement and body prosody, the visible flow of energy as movement. A lower or quieter voice reduces frequency and can assist clients to relax. A full range of prosody can be engaging and invite clients to energize and connect.

The power of rhythm to connect and restore the VVC's ability to shift us toward wholeness and social engagement, and closer to our usual range of social and relational capacities, is shared in these vignettes about Ahmed and the young men living on the streets of Haiti.

AHMED AND THE POWER OF RHYTHM

Ahmed's pivotal moment in therapy was when he connected the slow fluid movements the physio ball invoked to music from back home. Our dance between moving the ball and being moved by the ball elicited flow through the yield in his pelvic floor and legs, areas of the body central to grounding. It was at the very end of a session that he paused and grew very quiet, then said, "I'm remembering music as if I hear it." I asked some questions about the music—the names of songs, the artists, and when he listened to it. I learned he loved the complex polyrhythms of Middle Eastern drumming and admired doumbek drummers. He had managed to make some old-fashioned cassettes of some of his favorite rhythms and songs from a few neighboring countries, and we layered the music into our physio ball practice. First, we alternated listening to music with no music, just as we had done with chair and ball, and then initiated ball movement versus being moved. When we would debrief about the influence of the music on movement, Ahmed described the "deep connection" to his movement that the music created. Eventually, we ended up moving to music all the time while sitting on balls, with periodic pauses to talk about both his pre-captive history and the things he experienced in captivity.

It was during this time he recalled stories he had heard as a child. I encouraged him to bring the stories to our sessions. We would begin each session with his chosen story or poem. As culturally meaningful stories often inspire us to do, Ahmed began to revive and share more of his story. This is when I learned that he had witnessed his mother's torture, always right after he was tortured. In his remembering, he described a sense of helplessness so overwhelming that my body empathically felt an overpowering sense of helplessness. The flatness and stuckness I felt in my body offered somatic insight into Ahmed's depression. As he described the surges of hot, dark energy that filled him while watching his mother suffering, I sensed heat in my own body. He was physically so immobilized that this energy could not move. It was the source of his freeze. He described heartbreak and self-directed disgust at the ways he had to appease his perpetrators when they were violating his mother. He connected that to his current sense of having betrayed his parents and himself. His willingness to open and share this was liberating. It was the first time he emoted and cried. This was also when we connected his inability to step into his familial role to internalized guilt and shame, and how this related to his highly charged freeze. I also learned that he had masterminded their escape, and we bridged the guilt he felt at not saving his mother from torture with the relief he felt at their liberation. He finally saw that he had, in fact, reduced her suffering, not in those moments of violence but by freeing her from their abusers. This connection began to visibly ease some of his sharp, stiff pain and muscle tone.

He discovered the story he had known since childhood about the flute created from the hollowed-out tree branch. Its music was made possible by the empty space. When he decided to write a poem as closure for our work together, he asked me to invite another therapist he had connected with at the center, and to think of a way to help him write a poem, which he had never done. Remembering a poetry writing practice I learned in college, I suggested a writing procedure. We wrote this poem:

When the flute speaks, I soften.
When the flute speaks, join life.
When the flute speaks, I feel the snake dance.
When the flute speaks, it complains to go back to what it once was.
When the flute speaks,
  Sweetness,
  Mourning,
  Emptiness,

Sweetness.
When the flute speaks,
It brings calm to the soul.

Ahmed and I finished working together shortly after he wrote this poem. He would occasionally come in for a "checkup," as he called it. The connection of movement to music to rhythm to story to history to creativity was the path that liberated him from his frozen state to a more playful, socially connected sense of wholeness and belonging. As Chapter 7 describes, he resumed working, tended to his socio-familial and cultural responsibilities, and while he always felt some pain and the loss of his father, he described his life as "whole again."

RHYTHMIC POETRY PRACTICE

This practice can be used in individual, family, group, and community sessions. I've done this with individuals and with communities of close to a hundred people. Once the poem is written, it can be used in many ways. Clients can draw images inspired by the poems. Teens I've worked with will rap or drum the poems. Those inclined to dance can move to the spoken word. The words can be cut up and repasted into a word collage. I invite students to choose their favorite creative process or skill to create ways to use this process cross-modally. Here are the directions:

1. Have a piece of paper (I prefer large flip chart paper) and markers or another writing utensil.
2. Invite your client to come up with the theme of the poem. Ahmed's theme was "When the flute speaks," the story that reconnected him to his body. The rhythmic movement process used with the kids in Haiti, below, is another wonderful way to solicit material for a group poem.
3. The therapist or facilitator says the theme/word/phrase

for the poem and holds up one finger to solicit a single word or all five fingers to solicit a phrase of two or more words related to the theme.

4. The rhythm or cadence to the poem is as follows:

   THEME AS TITLE

   a. Theme + one word
   b. Theme + one word
   c. Theme + one word
   d. Theme + phrase
   e. Theme followed by
      i. One word
      ii. One word
      iii. One word
   f. Theme + phrase

With Ahmed, I said his chosen phrase, "When the flute speaks," and held up one finger three times in a row, then I repeated the phrase and held up five. After that, I held up my finger three times in a row after saying, "When the flute speaks" only once, and then repeated the phrase a final time, holding up five fingers to end.

To document the poem, follow Ahmed's poem format and cadence as a guide. Note how the theme is used repeatedly for the first three single-word inclusions and only once the second time single words are used. This can be adapted to other styles of poetry and prose.

Dancing in the Streets

The span of my work with young men living on the streets of Haiti included living there to direct a psychosocial program for survivors of organized violence and numerous short-term contracts with international nongovernmental organizations (INGOs), government organizations, and the Haitian National Police as well as local nonprofit and educational programs. Decolonizing humanitarian psychosocial work merits many books. One of the most compelling moments I experienced in my work there, which catalyzed the practices with drum and dance, occurred in 2010, after the earthquake. I was cocreating a staff support program with an INGO. The staff were discussing dance and how many of the people in the rural communities were mourning the loss of traditional areas (*lakous*, most simply translated as sacred and/or communal gathering places) for their ceremony and for social gatherings. They were also sharing how some drums were destroyed. Some community members were gathering the drums they could find and initiating drumming to call to Spirit for support, community, and healing.

I mentioned my love and appreciation for Haitian dance and asked about the team's comfort level with us introducing some more traditionally inspired dance and drum processes. There was a long pause, then one of the team members shared that many of them were conditioned to look down on their own traditions. They were raised in homes or communities where the many layers of colonial interference from governments, INGOs, missionaries, and innumerable other groups had relayed messaging that portrayed their traditional cultural practices as wrong and evil. Having witnessed the disrespectful messages toward Haiti's local wisdom and culture that these groups promoted, and the destructive impact these groups and their message had and have when they descend on Haiti to "fix" her (as they have been doing for well over 500 years), I was not surprised. I was, however, heartbroken.

While there is much to write just to begin to share the depth, beauty, and power of Haitian tradition, it is well beyond the scope of this book. What emerged from this moment was a renewed commitment to work with the young men who had been explicitly requesting drums, drum lessons, dance lessons, and a space to advance their love of their tradition. One group wanted to refine their performance troupe's skills.

This is when the core rhythmicity work adapted to local collective culture. Over many years, this drumming practice grew with the passionate wisdom of the young men, the staff support team, and other communities of Haitian artists, musicians, and wisdom keepers. Every program I worked with that supported the children on the streets soon owned drums and percussion instruments. This required a strong push in fundraising, grant writing, and partnerships. The richness of this ventrally mediated sociocultural restorative and respectful cocreative play is also worthy of an entire book. It would highlight the sociocultural-informed environment where the kids and team members oversaw developing the practices.

My role became one of support, and of deep listening and openness to learning. I worked with the different groups to document the ways drumming and dance could be used in the postearthquake environment. Inviting their cultural wisdom and intuitions to inform the ways we used drumming and dancing was akin to the previous ideas for making the office environment as safe as can be. The environment in Haiti was full of input and demands from well-meaning and not-so-well-meaning outsiders who insisted on imposing their worldview. For a polyvagal-informed approach to be more relevant and inclusive, that is, to suit the collective nervous system that exists in any place, the local culture must inform how safety is understood. It also must inform the rhythms, movements, and all activities that are appropriate to be included, and the very structure and format of all of the above. There is no other way to decolonize the use and integration of practices that have deep historical and cultural meaning and are constantly appropriated and/or disrespected and discarded by others.

Following are descriptions of two practices that are easy enough to document in written form. Restorative rhythm drumming is challenging to write up. A brief scaffold is included for those who work with or are inclined to learn drumming to be able to work with rhythm in this way. There are many ways this work is powerful: the complexity of drumming and dancing traditional rhythms mirrors the complexity and finesse of our own ANS and its unique role as conductor of the polyrhythmic orchestra and living orchestration the moving human body is. This is what engages the VVC's connective capacities that can restore flow to not just individual but also the collective ANS.

PRACTICE: MOVING HUMAN RHYTHMS

This practice works with six ways of moving (slow, fast, heavy, light, tight, loose) that can be expressed rhythmically. These terms come directly from words clients have used over the years to describe their neurophysiological and biochemical feeling states. It's a very dynamic, playful movement practice that can be adjusted for all ages and contexts. It also is a great way to harvest words and phrases that can be used for the group poem practice. Here are the directions:

1. Give everyone a way to document their cued movement through the six rhythms. I hand out a single piece of paper with the six words printed on it, as on the Rhythm Worksheet on the following page. Drawing images and symbols can also work for clients who have not yet learned to write. Sometimes I have people call the words out, and I scribe them on a whiteboard or flip chart, especially if I am working with a community that has not had the resources or access to provide everyone's literacy in writing and/or if paper is not available.
2. Have everyone find a place to stand in a room with ample movement space. Outdoors can work too.
3. For a baseline, invite everyone to walk at their natural pace, whatever that is in the moment, and notice and remember that. I also sometimes invite them to notice how comfortable they feel in the environment itself, to notice the other people, and notice if they tend to move toward or away from anything. The latter is a useful baseline to sense our present-moment neuroception of and relative safety in a place.
4. Let everyone know you are going to use word and verbal cues to change the rhythm of their movement in the shared space. I have also used preselected music to invoke the rhythms. I ask everyone to agree to keep themselves and everyone in the space as safe as possible and let

them know we will be transitioning quickly at times and that continuing is always optional. It's important that folks with movement limitations and/or mobility or other disabilities can participate as safely as possible, or; opt out and observe respectfully. I adapt the instructions and agreements so this practice is accessible to everyone in the community. Begin cueing the six rhythms in whatever way you intuitively think of. Here is an example of how I do it:

a. Say "Bring your walking baseline to a pause and reflect for a moment so you can compare your walking rhythms later."
b. Say "Now begin to move fast. Fast, fast, FAST, FAST!!!!! That's not fast enough!! Are you kidding, that's a snail's pace! The bus is leaving and you have 50 yards to run to get there or you miss it forever! You just saw your dearest friend of many years ago in a crowd, and if you don't hurry, you'll miss the chance to hug them again!" I use verbal cues that offer different contexts, that is, that vary from rushing in what may be a stressful encounter (missing a bus) to a joyful one (hugging a dear friend). Cues can be humorous, cheeky, or fun, and depending on the group's collective energy and familiarity with you, you may be able to push comfort levels.

5. Say "Find a way to transition out of this rhythm and pause. Take your time. Do whatever your body needs to shift out of FAST. Go back to your natural walking and notice if there have been any changes."
6. Do this for each of the remaining five rhythms. Depending on the community you are working with and your theoretical foundation and comfort level, you can change up the rhythms used and the way you invite the group to explore them.
7. When all six rhythms have been explored, invite everyone to take a walk through the space until they naturally

feel their pause. Remind them to revisit the pace of their walking and their relationship to the environment, including people, for a comparison.

8. If you prefer to use music, choose music that amplifies the rhythm. As an example, Vivaldi's "Spring" from the *Four Seasons* can work for light. Strong bass music can work for heavy. Tchaikovsky's "Russian Dance" from *The Nutcracker Suite* works well for fast. Obviously, these will need to be adjusted for cultural preference.

This practice can seed interesting conversations around how we move through life. The rhythm of our movement affects how we perceive the environment, other people in it, access to our social and relational capacity, and so on. Using the words, phrases, and/or images and symbols to describe individual experiences of these moving rhythms on either individual handouts or a large paper, a collective poem can be written according to the guidance above. Many clients find it useful to identify their "rhythm patterns" associated with fear, painful past memories, and trauma and the rhythms that help connect them to their strength, hope, and resilience. When they sense a subconscious, dysregulating state shift, they can consciously "call up" the images, words, internal sensations of the rhythms—and even the rhythm itself—to invoke a consciously recruited regulating state shift.

The following "Rhythm Worksheet" offers a template for an individual handout to help movers record their bio-rhythmic experiences. I do this by inviting them to pause, transition out of the rhythm we just played with, and go to wherever their paper is and jot down single words, phrases, and/or images in the area allotted for each rhythm. This helps build a restful transition into the practice. This written or drawn record serves as a reminder of clients' core bio-rhythms and their associated people, places, and experiences they can refer to when a conscious, regulating state-shift is helpful. These words, phrases, and images can also be used for the group poem. Sometimes, to save paper (and trees!) I use a large flipchart paper to record a selection of the group's words and phrases. I let them know in advance that I will only include the first 3–5 per rhythm that I hear, which adds an element of slightly competitive play to the practice because they have to shout them out quickly.

RHYTHM WORKSHEET

FAST	SLOW
HEAVY	**LIGHT**
TIGHT	**LOOSE**

PRACTICE: RESTORATIVE RHYTHMS DRUM PLAY

This practice requires drums. I recommend djembes, although congas, ashikos, and even doumbeks can be used. Every time I facilitate this process, I bring one or two of my djembes and include as many of the local culture percussion instruments as possible. I recommend at least one-third to one-half of the people have large drums, and the others can use shakers, rattles, rhythm sticks, and so on. Make sure to switch this around so everyone has a chance with big drums.

For those to whom drumming is brand new, if this work is appealing, take a few drum classes online or in person. One does not have to be a professional drummer. The lead facilitator needs to be able to demonstrate basic drumming technique and be able to solidly maintain a basic 4/4 rhythm for an extended time. Being comfortable leading some simple improvisational rhythms is also key. Having two to three rhythms you can play is essential. I always ask who is experienced in the group and invite them to be my improviser. Sharing leadership is another way group processes can contribute to a reciprocal alliance. If no one is experienced, I find someone who can hold a basic rhythm, and I will demonstrate improvising. It's important to note that improvisations, that is, changing the rhythm, means that the new rhythm is being played at the same time the group is maintaining the original rhythm. They must play a rhythm that riffs off the original. Otherwise, the sound gets muddy. It's also essential to remember that people new to drumming almost always accelerate the rhythm, so it's important to remind them to keep it at the slower end. Another way to share leadership is to invite other drummers to facilitate the second and third (and so on) shared rhythm explorations.

This URL to a news story centers restorative rhythm drumming in post-earthquake Haiti and demonstrates some of the "steps" included in this scaffold: https://youtu.be/wO2kt_BvVYI?si=npHMUTPUoquCiSK1.

The basic format is this:

1. Have everyone sit in a circle and rest their hands on their drum or instrument and "feel the vibe" to connect to it. Have everyone notice their breath and that we are breathing together.
2. Invite everyone to introduce themselves with a rhythm. A simple way is to say their name and then play the rhythm of it. The facilitator can direct which way the introductions move around the circle.
3. When introductions are complete, invite everyone to place their hands back on the drums. Then instruct them in basic drumming technique. I always remind people we are not putting the rhythm in the drum; we are drawing it out. Otherwise, people tend to hit the drum hard and leave their hand there, which flattens the sound. The drummer's hand should land on the drum and lift off, allowing the sound to be liberated from the instrument.
4. Pause. Have everyone sense their breath and then place a hand somewhere they can feel their heartbeat. They can also just sense it inside them. At the same time, cue everyone to play the rhythm of their heartbeat. It will be muddy at first. Allow it to keep going, offering verbal cues as needed (e.g., "Slow down, we're speeding up too much," "Play it a little louder"). Eventually the rhythm might entrain and synchronize. If it doesn't do this naturally, you can invite everyone to listen to one neighbor, and then another neighbor, and then all the drummers' heartbeats and begin to bring the rhythm together. This mimics the early formation of our own heart's rhythm and connects us to the rhythms and energetic fields of the hearts surrounding us. Research suggests that the heart's electromagnetic field is 60 times the amplitude of the brain's. This suggests we connect heart to heart before our brains connect ("The Science of HeartMath," 2015, p. 36).

5. Pause and see how everyone is and if anyone wants a refresher on playing the drums.
6. Invite the group to offer reasons why people gather, drum, gather to drum, gather to play, and gather in community—whatever you're moved to say.
7. Using the verbal responses from #6, decide three themes for the group to play. Examples might be love, community, sharing, fun, magic, mourning, and protest. I always co-decide with the group.
8. The facilitator always initiates the first rhythm by stating the theme (e.g., community) and choosing a very simple rhythm to play. Cue the group to begin to join and play along with the rhythm. Begin to vary the tempo and audibility by using your chosen hand signals for faster, slower, louder, and quieter. Also decide what gesture will signify "stop" and practice that several times in this first round, making sure you explore all the possible ways the rhythm can vary.
9. If there is a designated improviser, invite them to improvise. Invite others to join them, ensuring that a solid half of the group remains playing the basic rhythm with you.
10. Sometimes the group can get ahead of itself and get wild, muddy, or activated. I always have a previously agreed-upon pause. Often, it's a verbal cue to pause, such as saying, "Three-two-one!" and stop drumming, and then having everyone raise their hand up in the air, close enough to their neighbors' hands to "feel their energy" and breathing together a set number of times.
11. When this exploration feels complete, which is anywhere from 5 to 60 minutes, pause. Have everyone place their hands on their drum or instrument again and feel the rhythm that is still there. Almost always, energy is still pulsing. This can also be felt near their neighbors' hands or touching neighbors' hands if that's appropriate.

12. Repeating the second and third rhythms can invite vocalizing, singing, and dancing as well, depending on the group's comfort level.
13. Process the experience in any way typical for your work.

As our hearts are formed in utero, they begin to beat their—our—unique rhythm through a cascading developmental process. Biological folklore suggests that the heart begins with a single cell whose "beat" (likely a contraction or pulse) establishes the mother beat, and then another cell couples with it, entraining to pulse at the same rhythm. More recent research on when a human heart begins to beat estimates the actual heartbeat, defined as "the regular movement that the heart makes as it sends blood around your body" most likely initiates 20 to 35 days after fertilization (Männer, 2022, p. 20). Folklore describes couplets of heart cells joining to form the heart tissue and, eventually, the heart and each couplet entraining to the original formative cell's beat. This story may hold elements of both scientific and intuitive truth. That rhythm entrains humans into shared movement is well established and, in this spirit, restorative rhythm drumming offers a powerful process to literally unite hearts. In the spirit of being in service of evolution, perhaps this can build bigger shared fields of compassion and reciprocity.

Harvest

Not all clients successfully achieve full "ventrosity," a term I use to describe being in a ventrally mediated state. The social emphasis on privileging ventral is challenging, because it is our birthright to experience the inherent flow of the ANS. And, as long as there are those who continue to promote oppression, racism, violence, marginalization, othering, and more, our resilient ANSs will recruit from the evolutionary wisdom we all carry inside us to promote states that ensure our survival. "Dorsalocity" helps us remain invisible to predators and perpetrators; it is a huge burden to carry this legacy of being unseen, and many in the society I live in, where cultural and ethnic erasure is ongoing, must recruit this adaptive state shift to stay alive. The SNS ability to mobilize us to protect and/or defend ourselves and those we love will always be adaptive and necessary in societies where people must protect and defend themselves from violence and acts of racism and oppression.

The restorative process towards more ventrally mediated conscious state shifts, especially in communal settings, fosters reclamation of our own personal, and collective, biorhythms. This is how we can promote the restorative feedback loops that recalibrate our ANS and re-pattern the neurophysiological ground of our movement and body narratives and stories. Working creatively with rhythm can restore our inner polyrhythmicity, our own unique "beat," increasing our capacity to move, relate, and share more authentically, holistically, and reciprocally. Rhythm play naturally offers variety and complexity to bolster healing and restore dignity and as much a sense of belonging as possible. Loss, fear, and the recruitment of our biological wisdom will always be necessary and adaptive, albeit exhausting in the long term and unjust to have to sustain, for those of us whose environment regularly or almost always signals danger and life threat. This is our job, not just as therapists but as human beings and planetary stewards, to contribute to an environment that welcomes and offers a multiplicity of rhythms, movements and dances; and an environment that potentiates a regulated and freely humming ANS is possible for all.

CHAPTER 11

Full Circle

VAGAL PATHWAYS TO NOURISHMENT

When you learn something from people, or from a culture, you accept it as a gift, and it is your lifelong commitment to preserve it and build on it.

—YO-YO MA, JUNE 9, 2019

Rest might be thought of as a lost art in fast-paced societies. It may seem paradoxical that rest is essential to cultivate strength and to nurture our resilience. In the complete peak and trough cycle of daily life, it's the trough, the lowest point in the cycle, that resets our ANS and replenishes our bodies, hearts, minds, and spirits. Rest is our capacity to pause, to nap, to sleep, to be still, to root, and to ground. Rest is essential to nourishment. It is one of the most restorative things a human being, any living being, can do. Rest is also an aspect of our humanity that is undermined by interpersonal and collective trauma, intentional abuse, long-term oppression, and human rights violations.

In sadistic forms of human rights abuse, abusers intentionally undermine and destroy the capacity for people to rest, settle, and digest because that is what nourishes resistance and resilience. This is key to how they maintain control of the person. For most sadistic abusers, especially for the survivors of political torture whose stories inform this book, a primary intent of the abuse is to let the victim know that the perpetrator exerts total control, always. Disrupting our natural core biorhythmicity is how they do this.

The DVC promotes states that invite and allow rest. As the older branch of the vagus nerve, it governs our ability to be still. Its primary action of shutdown is terror-induced. It can also be recruited in relatively safe environments and contexts, and when it is, it contributes to our capacity to rest and settle, rest and digest, and surrender to deep quiet. Rest states are what help restore homeostasis, which is a primary role of the parasympathetic nervous system that the DVC is part of. It does this in tandem with the more modern, highly myelinated VVC. That moment just before sleep when your eyelids feel as if they are weights yielding down into your eyeballs, that instant of drifting at the edge of sleep, is connected with the DVC's contribution to our capacity to yield and be receptive to nourishment. This happens because the VVC is also engaged enough to promote a sense of enough safety to allow our body to rest into the support and welcome of our bed as we drift off. Just as our bodies require stillness and often prefer solitude to digest, we also need deep rest to integrate information and activities and anything we are exposed to that might contribute to our knowledge base and wisdom. It's only in rest that new neural pathways created by new activities, be they moving or contemplative, are more permanently etched into our brains (and possibly our hearts).

The emerging research for the heart, once described as a pump of involuntary muscle, suggests that the heart has its own neural circuit and transmits information to the brain via the afferent vagal pathway (Fedele & Brand, 2020, p. 1). It seems possible that the heart also has plasticity to change, grow, and heal. Bioplasticity, a term coined from the various wisdoms informing this work, posits that our whole body can change and grow in response to experience. Being alive is not static, and there is a considerable old wisdom that recognizes that our interconnectedness with all forms of life shapes and reshapes us. Certainly the human nervous system, and possibly the heart, are evidence of this. Perhaps being open-hearted really means that our hearts have a true capacity to connect, grow, and expand in service of compassion and reciprocity.

That all three ANS circuits influence our heart's rhythm is core to how the ANS influences our own polyrhythmicity. When our ANS is humming and the pathway between DVC and VVC is open, the VVC is inhibiting the activation energy of the SNS at the sinoatrial node I call "Kiss of the Beloved." Our SNS still supplies energy for movement so the DVC and VVC coupling can promote the sense of nourishment we get from sharing food, resting, and relationship.

Section II of this book follows the flow of our phylogeny. This evolutionary hierarchy gifted us the multibranched ANS that guides us between inner and outer spaces. Coming full circle, we return to the roots of evolution and the vagal pathways that evolved. This is a homecoming in our human lineage of hierarchical species evolution. This hierarchy is a map to guide our moment-to-moment navigation of inner and outer landscapes of humans, or environments. The hierarchy inherent in the evolutionary path that created these circuits and the primary, hybrid, and blended states they create is really a spiral. Within the hierarchy, there are feedback loops that connect to what's past and pattern, and emergent and possible, at once, ongoing.

Potent Pausing

Rest has been one of the hardest things for many of my clients to find. Whether they are inclined toward immobilization, mobilization, or any hybrid or blend of primary states, rest is elusive. The myriad states and actions that appear as hypervigilance, defensiveness, protectiveness, arousal, shutdown, and dissociation that arise from exposure-induced ANS imprints and the trauma feedback loops they become can make rest elusive. Clients who sleep a lot often don't experience a sense of nourishment or refreshment because their sleep feels weighty, heavy, or so lengthy (and often multiple times a day) that they feel themselves sinking deeper into lethargy, misery, and loneliness. Those who are agitated and/or activated and vigilant in constant mobilization describe not being able to settle enough to maintain sleep and rest states and activities. All describe awakening exhausted. Restoring our capacity to rest reestablishes the bridge between movement and pause, which is what transition is.

This is one influence on the idea of potent pausing. Not original, this concept of taking a conscious longer pause, long enough to breathe several times and pay attention to something in the space with full attention, derives from many contemplative and sacred traditions such as meditation, yoga, and contemplative dance.

MIRIAM'S PAUSE

Before Miriam began sleeping on the couch in our waiting area, I often experienced a drain in my own energy when working with her. Her moments of SNS activation were always couched in bitterness and negativity. She spoke and acted like a miserable person, which contributed to her isolation. She suffered horribly and alone in her home country. Her life was truly hard as a pain-ridden single mother of three in a brand new, very different culture where she could not speak the language.

She stopped going to English classes because none of the lessons stuck. She was convinced she couldn't learn anything new. She resisted anything I asked or invited that was insight oriented, and when I pushed, she snapped, "Why bother? Nothing will ever change."

Yet somehow in our shared persistence of weekly sessions, our ANSs were coregulating. Her naps and eventual rest in my office and sleep at home were the fruit of this coregulation. In Chapter 9, I describe how progressive and pancake pandiculation, with its emphasis on noticing the first thing she awoke to, helped ease the transition to wakefulness in a more playful and more pleasant way. This helped her wake up without her SNS startle pattern, though it usually didn't last long. She would be grumpy and complain again, until I learned about her love of and expertise with plants.

One day she was beginning to sit up from a nap, and the first thing that caught her eye was my three plants. As she slowly tracked them with her eyes and lifted herself toward them, a smile appeared on her face. She paused, hovering, and breathed in more deeply than I'd ever heard her inhale. I asked her what she was noticing and invited her to pause even longer there, which she did, supported by several cushions behind her back. Then the smile left her face, and she popped up and said, "You need bigger pots for your plants. They are sick." Since they looked okay to me, I asked her to say more while committing to revisiting that suspended pause, when I noticed her face soften in ways I'd never seen before.

I learned that she was not only very fond of plants, but she had also been known back home as a plant doctor. She would welcome friends' and neighbors' sick plants into her home and nurse them back to vibrancy, restoring their life. Since my plant knowledge is limited to watering them weekly, I asked her if she would help my plants.

Recognizing client expertise and inviting clients into leadership roles rooted in their expertise fosters reciprocal alliance. She left that day with all three of them, and they were each returned, much healthier (and in bigger pots, which I purchased at her instruction). This simple act of noticing and of inviting her passion into our work was transformative in several ways. Her energy increased, and she was more frequently excited and playful versus her previous intense surges of angrily expressed activation. She had kept one of the plants in her bedroom, and this became her consistent object of focus when she remembered to awaken slowly, gently stretching into her day. I challenged her to lengthen her first pause by 30 seconds each day, and she did. It was easy for her to rest her eyes on plants. As part of this potent pause, I invited her to breathe however she was already breathing and then deepen it a little more, never to the point of uncomfortable activation, but powerful enough to feel the exchange with the plant. She valued plants for their oxygen and knew they tidied up the planet's excess carbon dioxide. She loved plants for their colorful beauty.

She soon relished these long pauses and described brief but restorative moments of extended free stretches, refreshing breaths, and a softened gaze. She began to soften the previous furrow in her forehead and rub it, so her face would, in her words, "shine more love." This became the impetus for the brow-softening practice and the soft gaze of compassion, described later in this chapter. Potent pausing became a consistent part of our time together.

When she decided she was done with therapy, we had not engaged in any depth work or trauma processing, because she didn't want to. She wanted to get busy doing things she loved. I mentioned this at a staff meeting of the resettlement agency where she received support services. She had had no plants of her own at home, and she felt both overjoyed and proud to have helped my plants and sad to see them go. Within a week, volunteers had donated over 20 plants to Miriam, as well as soil, tools, and pots for her to begin a small plant garden in her tiny yard. She had ample space for indoor plants, and this restoration of social and relational capacity with the plants with which she enjoyed prolonged pauses was full circle for Miriam.

An essential and ongoing lesson of this work is letting go of the usual idea of therapeutic outcome and recognizing—and weaving into treatment and closure—the socio-historical, cultural, economic, and other influences on clients' worldviews and ways of being. It is also common in work with newcomers that they stop coming to sessions abruptly or with little time for closure because of sudden changes in their lives that they don't have much or any control over.

MELISSA: FAMILY, LOVE, AND NOURISHMENT

I experienced one profound exception to this sudden attrition with Melissa, the women's rights activist of Chapters 4 and 8.

Once Melissa began to leave her home, her progress toward a level of independence happened rather quickly. First, she could drive herself and a new friend to classes. This was after the first eight months of our work and play together focused mostly on the postures of preparation. Her assigned home play was to travel to another room, then out the door, then outside, and onward, until she was moving around to walk, shop, and exercise in public more freely. During that time, our posture play became more free-form to embody the idea of freedom. This is when I taught Melissa the Moving the Three Dimensions of Breath practice. Eventually, as her ANS calibrated and as she connected more with me and with others in her daily home play explorations, she also noticed her ability to not only tolerate but enjoy longer sustained moments of quiet and rest between postures.

Initially, like Miriam and Ahmed, her transitions were fast and would seem to trip her out of the conscious state shifts we were practicing. She reverted to subconscious state shifts arising from her fear patterning. To disrupt these patterns, we incorporated potent pausing into our work, inviting her to sense the breath inside her. This facilitated the Sensing Breath practice described next, which has become a teaching staple for students to understand the power of breath as an efficient ANS regulator and neurophysiological state shifter. It also connected her to the idea of interoception, which I had tried to introduce before as "listening to the wisdom inside you" when she expressed self-doubt.

Because our posture explorations often reminded her of prayer, she would begin to feel the same contentment, relative safety, and expansion she once felt in prayer. Prayer had been hard for her since coming to the United States, and she fretted that she wasn't being a "good enough Muslim." Her sociocultural and spiritual roles as mother, wife, lover, and Muslim were the most important things for her.

During this time, I learned much more about her activism, her home and family life, and her strong belief that she could make a meaningful contribution to this society if she could liberate herself from the fear that kept her at home. In one session, when she was pausing for several minutes with her breath and listening inside, she said, "I think I feel the peace you have been talking about. I feel like prayer." I asked her to describe what she was sensing inside herself, how her body was communicating peace and prayer to her. Asking a version of the question "How is your body letting you know what you are feeling?" has helped many clients connect to their bodies. She said, "I am as expanded as the dawn and the dusk. Inside me feels like this time when we do our prayers. It is at this time that Allah [God] is closest to us. My inside body softens, and I feel myself smile." She stayed there for several more minutes, and then I invited her to check in. She shared one of her favorite facts about prayer: In her religious tradition, prayers are most potent at dawn and dusk because that is when God is closest. She offered both a spiritual and a scientific rationale for this.

After this session, Melissa began to signal that she felt that we were approaching the end of our time together. She was one of the first clients to do this, and she requested that we plan how we would finish our work. Melissa expressed relief and joy at being reconnected to her liberated self. She also shared how grateful her family was and how she had told them quite a bit about both the content and the process in our sessions. Both her husband and her children asked questions about the therapeutic process. We planned to end two weeks later, so we could commit the following session to reviewing her entire flowing series of postures and other practices we had done together. At that session, she informed me that her entire family would be coming to the final session to thank me. This was a first, and I was delighted. The strain on her marriage and intimacy with her husband and the tension she described in mothering when she felt locked in her fear imprint and patterning were primary reasons she sought therapy, along with feeling isolated and disconnected at home.

When she arrived for our final session, husband and children in tow, the two young girls carried a chocolate cake, my favorite, with "Thank you" written on it in both of our spoken languages. The family had baked it together after she sneakily learned what my favorite flavor was, and they wished to share it together. Then I was to take the remainder home to my family. We picnicked on a rug in my therapy space, and the husband and children took turns sharing the changes they observed and appreciated in Melissa.

Sharing food is an act of nourishment in many ways. We literally nourish our cells, bodies, and all their intricate needs by eating, and we nourish our biological need for connection in restful, calm environments. Eating together is a ventrally mediated action that connects the entire vagal nerve pathway because digestion is dorsally mediated. Places that still practice siesta understand very well the need for a long enough solitary rest to properly digest in service of true nourishment.

This shared gesture and process was a full-circle moment for Melissa, who was beginning to fully reconnect with her role as Muslim, mother, wife, and active woman. Food sharing, especially if food is a client's gift, can be discouraged in old-school behavioral approaches to psychotherapy. With Miriam and many other clients, food sharing was a culturally meaningful way to integrate our bodies into the restorative process. Including rest in all its forms, from contemplative practices or reflection to digestion to sleep, is restorative of our core biorhythmicity and our humanity.

PRACTICE: SENSING BREATH

This is the third practice that evolved out of the Three Dimensions of Breath practice. Structure and Function has been the most accessible and helpful to clients. Moving the Three Dimensions also has been helpful for clients wanting to engage with playfulness, and it is especially useful with younger clients. Sensing Breath is a practice I use often for teaching and less often in clinical work until the timing is right. The client and I must have a strong enough alliance, and both self-regulation and coregulation must be established. Here is the Sensing Breath exercise:

1. Find a place to lie down. This practice can be done sitting, and because it's a deeply sensory practice that can invite inner awareness and a sense of VVC/DVC hybrid rest and settle connection, lying down in horizontality tends to be the most supportive way to do it. Students usually lie down; many clients prefer to sit.
2. Practice Shifting to Comfort.
3. Take a baseline of your breath. This is another practice where noticing the relative length of inhale and exhale can be interesting and informative.
4. Take a moment to sense your breath inside you. Sometimes it's a temperature, sometimes a texture. Sometimes we hear or taste it. Using any of your senses to connect to your breath is an expanded baseline.
5. Now notice the horizontal dimension specifically. I cue this: "Notice if you can feel your chest [lungs, torso, body, etc.] widening you inside each time you inhale. Notice how your inner shape changes again when you exhale."
6. Depending on the context (class or session) and the strength of our Reciprocal Alliance, I may invite this exploration for two or three breaths, two to three minutes or longer. Use your clinical intuition. Inviting clients to let you know when they are done supports their self-regulation capacities from this co-regulated space.
7. Let your sensing of the horizontal, widening dimension go, and rest. Rest offers integration. Contemplative practices that consciously engage the body and our awareness of a neurophysiological and biological process are powerful state shifters and promote neuroplasticity, and possibly bioplasticity, which means we create new neural pathways with helpful associations or reassociations to counter the pathways associated with the ANS bias for negativity when we are under strain, exhausted, afraid or traumatized.
8. Compare your breathing now to your baseline.

9. Repeat for the vertical (lengthening) and sagittal (forward/back) dimension. Compare your breath after each round to your baseline. Notice how you feel. It's not uncommon, especially when we are resting and digesting, that clients drift off into a nap when doing this. That moment of rest is a potent pause that restores flow in transitions from breathing, sensing, moving, feeling, and thinking. This combined VVC/DVC homecoming is restorative, restful, and reconnecting.

MARIA: BREATH AND BOUNDARY

Maria and I did a lot of trauma processing work in the time between Javier joining our sessions and their return to intimacy. The Three Dimensions of Breath in all its forms was one of the practices we relied on in our sessions to navigate the memories we worked with, and the way they still held her body captive. We began with Structure and Function using props, similar to Mo, so that she could experience a sense of her skin boundary. For many clients whose bodies are violated multiple times, no matter how they define their boundaries (which are not always at the skin), the sense of rupture at the level of skin can create intense reactivity to touch. We used the props, usually something soft like a "slo-mo" pilates PVC ball or a soft toy or a folded piece of cloth, to increase her capacity to tolerate contact. She would hold the object away from her skin and slowly move it toward her skin, using one of the dimensions of breath to expand her body to meet the object. As her tolerance for contact grew, we integrated Sensing Breath. This allowed her internal space to become part of her joining the object. This exploration of many months was accompanied by trauma memory processing, and we paused frequently to recalibrate by grounding or moving. Maria arrived at one session with a new brightness in her eyes that appeared like light and tears at the same time. When

I observed this aloud, she responded, "I am pregnant. We are going to have another baby."

Maria's work began with changing her home environment to create cues of relative safety so she could neurocept and perceive a more homelike space and reengage with activities that she loved. Including Javier, and how he spoke, moved, and connected to her allowed her to reassociate her home and relationship as safe enough. Incorporating breath, first externally and then internally, helped Maria reestablish boundaries that welcomed the nourishment of intimate physical contact. Maria came to session several more times and then chose to stay home and rest to ensure her baby's development was as supported as possible by the love she once again experienced there.

Nourishing Hearts

The Kosovar women's group shifted after our elder invited movement, and we stretched together. The integration of "bread, salt, and heart" as part of opening and closing rituals, and the incorporation of movement and creative processes in every session contributed to a new and different sense of bonding. Previously, the women bonded around their shared stories, losses, and traumatic memories of war. Now they were beginning to connect around activities that were social, engaging, and playful. They were creating new stories and memories together, and a natural order of leadership that built on eldership, youth, talents, and skills emerged. The group was becoming a source of inspiration, education, connection, and nourishment.

When our time ended, the women did not want to stop meeting, and our resources were such that we could not continue the group as it was. In the last two sessions, one of the themes that emerged was about food: longing for culturally relevant foods and the places where they grew or were bought. It so happened that I had been deployed to Kosovo during the New Year's holiday, which landed a few weeks before our last sessions when we ate their traditional bread. At one women's center in Pristina, I had also participated in making it. I shared that with the women, and they decided that we would meet at someone's house to make and share the bread together.

The Bread, Salt, and Heart ongoing women's gatherings were born. My colleague and I helped organize and participated in the first few, at their request. One of their most pressing concerns when they began to meet was where to get the ingredients they were used to that were not easily available in the United States. Our program had a thriving volunteer community, and one of our volunteers, Joanna, was a nutritionist. We invited her to our first meeting, and the women loved her. She gathered a list of all their favorite and most culturally meaningful and nutritional foods and did some research. Within a month she had identified stores where these ingredients could be purchased, or substitutes based on flavor, nutritional value, consistency, and so on. We handed the group off to Joanna after a closing celebratory meal together, and she and the women met for several years. Each meeting included a "shopping spree" (the volunteers' religious community supported the grocery bills) and a gathering to cook and eat together at a different woman's house each time. Joanna received support through our volunteer program, so we heard, secondhand, how appreciative the women were to have an opportunity to gather in an environment they described as "nourishing to our hearts, and happy for our bellies."

Wholism is an expression of social engagement. Somatic and creative arts–based therapeutic approaches recognize that relating and relationship include the whole body. As the field of mental health expands to welcome and include somatic and movement-based approaches—as well as creative arts approaches that center dance, art, music, poetry, and drama—the entire body will necessarily be included. As a somatic psychotherapist and a dance/movement therapist, I am trained to integrate awareness of the body and sensations, movement, and nonverbal and verbal creative processes into my work. I also integrate other elements of bodily experience that are integral to our sense of well-being, wholeness, and flow, such as nourishment, sleep, exercise, and prayer. These are within the very clear and defined boundaries of my role and agreement with clients.

The Brain-Gut Axis

The brain-gut axis is one of the most revolutionary current applications of Polyvagal Theory. Dr. Porges writes, "Vagal pathways support the homeostatic functions of visceral organs including the heart and gut via more efficient digestion and flow of oxygenated blood through the body" (2024, p. 7). A body that suffers frequent sympathetic activation is more prone to inflammation and hot conditions, such as fever and rashes. PVISDMP integrates current research through grounding and earthing structured practices like Grounding to Earth and Grounding to Sky, which combine breathing and muscle contraction and release to promote oxygenation. Movement processes that invigorate the pelvic floor and belly area and invoke fluid sacral and hip movements like Slow Flow all support the brain-gut axis because movement supports digestion. The work of B. G. Mancini (n.d.), of the Brain and Gut Institute, emphasizes how nutrition and movement are core to true nourishment and to countering the inflammatory and painful physical and psychological impacts of toxicity in any form—physical or emotional. Mancini writes:

> The Brain-Gut axis highlights how our physiology is guided by the rhythms and responses within the nervous system, microbiome, and sensory processing. Professionals and families that recognize how these interconnected systems communicate, often beneath conscious awareness, shaping emotional regulation, resilience, and overall well-being have a lens to understand themselves and each other that more closely aligns with the truth of our experience. By understanding and supporting the natural rhythmic patterns of safety and adaptability in the Brain-Gut connection, we can reduce chronic threat responses, restore balance in the autonomic nervous system, and create more capacity for connection, healing, and growth. (personal communication, 2025)

What this means is that what we eat, the time we allow for digestion, the time we spend engaged in enjoyable activities with those we love and are close to, and the extent to which we control our exposure to environmental toxicity and stressors (which circles back to what we eat), are all potent influences on our well-being and sense of flow and wholeness. It bears noting that many people are constantly exposed to physical and psychological toxicity, violence, insecurity, and so much more with no ability to control it. Mancini's work with the vagus nerve is changing the field of mental health and psychotherapy in ways that can support mental health professionals and our clients to include this knowledge. The practices she teaches amplify our impact. Just as diversity in diet ensures healthy biomes, biodiversity ensures longevity and health for our planet. Human diversity is similarly a sign of collective health. We are complex organisms and systems and need the complexity of our species and the planetary web to feed and mirror this. We know diversity in all species ensures ongoing evolution and creation. This is what bioplasticity acknowledges and celebrates.

Starting with the basics, the inclusion of nourishment in simple ways, like having snacks and tea available in our psychotherapy spaces, is survivor-centered, polyvagal-informed, and very practical. Some, not all, traditional psychotherapies have discouraged sharing meals with or accepting or even offering food to clients. My clients who do not pay but are covered by insurance will bring homemade treats as an offering of gratitude, and my acceptance of them is a heartful gesture that promotes respect, compassion, and reciprocity. To reject it would be detrimental to the restorative process and the reciprocity that this process endeavors to cultivate.

Working in a diverse multicultural context necessitates creative approaches inclusive of a variety of global traditions around cooking and sharing food. Chapter 4 describes my integration of ritual at a client's request and an interpreter's urging. The women from Kosovo taught me many valuable lessons, including how cooking and eating together are restorative because they are collective rest that helps us settle into relationship with others. What could be more coregulating than a room full of happy, satisfied bellies?

The Heart of Belonging: The Afghan Women's Fresh Minds, Good Hours Group

In 2016 another refugee resettlement agency invited me to offer a creative arts and dance movement therapy group with recently resettled Afghan women who had arrived alone, or with their children only. All the women had lost their husbands. They were settled later than many other groups because most of them had never worked and/or had not attended a typical school. They did not know each other and were all visiting the resettlement agency office complaining of loneliness, isolation, distress, and fear. They all described their individual experiences of feeling completely lost and unsafe.

I instantly recalled the patience and leadership of the Kosovar women. I countered with a proposition: I would cocreate, with an art therapist colleague, a polyvagal-informed women's group to reduce isolation and to promote connection. I cowrote the grant so that PVISDMP would be the central theoretical framework, with the rest to be designed with the group participants. The women's involvement in the actual group design was nonnegotiable. Funders often require a program to be described in its entirety to consider funding it. This is a flawed, exclusive approach to philanthropy. Because this community had already expressed stigma around anything having to do with mental health, we decided to invite women through written, conversational, and word-of-mouth pathways, and while our grant required us to preset goals, structure, and format, we left it open so that the women could be included in support of dignity, reciprocity, and belonging. It's been my experience with group therapy with a diverse community that is designed without any flexibility to incorporate and include multiple cultures and worldviews that dropout rates are high.

My colleague Anita and I invited the women to an informational and planning session. We had decided to use a public health research technique called "free-listing" from my work in that area with colleague Dr. Paul Bolton (Bolton et al., 2012, p. 5). This research sought to identify local idioms and ways to understand and describe mental health for violence-affected communities in Mexico and Haiti, based on their community-specific needs. Rather than translate mental health terms, we used open-ended questioning to get to the heart of what mattered for their healing. Using the free-listing method, the answers, or data, are reorganized according to similarities in meaning and themes.

The preliminary goals the resettlement agency, Anita, and I established for funding purposes were to reduce isolation and offer a space to learn relevant skills and increase social connection with other members of their community. Promoting social engagement, fostering community through many pathways, and enhancing resilience through relationships were also goals. Designed as a pilot program, we agreed to track symptoms if relevant and if the women agreed. We also agreed to be open to changing what we tracked based on what mattered to the women. We asked questions to respectfully elicit information about the women's social and relational activities in Afghanistan. We began with open-ended questions, and then we used more refined questions to probe for more culturally relevant information. Anita and I took turns asking the questions and writing down the responses.

Some of the questions and probes were:

- Do women get together on a regular basis in Afghanistan?
- What kinds of things did you love doing back home?
- Were there things you especially loved doing with other women back home?
- Are there things you miss doing? If so, what are they? When did you do them?
- What kinds of things would you all like to do together?
- Why do you think it's important, helpful, or meaningful to engage in activities together?
- What ideas do you have now for our proposed group?

After the first planning meeting, the women were so enthused that they asked if we could hold a second meeting so they could invite others who had been unable or were wary of joining. We repeated the same questions, and in this second session, we shared our free-listed clusters of shared themes and answers. We organized the list while they socialized.

We used this information to design the group content, format, and processes. With the women, we agreed to hold eight sessions monthly instead of the usual weekly format of therapy, per the women's scheduling preferences and needs.

The women initially explicitly stated that they did not want therapy, and after our planning meetings they asked that the group offer a space to "share the things that bother us so we can help one another." The women requested that we use our expertise to help structure the group. Together, we decided to integrate a cultural or creative activity based on their interests and allow time for preparation and follow-up. Choosing a cofacilitator who used a different creative arts therapy was intentional. This dimensionalized the possibilities for our activities. It was the women's idea to make sure that we included time to share their feelings about what we did together and their lives in general. The women also requested the group be held in a central, easy-to-access location and that children be welcome. We ended up moving around according to the activity and finding ways to include the children who came. This is atypical of group therapy, yet this honoring of their sociocultural worldview on what it is to be socially engaged was essential. The women created this list in response to the question, Why is it important to come together in a group?

- A fresh mind
- It makes your heart softer, makes you feel better
- To learn about American culture
- To learn how to play
- To get to know each other, see each other, rely on each other
- To enjoy each other and be in community
- To help each other
- To practice English
- They are the good hours of life
- Sharing problems and good moments
- Problem solving
- Resettlement issues and the painful challenges of adjustment
- Create space to share and to process feelings together

Based on these responses, which helped name the group the Fresh Minds, Good Hours Group, we reviewed their responses and looked for repetition of shared themes. Together, based on these themes, group members ended up deciding these were the activities we would do because they were either culturally familiar, collaborative, socially engaging, skill-building, or confidence-enhancing:

- Cooking both Afghan and American food
- Playing soccer
- Bowling
- Creating art
- Dancing
- Going to a local family fun center

Each group began with a polyvagal-informed somatic movement practice related to the activity. We would then engage in the activity, followed by processing time as the women requested. During the processing time, we initiated sharing with questions Anita and I came up with. We also ended with an emergent practice one of us came up with spontaneously, inspired by the group.

The women decided we should begin with cooking Afghan food. Our first practice was Grounding to Earth with hands on our bellies to welcome the food and prepare to digest it well. At the women's suggestion, we rubbed our bellies and laughed so they would be "ready to be full and happy." After our shared meal, we gathered in our circle, and each woman shared a bit about what they had prepared, and we asked this question: "What are your tips for making this dish delicious, every time?"

Each one of us responded, and apparently my trademark brow furrow appeared on my face while I shared how my husband "took over" my brownie baking. One of the women paused me and told me to soften my brow. She said, "The most important ingredient is love, and you are not loving the food if you look like this," at which point she imitated my face. After a few giggles, I shared a bit about the VVC and referred to it as a neural pathway of love, connection, and kindness based on what the women were sharing about having a soft brow to cook. We ended with a collective phrase to synthesize our responses: "The most important ingredients for nourishing, delicious food are seasonings and *love*. Talk to the food, infuse it with *love*. Then it will nourish you and everyone who eats it. And keep your eyebrows soft."

After that we integrated belly hugs and softening our eyebrows into every practice. To end each session, we repeated Grounding to Earth with one hand on our belly, "loving our digestion," and we used the other hand to massage between our brows and remove the furrow there, softening our brow area, which is innervated by cranial nerve 7 and changes our facial expressivity. This became a practice the women referred to as "sharing love and nourishment."

Numerous studies show hugging can increase our oxytocin levels, which helps us feel good. While self-hugging may not elicit as potent a feel-good response as hugging another person or pet or even a comforting blanket or plush toy, many clients report a sense of comfort and calm with self-hugging. There are oxytocin receptors in the area of the belly, heart, and face. Hugging the face may not feel as good, so hugging your belly or chest is recommended.

PRACTICE: SOFTENING-BROW AND THE OXY HUG

Here's a simple way to do the Oxy Hug, the name that emerged from the belly-hugging and softening-brow practices:

1. Find a mirror (or imagine you are looking in one) and notice your brow. Many of us have a scowl from thinking, looking at a screen, or being outdoors.
2. Take a moment to sense into yourself and notice how you feel. You can Shift to Comfort if that's helpful and notice again how you feel.
3. Place your hands on your belly or chest and hug yourself. You can also rock.
4. Notice if you feel different, that is, a state shift.
5. Pause, rest, integrate.

6. Place your hands on your forehead and gently rub your brow area, "erasing" the lines.
7. When you breathe, feel every exhale releasing air from your body, softening your face and imagining the skin of your face relaxing.
8. Do the hug and the brow softening as long as you want. Recheck how you feel.
9. You can swap the order if you prefer to start with the brow softening.

The group ended up not playing soccer or going to a family fun center because those were planned toward the end of our time, which ended up being right after the 2016 election. With the Muslim ban in place, the women did not want to risk tainting our time together by being in an environment that cued hostility. The women were bonding and forming close friendships and beginning to do things together. It was not the time to undermine their collective ANS sense of relative safety. Instead, the women had heard about a community garden the resettlement agency had started and wanted to go there. This was our second-to-last session, and it was one that, like our first cooking class, was pivotal.

When we first arrived at the garden, we stood on the earth near ancient acequias, canal-like structures pervasive in arid New Mexico. Many of these acequias have existed for centuries. The program coordinator shared the history of the local land and the origin of the acequias, and one of the women guided us in her adaptation of Grounding to Earth. Inviting group members to share a taught practice in their own style is empowering, and sharing leadership contributes to a sense of individual and collective belonging. Afterward, each woman was given a few seedlings, then chose an area to plant them. The group grew quiet as the women, hands in earth, placed their little plants. Many of them were crying.

During our processing time, we asked the question, "What is it like for you to work in the earth?" Each woman shared a heartbreaking story of loss of land back home. Many of them came from families who had lived on land as far back as 10 generations and more. They spoke of their connection to land, of how sensing and touching earth simultaneously brought up grief and deep contentment and calm. One woman said, "My heart was calm, and I feel calm. When I touch the earth, close my eyes, I feel calm and happy." As she spoke, her receptive yield into earth was palpable. She had not felt this way since before her flight from Afghanistan.

The nourishment the women described was like an umbilicus to their shared histories, not just in this time and place but to that shared history and to the new relationships and possibilities they as a group represented. It was a wordless shared experience, and for this group, it was also the impetus for them to find a way to continue meeting beyond our group, which they did.

As each woman spoke, my own body felt how deeply the moist soil communed with their flesh. The meaning of the word "loam" transformed for me; I could sense the earth regenerating, reminding, and co(mmunity) regulating our collective through every pore. Our collective ANS seemed to inhale, exhale, sigh, and yield together. It was as if I was witnessing the rejoining of long-lost lovers. The soil seemed to welcome the women, and they reciprocated by offering their tears as water, massaging her rich flesh and gifting their plants to her care. While they shared, a lesser goldfinch appeared. First, it flew over us several times, perching in a nearby branch and vocalizing. The women continued sharing stories from their hearts about legacy, lineage, ancestry of both human and land. They spoke of their connection as a relationship of deep eternal reciprocity. One of them said, "We miss the earth back home, and we can touch it here. Touching this earth, I feel my home." As they spoke about their longing for earth, the lesser goldfinch landed in the middle of our circle, and paused. It made its own tiny circle, chirping a bit and looking at us. Then it flew off.

Witnessing the women, and the bird, I experienced a sense of how all the "-ceptions" contribute to our neuroception, of how we are shaped by and shape the environment in a present moment as individuals and as a shared collective. This is what bioplasticity means. It is a more holistic concept of neuroplasticity. Neuroplasticity privileges the brain. It seems plausible that our ability to use our sensory capacities to feel our belonging and connection to earth is an experience that, like the meditation practices or physical exercises often cited in neuroplasticity research, can increase our gray matter and create new neural pathways. Bioplasticity suggests that not only the brain but all of our tissue, our fascia, our noble pathway of brains, anywhere there are nerve pathways, can grow. Our lesser goldfinch certainly knew we were there. We all agreed that it seemed to sense us and to have joined us with intention. We all felt gratitude for being seen and witnessed by this tiny, bold being.

Polyvagal Theory is changing and growing as new pathways of professions, practitioners, and experiences illuminate its relevance in many spheres. This dual-branched nomadic nerve is both hierarchically evolutionary and ever emergent and is part of the ANS that regulates us internally and can extend beyond us like a beacon to the world around us.

PRACTICE: THE SOFT GAZE OF COMPASSION

The Soft Gaze of Compassion was one of the women's favorite practices. It emerged from several influences. The Soft Brow practice we cocreated is one. An optometrist's advice to rest my computer-weary eyes by standing outside in the warmth of the sun and allowing the warmth to permeate my closed eyes is another. The third, humpback whales, is perhaps the most influential. That the ocean is the origin of all life, as is widely believed, and that humpback whales followed the evolutionary path from ocean to land and then returned to ocean, merits inquiry. The question of why has never been conclusively answered. From a polyvagal perspective, it's interesting to be in inquiry with what adaptations they made to return to the ocean. Ocean is an ancestor and returning to it, for cetaceans, a homecoming. To adapt to the big blue environment, having lost their gills, they evolved blowholes, which required their nostrils to migrate backwards and upwards to the top of their skull. They reclaimed aquatic tails. This, and water, changed their spines and their movement. Their eyes moved farther back to be able to see more of their watery environment, to see more expansively.

Whales can stay submerged for anywhere from 20 minutes to three hours before they resurface to consciously exhale forcefully and inhale more air. It seems possible that this change in breathing required some significant adaptations because they breathe consciously all the time. How did their ventral vagal nerve pathways adapt for this changed oxygen demand? Perhaps this adaptation boosts their intelligence, expanding their heart-brain connection, something my teachers and Elders teach me as the "HeartMind," the deeper wisdom that arises from this connection. Whales are often cited as being quite possibly more intelligent and compassionate than humans. They are known to be altruistic among themselves and with other species. Perhaps their bio-intelligence and altruistic, compassionate nature are connected to all these adaptations. The Soft Gaze of Compassion is a practice that invites the possibility that if we expand our way of seeing to be more inclusive of everything around us, less myopic and forward focused, we might other and objectify less. We might see, and be seen, for where and how and who we truly are.

1. This practice can be done in any posture. Choose your preferred posture and Shift to Comfort.
2. Take a look around the space you are in and notice what you see. This is your baseline.
3. Rub your hands together until your palms are very warm.
4. Close your eyes and rest your closed eyes on the palms of your hands. Let your head rest into your hands so your neck is more relaxed.
5. Do this as many times as feels good.
6. Open your eyes and look around you. How does the space or environment you are in look to you now? Has anything changed?
7. How do you see the world now? Consider this: Our eyes reflect what we feel in our hearts. How might others, the world, see you?

Harvest

Holism in this framework means to be as present as possible in our bodies, hearts, minds, and spirits. It is less about being broken and then fixed and more about appreciating the inseparable braid of trauma and resilience that life is. Staying resilient in the wake of a traumatic experience can feel exhausting. The imprints of traumatization and the patterning of the ANS are always adaptive, even when they wear us down. Our bodies are a wilderness of emergent possibility. We learn, and pattern in service of our survival. We innovate and emerge in new ways in service of ongoing life.

Being whole also means to reconnect to our place, to our sense of belonging, in the world of all things. Our natural environment has always held and offered many things, some dangerous and worthy of caution and respect, others a source of nourishment, offering food and medicine, and providing spaces that inspire awe and joy for the vast diversity of landscapes in our shared earth home—majestic, serene, colorful, wild, biodiverse—that surround and hold us.

Nourishment is an antidote to exhaustion, fear, uncertainty, oppression, and trauma. The deepest source of nourishment is experienced in our own body however we define and inhabit it. We nourish ourselves literally as bodies, breaking down food to become nutrients that keep us moving. We nourish ourselves physically, emotionally, psychologically, spiritually, communally, and collectively in many ways: dance, yoga, exercise. Rest. Prayer. Sharing meals, hikes, books. Pausing to appreciate beauty. Loving our family, pets, and our wild relatives. Ritual and ceremony. The list is extensive. The vagus nerve is a trail and a pathway that navigates, instigates, maps, and connects all of this. It is a hub and a center for what we sense, feel, and move. When enough safety and comfort allow our smart, integrative, governing VVC to metaphorically buoy in the ancient sea of our DVC, we can move and flow towards connection and compassion that nourishes our personal and collective wholeness.

EPILOGUE

The Gift

Faith is a bird that feels dawn breaking . . .
and sings while it is still dark.
—RABINDRANATH TAGORE, 1916, *FIREFLIES*

The Bird

The Afghan Women's Fresh Minds, Good Hours Group met one last time after our time at the garden. We met in one of the women's homes, and Anita, who had photographed all our sessions, brought poster board and enough copies of photos of our time together that each woman could create a collage of memories to take with her. In our closing sharing circle, each one of us shared our memories and our harvests.

One woman paused for a long time before speaking and then said, "The bird was a gift. She came to see us. She saw us with kindness and caring. I felt compassion."

She paused. "Our gift had wings, and," she gestured from her place in the circle to every one of us there, individually, "we sent her off to fly to others we love in the world, to everyone in the world, to share this gift."

References

Abbott, E. (2011). Haiti: a modern history. Richmond ENG, Duckworth Publishers.

American Psychiatric Association (1980*). Diagnostic and statistical manual of mental disorders, 3rd edition*. APA Publishing.

Aposhyan, S. (2004). *Body-mind psychotherapy: principles, techniques and practical applications. New York: W. W. Norton & Company.*

Arain, M., Haque, M., Johal, L., Mathur, P., Nel, W., Rais, A., Sandhu, R., & Sharma, S. (2013). Maturation of the adolescent brain. *Neuropsychiatric Disease and Treatment, 9*, 449–461. https://doi.org/10.2147/NDT.S39776

Baenninger, R. (1997). On yawning and its functions. *Psychonomic Bulletin and Review, 4*, 198–207. https://doi.org/10.3758/BF03209394

Berrol, C. (1992). The neurophysiologic basis of the mind/body connection in dance/movement therapy. *American Journal of Dance Therapy, 14*(1), 19–29.

Bolton, P., Surkan, P. J., Gray, A. E., & Desmousseaux, M. (2012). A qualitative study in northern Haiti: The mental health and psychosocial effects of organized violence. *Transcultural Psychiatry, 49*(3–4). http://tps.sagepub.com/content/early/2012/01/06/1363461511433945

Brown, K. (2000). *Tending the helper's fire* [Unpublished master's thesis]. Naropa University.

Caldwell, C. (1996). *Getting our bodies back: Recovery, healing, and transformation through body-centered psychotherapy*. Shambala.

Caldwell, C. (2018). *Bodyfulness: Somatic practices for presence, empowerment and waking up in this life*. Shambala.

Caldwell, C. (2024). *Conscious moving: An embodied guide for healing, learning, contemplating, and creating*. North Atlantic Books.

Casimir, (2020). The Haitians: A decolonial history. The University of North Carolina Press.

Cohen, B. B. (2012). *Sensing, feeling, and action: The experiential anatomy of Body-Mind Centering*. Contact Editions.

Conrad, E. (2007). *Life on land: The story of Continuum, the world-renowned self-discovery and movement method*. North Atlantic Books.

Cottingham, J., Porges, S., & Lyon, T. (1988). Effects of soft tissue mobilization (Rolfing pelvic lift) on parasympathetic tone in two age groups. *Physical Therapy, 68*(3), 352–356.

Damasio, A. R. (1994). *Descartes' error: Emotion, reason, and the human brain (Rev. ed.).* Putnam.

Dana, D. (2018). *The Polyvagal Theory in therapy: Engaging the rhythm of regulation.* Norton.

Farmer, P. (1994, 2003, 2004). The uses of Haiti. Monroe, Maine: Common Courage Press.

Fedele, L., & Brand, T. (2020). The intrinsic cardiac nervous system and its role in cardiac pacemaking and conduction. *Journal of Cardiovascular Development and Disease, 7*(4), 54. https://doi.org/10.3390/jcdd7040054

Geller, S. M., & Porges, S. W. (2014). Therapeutic presence: Neurophysiological mechanisms mediating feeling safe in therapeutic relationships. *Journal of Psychotherapy Integration, 24*(3), 178–192. https://doi.org/10.1037/a0037511

Gershon, M. (1999). *The second brain: A groundbreaking new understanding of nervous system disorders of the stomach and intestine*. Harper Perennial.

Gray, A. E. (2010). Trauma Resources 501c3. Haiti Drum Circle. You Tube. https://youtu.be/wO2kt_BvVYI?si=yVzGQXaRhHO-fIo2

Gray, A. E. (2015). What language does your body speak: Some thoughts on somatic psychotherapies in international contexts. *Somatic Psychotherapy Today, 5*(4), 30–37.

Gray, A. E., & Porges, S. (2017). Polyvagal-informed dance/movement therapy: Restoring core rhythmicity. In C. Malchiodi & D. A. Crenshaw (Eds.), *What to do when children clam up in psychotherapy: Interventions to facilitate communication* (pp. 102–136). Guilford Press.

Gray, A. E.(2018). "Dance/movement therapy and survivors of torture." American Dance Therapy Association. https://www.youtube.com/watch?v=Cm4aTzWyKDE

Gray, A. E. (2018). Roots, Rhythm, Reciprocity: Polyvagal informed dance movement therapy for survivors of trauma, In *Clinical Applications of the Polyvagal Theory: The Emergence of Polyvagal-Informed Therapies* S.W. Porges & D. Dana (Eds) Norton.

Grof, S. & C. Grof, (2010.) Holotropic breathwork: A new approach to self-exploration and therapy. State University of New York Press.

Hackney, P. (2015). *Making connections*. Routledge.

Harris, D. (2002). *Mobilizing to empower and restore: Dance/movement therapy with children affected by war and organized violence* [Unpublished master's thesis]. Medical College of Pennsylvania and Hahnemann University. https://doi.org/10.17918/etd-2649

HeartMath Institute. (2015). The Science of the heart: Exploring the role of the heart in human performance. HeartMath Institute.

Herman, J. (1992). Complex PTSD: A syndrome in survivors of prolonged and repeated trauma. *Journal of Traumatic Stress, 5*(3), 377–391.

Herman, J. (1997). *Trauma and recovery.* Basic Books.

Hindi, F. S. (2012). How attention to interoception can inform dance/movement therapy. *American Journal of Dance Therapy, 34*(2), 129–140.

Johnson, R., & Ndefo, N. (2021, January 26). When agreement is not consent: Appeasement is the trauma response no one is talking about. *Medium*.

Kaplan, I. (2020). *Rebuilding shattered lives: Integrated trauma recovery for people of refugee background*. Victorian Foundation for Survivors of Torture.

Klimecki, O. M., Leiberg, S., Ricard, M., Singer, T. (2014). Differential pattern of functional brain plasticity after compassion and empathy training. Social Cognitive and Affective Neuroscience. ;9(6):873-9. doi: 10.1093/scan/nst060

Kolaitis, G., & Olff, M. (2017). Psychotraumatology in Greece. *European Journal of Psychotraumatology, 8*(Suppl. 4), 135175. https://www.ncbi.nlm.nih.gov/pmc/articles/PMC5632764/

Konie, R. (2011). A brief overview of laban movement analysis. Psychomotorischetherapie.info. (https://psychomotorischetherapie.info/website/wp-content/uploads/2015/10/LMA-Workshop-Sheet-Laban.pdfP

Kroll, E. (2025). The science of safety in birth: Integrating Polyvagal Theory and limbic dominance for childbirth education and labor support [Unpublished manuscript].

Lanius, R. (2024, October 4). Easy to understand summary: autobiographical memory and recalling traumatic memories. https://www.ruthlanius.com/autobiographical-memory

Levy, F. (2005). *Dance/movement therapy: a healing art. 2nd Revision.* American Alliance for Health, Physical Education, Recreation, and Dance.

Linklater, R. (2014). *Decolonizing trauma work: Indigenous stories and strategies.* Fernwood.

Mancini, B. G. (n.d.). Brain and Gut Institute. https://www.braingutinstitute.com/about.

Männer, J. (2022). When does the human embryonic heart start beating? A review of contemporary and historical sources of knowledge about the onset of blood circulation in man. *Journal of Cardiovascular Development and Disease, 9*(6), 187. doi: 10.3390/jcdd9060187

McGonigal, K. (2013, September 4). How to make stress your friend [Video]. YouTube. https://youtu.be/RcGyVTAoXEU

Menaken, R. (2017). *My grandmother's hands: Racialized trauma and the pathway to mending our hearts and bodies.* Central Recovery Press.

Mullan, J. (2023). *Decolonizing therapy: Oppression, historical trauma, and politicizing your practice.* Norton.

Mynasny, B. (2009). Understanding the process of fascial unwinding. *International Journal of Therapeutic Massage and Bodywork, 2* (3), 12.

New Perspectives. (n.d.). *The history of psychological trauma.* https://newperspectivesinc.com/the-history-of-psychological-trauma/

Okun, T. (2021). White supremacy culture. White Supremacy Culture. https://www.whitesupremacyculture.info/

Cottingham, J., Porges, S., & Richmond, K. (September 1988). Shifts in pelvic inclination angle and parasympathetic tone produced by rolfing soft tissue manipulation, *Physical Therapy, 68*(9), 1364-1370.

Porges, S. W. (2011). *The Polyvagal Theory: Neurophysiological foundations of emotions, attachment, communication, and self-regulation.* Norton.

Porges, S. W. (2017). Vagal pathways: Portals to compassion. In E. M. Seppälä, E. Simon-Thomas, S. L. Brown, M. C. Worline, C. D. Cameron, & J. R. Doty (Eds.), *The Oxford handbook of compassion science* (pp. 189–202). Oxford University Press.

Porges, S. W. (2021). *Polyvagal safety: Attachment, communication, self-regulation.* Norton.

Porges, S. W. (2023). *Our polyvagal world: How safety and trauma change us.* Norton.

Porges, S. W. (2024). Disorders of gut-brain interaction through the lens of polyvagal theory. *Neurogastroenterology and Motility, 37*(3), e14926. doi: 10.1111/nmo.14926

Porges, S. W. (2025). *The autonomic cost of surviving mortal threat: Polyvagal perspectives on survival and healing.* Polyvagal Institute. https://www.polyvagalinstitute.org/

Prummel, K. D., Nieuwenhuize, S., & Mosimann, C. (2020). The lateral plate mesoderm. *Development, 147*(12), dev175059. https://doi.org/10.1242/dev.175059

Rifkin, J, (2010, August). The empathic civilization. [Video]. TED Conferences. https://www.ted.com/talks/jeremy_rifkin_the_empathic_civilizationutm_campaign=tedspread&utm_medium=referral&utm_source=tedcomshare

Rosenberg, S. (2017). *Accessing the healing power of the vagus nerve: Self-help exercises for anxiety, depression, trauma, and autism.* North Atlantic Books.

Rothschild, B. (2002, July/August). Understanding dangers of empathy. *Psychotherapy Networker,* 2–6.

Salter, A. C. (1995). *Transforming trauma: A guide to understanding and treating adult survivors of child sexual abuse.* Sage.

Sanders, M. R., & Thompson, G. (2021). *Polyvagal Theory and the developing child: Systems of care for strengthening kids, families, and communities.* Norton.

Seppälä, E. M., Simon-Thomas, E., Brown, S. L., Worline, M. C., Cameron, C. D., & Doty, J. R. (Eds.). (2017). *The Oxford handbook of compassion science.* Oxford Library of Psychology. https://doi.org/10.1093/oxfordhb/9780190464684.001.0001

Sneijders, C. (2024, March 13). Unlocking the power of your heart and gut: The science behind your three brains. *Qantastic Journal.* https://medium.com/the-quantastic-journal/the-3-brains-head-heart-and-gut-science-4eb075bbc08e

Sunseri, J. (2019, August 27). Deb Dana interview: Story follows state, climbing the ladder and diagnosis [Interview]. Justin LMFT. https://www.justinlmft.com/post/debdanainterview

Terr, L. (1992). *Too scared to cry.* Basic Books.

Tobey, H. (1999). *Secondary trauma and resiliency.* Vital Hearts. https://www.vitalhearts.org/training-schedule

van der Kolk, B. (2015). *The body keeps the score: Brain, mind, and body in the healing of trauma.* Penguin.

Index

Note: Italicized page locators refer to figures; tables are noted with a *t*.

About the Author

Photo by Genevieve Russell

Dr. Amber Elizabeth L. Gray, PhD, MPH, LPCC, BC-DMT, (Muxkwudeheenawxkway; Saa'am So Otsi) is a dancer, therapist, activist, author, and teacher whose work lives at the intersection of movement, healing, human rights, and planetary rights. Since 1999, she has been learning, practicing, and sharing embodied approaches to trauma, and has taught polyvagal-informed therapies since 2001. Amber works globally with survivors of human rights abuses, historical trauma, and oppression, integrating dance/movement therapy, somatic psychotherapy, yoga, Continuum, Spirit, and wild wisdom into her practice.

Her teaching, consulting, and writing center a survivor-led, culturally responsive, and justice-rooted approach to the restorative process. She is the creator of the Right-to-Embody framework and leads Body of Change eco-somatic retreats for therapists, artists, and changemakers worldwide. An inaugural editorial board member of the Polyvagal Institute, Amber continues to explore how movement, creativity, and relationship support restoration, resilience, and collective transformation.